THE BATTLE OF THE DENMARK STRAIT

THE BATTLE OF THE DENMARK STRAIT

AN ANALYSIS OF THE BATTLE AND THE LOSS OF HMS *HOOD*

DANIEL KNOWLES

FONTHILL

Fonthill Media Language Policy

Fonthill Media publishes in the international English language market. One language edition is published worldwide. As there are minor differences in spelling and presentation, especially with regard to American English and British English, a policy is necessary to define which form of English to use. The Fonthill Policy is to use the form of English native to the author. Daniel Knowles was born and educated in United Kingdom; therefore, British English has been adopted in this publication.

Fonthill Media Limited
Fonthill Media LLC
www.fonthillmedia.com
office@fonthillmedia.com

First published in the United Kingdom and the United States of America 2020

British Library Cataloguing in Publication Data:
A catalogue record for this book is available from the British Library

Copyright © Daniel Knowles 2020

ISBN 978-1-78155-786-0

Typeset in 10pt on13pt Sabon
Printed and bound in England

Contents

Introduction

The loss of the battlecruiser HMS *Hood* on 24 May 1941 in the Denmark Strait following action with the German battleship *Bismarck* was a naval disaster that shook the British public and the Royal Navy to its core. The loss of 'The Mighty *Hood*' was the single greatest loss of life for the Royal Navy during the Second World War; out of a crew of 1,418, only three — Midshipman William Dundas, Able Seaman Robert Tilburn, and Ordinary Signalman Albert 'Ted' Briggs—survived.

The sinking of the *Hood* was one of the most traumatic events experienced by the Royal Navy and the British Empire during the Second World War. The events surrounding the loss of the *Hood* have been widely scrutinised, analysed, deeply dissected, and hotly debated with much misinformation, often unknowingly, being propagated.

Related to this, the Battle of the Denmark Strait is perhaps one of the most famous and important naval battles of the Second World War and is one of the most documented, yet despite this, in the decades following the battle debate has raged over what happened.

Since the *Hood* sank, debate has raged over the ship's loss. The debate that has continued to this day has centred on how it was that the ship was lost in such a catastrophic manner with the result that almost all hands were lost. It is not the intention of this work to be morbid or offensive, but the purpose of this work is to provide plausible theories on why the *Hood* sank and to provide truthful answers as to why she sank. The questions that this work seeks to provide an insight into are why was it that the *Hood* was lost and why did so many men die—or, perhaps more fittingly, how was it that anyone survived?

In addition to analysing the loss of HMS *Hood*, this book will also analyse the Battle of the Denmark Strait itself, the actions of the vessels involved, and the way in which the battle was fought. This work began as a project dedicated to analysing the loss of the *Hood* alone at dawn on 24 May 1941, but while conducting research into the ship's loss, it quickly became apparent that one cannot analyse the loss of the *Hood* without looking in depth at the Battle of the Denmark Strait for the two are so intertwined as to be almost inseparable.

The picture that is presented here of the loss of the *Hood* as well as of the Battle of the Denmark Strait itself is derived from a variety of sources which are clearly outlined in the bibliography. This work not only considers the merits of different sources but looks and considers different viewpoints, taking into account the thoughts and views of those who witnessed events, those who have spent considerable time analysing events through printed works, and those who have put forward their views in exchanges on internet forums and in private correspondence. Every effort has been made to analyse and understand different points of view, especially those that differ from the views of the author.

Operation Rheinübung

The German Naval Command fully recognised that Britain was an island nation dependent upon merchant trade bringing in food and essential raw materials. Protecting this vital lifeline was one of the highest priorities for Britain. If Britain's lifelines were severed, she would have to either sue for peace or negotiate an armistice.

Grand Admiral Erich Raeder, the commander of the German *Kriegsmarine*, believed that the goal of defeating Britain by severing her lifelines was achievable. Indeed, a campaign of unrestricted submarine warfare around Britain by German U-Boats during the First World War had almost succeeded in bringing Britain to her knees in 1917. Raeder believed that the primary method to achieve the severing of Britain's lifelines was to use traditional commerce raiding tactics executed by battleships and cruisers supported by U-Boats. Raeder succeeded in convincing the *Oberkommando der Wehrmacht* (High Command of the Armed Forces) and Hitler that if her maritime lifeline was severed, Britain would be defeated.

Operation Rheinübung (Rhine Exercise) was the latest in a series of operations against Allied shipping undertaken by the surface units of the *Kriegsmarine*. It was preceded by Operation Berlin, a highly successful commerce raid in which the battleships *Gneisenau* and *Scharnhorst*, commanded by Admiral Günther Lütjens, sailed from Kiel on 22 January 1941, transited the Denmark Strait whereupon they reached the North Atlantic, and conducted operations against merchant convoys. The first convoy intercepted by the *Scharnhorst* and the *Gneisenau* was Convoy HX-106. The attack on the convoy was aborted when the battleship HMS *Ramillies* was sighted as Lütjens was under orders to avoid action with enemy capital ships. The *Scharnhorst* and the *Gneisenau* made good their escape and happened upon an empty convoy that was *en route* to the United States. Over the course of twelve hours, five merchant vessels were sunk before the battleships moved an area around the Azores to intercept convoys sailing between West Africa and Britain. One convoy was sighted but not engaged owing to the presence of HMS *Malaya*, which prompted a move back to the western Atlantic, where a solitary freighter was sunk. Having arrived back in the western Atlantic, two unescorted convoys were engaged and sixteen merchant ships were sunk or captured; during this, the presence of the German raiders was revealed by one of the merchant ships. During the action in which the *Gneisenau* engaged the merchantman *Chilean Reefer*, HMS *Rodney* appeared having received the distress signal, but the *Gneisenau* succeeded in bluffing her way to safety and the two battleships made good their escape once more.

Subsequently, the *Scharnhorst* and the *Gneisenau* were ordered back to Brest, where they docked on 22 March. Against the backdrop of the successful sortie undertaken by the *Gneisenau* and the *Scharnhorst*, the German Naval Command decided in spring 1941 that the time was right for a far more ambitious operation using the most powerful commissioned ship in European waters, and new flagship of the *Kriegsmarine*—the *Bismarck*.

Laid down on 1 July 1936 and launched on 14 February 1939, the *Bismarck* was built to be superior to any other warship afloat. The *Bismarck* was named after the 'Iron Chancellor', Otto von Bismarck, and was launched by the former chancellor's granddaughter. Built in complete violation of the naval restrictions placed on Germany following the First World War, displacing 50,300 tons at full load with an overall length of 823 feet and with a beam of 118 feet, the *Bismarck* was relatively wide in comparison with her length, which increased her value as a gun platform.[1] Placed under the command of Captain Ernst Lindemann, the *Bismarck* was armed with eight 15-inch guns in four twin turrets, two of which ('Anton' and 'Bruno') were mounted forward, while the remaining two ('Caesar' and 'Dora') were mounted aft. Unlike on other warships, the gun turrets of the *Bismarck* were not fixed into position, rather such was their weight that gravity alone kept them in place. The guns had a maximum firing range of 22 miles. The *Bismarck* also carried a formidable secondary armament in the form of twelve 6-inch guns housed in six turrets that were evenly divided on either side of the ship. The ship was equipped with 12.6-inch-thick belt armour and up to 14 inches of armour on her main battery turrets. The *Bismarck* had a maximum speed of 30 knots, a maximum range of 8,870 nautical miles, and a complement of 103 officers and 1,962 other ranks. For reconnaissance, the spotting of shot and liaising with friendly aircraft, the *Bismarck* was equipped with four Arado Ar 196 aircraft, which in addition to their reconnaissance role, could also be utilised as light fighters.[2] Thus, the *Bismarck* was a very formidable weapon of war and was a ship that struck fear into the heart of the British Admiralty. A further headache for the Admiralty was the fact that the *Bismarck* had a sister ship under construction—the *Tirpitz*.

The *Kriegsmarine* intended to send a powerful battle group comprised of the *Bismarck*, *Tirpitz*, *Scharnhorst*, and *Gneisenau* into the Atlantic to attack Allied shipping. However, the *Scharnhorst* and the *Gneisenau* were tied up in the French port of Brest and had been since the conclusion of Operation Berlin. Furthermore, the *Scharnhorst* was in dry dock undergoing machinery and repairs to damage she had sustained as a result of nightly RAF raids on the port to destroy the ships. As such, she was unserviceable until June at the earliest. The *Gneisenau* had also sustained damage thanks to the efforts of RAF Bomber Command and was also undergoing repair work. The *Tirpitz*, meanwhile, had yet to undertake her sea trials, meaning that it was highly unlikely that she would be ready for the spring when the *Kriegsmarine* intended to launch its newest sortie into the Atlantic.[3] Even with the *Scharnhorst* and the *Tirpitz* not ready for operations, it was decided that a sortie should still be undertaken against Allied shipping in the Atlantic.

Under the codename Operation Rheinübung, it was decided that the *Bismarck* would put to sea accompanied by the heavy cruiser *Prinz Eugen*. Larger than contemporary heavy cruisers in service with the Royal Navy, the *Prinz Eugen* was an Admiral Hipper-class cruiser. Laid down on 23 April 1936, launched on 22 August 1938, and commissioned on 1 August 1940, the *Prinz Eugen* displaced 19,050 tons at full load and was 697.2 feet long. Capable of 32 knots, the ship was armed with eight 8-inch guns in four twin turrets arranged forward and aft.

Under the command of Admiral Lütjens, Operation Rheinübung envisaged the *Bismarck* and the *Prinz Eugen* breaking out into the Atlantic via either the Denmark Strait, the Iceland–Faroes Gap, the Shetland–Faroes Gap, or the Shetland–Orkneys Gap where they would begin preying on merchant convoys. In particular, according to the orders issued to Lütjens by Grand Admiral Eric Raeder, the objective of the *Bismarck* was not to defeat enemies of equal strength but to tie down Allies escort vessels while preserving her combat capability in order to allow the *Prinz Eugen* to ravage enemy convoys. Raeder went on to order that, 'The primary target in this operation is the enemy's merchant shipping; enemy warships will be engaged only when that objective makes it necessary and it can be done without excessive risk'.[4] To support and provide the raiders with the facilities to refuel and to take on provisions, a network of tankers and supply vessels were dispatched to the operational area. In total, seven tankers and two supply vessels were sent as far afield as Cape Verde in the south and Labrador, Canada, in the west.

Lütjens requested that that Rheinübung be delayed long enough for either the *Scharnhorst* or the *Gneisenau* to have their repairs completed and be made combat worthy for a rendezvous or for the *Tirpitz* to complete her sea trials so as to be able to accompany them on the sortie. In spite of the request by Lütjens, Raeder refused and ordered the operation to go ahead as planned.

The principal force tasked with meeting the threat posed by German surface raiders in the North Sea and North Atlantic was the Royal Navy's Home Fleet under the command of Admiral Sir John Tovey, which was based at Scapa Flow in the Orkney Islands. In order to prevent the breakout of the *Bismarck*, and indeed any German surface raiders into the Atlantic, Tovey was authorised to use all of the forces at his disposal, including numerous destroyers and cruisers plus several capital ships, such as the King George V-class battleships *King George V* and *Prince of Wales* (which were the most modern battleships in the Royal Navy); the battlecruisers *Hood* and *Repulse*; and the aircraft carrier *Victorious*. It is worth briefly noting that at the time, the *Repulse* and the *Victorious* were not assigned to the Home Fleet, having been detailed to provide an escort to convoy WS-8B as it sailed to the Mediterranean. With the threat from the *Bismarck* present, however, the *Victorious* at Scapa Flow and the *Repulse* on the River Clyde were ordered off escort duty by the Admiralty and placed at Tovey's disposal.

During the second week of May 1941, British suspicions regarding likely German actions were aroused. The British observed an increase in the number of German aerial reconnaissance flights that were undertaken between Greenland and Jan Mayen Island. To the British, it appeared highly probable that the reconnaissance flights were being undertaken in order to ascertain the current limits of the pack ice in the region. However, exactly why the Germans wanted this intelligence was unknown to the British. There were two possibilities as to why the Germans were studying the limits of the pack ice: it was possible that they were planning raids against Jan Mayen Island or Iceland, or that these reconnaissance flights were a precursor to a breakout into the Atlantic by German surface raiders. Whatever the Germans were planning to do—be it a raid against Iceland or a breakout attempt into the Atlantic using surface vessels—the action would form part of a growing list of British military crises.

On 14 May, Admiral Tovey sent out a request to the British flag officer in Iceland for a report on the prevailing ice conditions as well as for an assessment of the motive behind the German reconnaissance flights; the flag officer in Iceland reported that, in his opinion, the flights were being undertaken because the Germans were likely planning a breakout into the Atlantic. Meanwhile, Admiral Lütjens and his staff embarked upon the *Bismarck* and began to execute a number of exercises with the *Prinz Eugen*. During one exercise, the *Bismarck* suffered a minor technical malfunction, meaning that the departure of the two German warships was postponed while repairs were undertaken. Finally, on 16 May, Admiral Lütjens informed the *Kriegsmarine* High Command that both the *Prinz Eugen* and the *Bismarck* were ready for action. Therefore, the date for the commencement of Operation Rheinübung was set for 18 May.[5]

During the morning of 18 May, Lütjens inspected the *Prinz Eugen* at Gotenhafen before holding a commanders' conference on board the *Bismarck*. At the conference, Lütjens finally revealed the details of Operation Rheinübung to both Lindemann and *Kapitän zur See* Helmuth Brinkmann of the *Prinz Eugen*. At 11.30 a.m., Operation Rheinübung officially began. Both the *Bismarck* and the *Prinz Eugen* left their berths at Gotenhafen to anchor at the roadstead where they took on supplies. While there, the *Bismarck* began taking on fuel. However, during the refuelling operation, a fuel line was ruptured with the result that the *Bismarck*'s tanks could not be brimmed to their full capacity, leaving her approximately 200 tons light of her full fuel capacity.

During the course of the afternoon, the *Bismarck* left the roadstead to conduct a brief exercise in the Baltic before returning to the roadstead. At 9.18 p.m., *Prinz Eugen* weighed anchor and departed Gotenhafen, sailing west. She was followed at 2 a.m. on 19 May by the *Bismarck*, which immediately set a course for Danish waters. The two ships rendezvoused off Rügen Island at around 11.25 a.m. before Lindemann broadcast to the crew of the *Bismarck* that they were to venture out into the North Atlantic on a commerce raiding operation. Escorted by a handful of destroyers, the *Bismarck* and the *Prinz Eugen* approached the Green Belt at 10.34 p.m. before continuing on into the Kattegat with the German-occupied Danish Peninsula on one side and neutral Sweden on the other, which was reached the following morning.

Despite being neutral, Swedish sympathies lay with the Allies. Lütjens was worried that any of the Danish or Swedish fishing vessels might report seeing the German battle group and alert the British to a German operation. It was at noon on 20 May when Lütjens knew for certain that the presence of his two ships at sea would be brought to the attention of the British as the Germans encountered the Swedish seaplane cruiser HSwMS *Gotland*. With this encounter, Lütjens knew for certain that the sighting of a battleship accompanied by a heavy cruiser heading out towards the North Sea would be radioed to Stockholm and would eventually be passed on to the British. By evening, the British Embassy in Stockholm had been informed of the sighting of the German ships, and in London, the Admiralty was subsequently notified. Meanwhile, the *Bismarck* and the *Prinz Eugen* had ventured out into the rough waters of the North Sea.[6] In London, the Admiralty passed on the information that a battleship accompanied by a heavy cruiser had been sighted venturing out towards the North Sea to Admiral Tovey at Scapa Flow.

Interception

The German ships continued north during 20 May, and on 21 May, the *Bismarck* and the *Prinz Eugen* reached Bergen, Norway. At 11 a.m., the *Bismarck* dropped anchor 200 yards from shore in Grimstadfjord, a small inlet of the Korsfjord located just to the south of Bergen, while the *Prinz Eugen*, accompanied by three destroyers, anchored slightly further to the north in Kalvanes Bay. As a measure of precaution, two merchant ships were laid along both sides of the *Prinz Eugen*. The two merchant vessels were intended to act as torpedo shields and protect the heavy cruiser.[1] As the *Bismarck* was dropping anchor in Grimstadfjord, at the request of the Admiralty, RAF Coastal Command began scouring the Norwegian fjords between Stavanger and Bergen for the reported German warships.

On the morning of 21 May, two Supermarine Spitfires of the photographic reconnaissance unit took off from the airfield at Wick on the north-east coast of Scotland and flew across the North Sea to scour the coastline and fjords of Norway for the German ships. Flying Officer Greenhill was instructed to cover southern Norway up to Oslo while Pilot Officer Michael Suckling had been detailed to fly over south-western Norway down as far as Bergen. At 1.15 p.m., near Bergen, Suckling winged over Korsfjord and sighted what he believed to be a cruiser in Grimstadfjord while another cruiser appeared to be at anchor in Kalvanes Bay. From an altitude of 26,200 feet, Suckling photographed the German ships in the fjord system below before returning to Scotland, where he touched down at Wick at around 2.15 p.m. No sooner had Suckling come to a stop than a technician met his aircraft and began to remove the cameras to develop the photographs.[2] Once developed, the photographs were passed to a team of photographic interpreters who confirmed that anchored in Korsfjord were an unidentified Admiral Hipper-class heavy cruiser and a Bismarck-class battleship. Norwegian resistance had also reported spotting the German battle group heading north as it sailed towards Bergen.

These reports, coupled with the report from the *Gotland* were unfortunate for the *Kriegsmarine*.

During their stay in Bergen, both the *Bismarck* and the *Prinz Eugen* had their Baltic camouflage painted over with outboard grey. While at anchor, the *Prinz Eugen* took the opportunity to replenish her fuel, but for reasons unknown, the opportunity was not taken to refuel the *Bismarck*. By 5 p.m. on 21 May, the *Prinz Eugen*'s fuel had been replenished, and at 7.30 p.m., the German ships weighed anchor. It was at this time that an intelligence report from Germany was passed Lütjens and Lindemann on the bridge of the *Bismarck* alerting them to an intercepted British radio message stating that British aircraft had been instructed to be on alert for a battleship and a heavy cruiser accompanied by three destroyers proceeding on a northerly course.

Shortly before nightfall, at 8 p.m., Lütjens made the decision to take his ships out of Norwegian waters and attempt to break-out into the Atlantic under the cover of fog that had rolled in and blanketed the coast. Lütjens favoured the route through the Denmark Strait and so decided that it would be this route that he and his ships would take.

Meanwhile, back in Scapa Flow, Admiral Tovey was considering the best means of covering a break out attempt by the German vessels. On 18 May, Tovey had sent out an order to the heavy cruiser HMS *Suffolk*, which was on patrol in the Denmark Strait to keep a vigilant watch on the passage close to the ice pack. On 19 May, the sister ship of the *Suffolk*, HMS *Norfolk* (which was flying the flag of Rear-Admiral Frederic Wake-Walker, the commanding officer of the First Cruiser Squadron), was ordered to proceed from Hvalfjord, Iceland, to relieve the *Suffolk*, which was to return to Hvalfjord to refuel before resuming her patrol of the Denmark Strait. Tovey was fully aware that the most likely route that the German vessels would take into the Atlantic would be either through the Denmark Strait or the Iceland-Shetland Gap, which were the safest routes being farthest away from the airbases of the RAF and from Scapa Flow.

When news of the sighting of the German ships reached the British, it was passed on to Churchill who had embarked upon a week's stay at the prime minister's country retreat, Chequers, with his wife Clementine, his daughter Sarah, her husband Vic Oliver, and Major General Hastings 'Pug' Ismay, who was Churchill's chief of staff as the Minister of Defence. Churchill had also invited President Franklin D. Roosevelt's special representative, Averell Harriman, to spend the week. Before dinner on the Tuesday night (20 May), Churchill pondered through a stream of unwelcome reports on the German operation to seize Crete when news of the sighting of *Bismarck* reached him. The detection of the *Bismarck* raised his hopes that better tidings might be on the cards for the British.[3]

Based on the assumption that the German ships were to attempt a breakout into the Atlantic, Tovey issued orders to the ships at his disposal, sending them to cover all possible routes into the Atlantic. The *Suffolk*, which was by now refuelling in Hvalfjord, was ordered to delay her sailing to rejoin the *Norfolk* in order to coincide with the earliest possible time of arrival of the German ships in the Denmark Strait. HMS *Arethusa* (a 6-inch gun cruiser, which was on her way to Iceland) was ordered to remain at Hvalfjord at the disposal of Vice-Admiral Wake-Walker. The light cruisers *Birmingham* and *Manchester*, which were patrolling the Iceland–Faroes Gap, were ordered to make for Skaalefjord to replenish their fuel stocks before resuming their patrols. When issuing orders to the various ships at his disposal, Tovey sent out a variety of signals, including one to HMS *Hood* that read, 'Raise steam with all dispatch and be prepared to leave harbour 00.01 on May 22'.[4]

HMS *Hood* was a 15-inch gun battlecruiser and the pride of the Royal Navy. Launched in 1918 and commissioned two years later, the *Hood* was the only ship of her class and was considered well-built for her day. At 860 feet long, she had been capable of 32 knots and held the distinction of being the largest ship in the world. Having entered service too late to see action in the First World War, the pinnacle of British naval power spent the inter-war years on good-will missions, 'showing the flag', and representing Great Britain around the world as the flagship of the Royal Navy's battlecruiser squadron. In 1923, the *Hood* had been accompanied by the Renown-class battlecruiser HMS *Repulse* on an eleven-month world cruise. Having seen service with both the Royal Navy's Mediterranean and Atlantic fleets, the commencement of hostilities in 1939 found the *Hood* assigned to the Home Fleet before forming part of Force 'H' in the Mediterranean. Following the attack on Mers-el-Kébir, the *Hood* returned to Britain to bolster the Royal Navy's Home Fleet. By 1941, however, the *Hood* was an aged battlecruiser; her design had sacrificed protection for speed. She had adequate protection in some key areas but not over all of her vital areas. Due to her machinery, she was filled with large, open spaces. Through various minor refits (which included adding further armour plating) and years of service, her speed had been reduced to 27 knots. She was, however, in dire need of a major refit and overhaul. Unfortunately, the nature of the war meant she could not be spared from service for long enough to undergo the refit that she needed.

The eight 15-inch guns of the *Hood* were deadly, capable of firing a shell weighing 1,920 pounds (870 kg) a distance of 17.14 miles. Although the *Hood* suffered from outdated gunnery systems, she did boast modern radar equipment, but her crew had not had time to become proficient in its use. On 12 May 1941, Vice-Admiral Lancelot Holland had been appointed the commanding officer of the Battlecruiser Squadron and commenced flying his flag from the *Hood*.

Under Tovey's orders, the *Hood*, accompanied by the newly commissioned battleship *Prince of Wales* and six destroyers were to sail to Hvalfjord where they would be in a position cover both the Denmark Strait and the Iceland–Faroes Gap.

HMS *Prince of Wales* was a King George V-class battleship. Equipped with ten 14-inch guns and capable of 28 knots, she had been launched on 3 May 1939 and commissioned on 19 January 1941. During the spring of 1941, when contemplating how the Royal Navy might contain the threat posed by the *Bismarck*, Churchill continued to view the King George V-class of battleships with dismay. This was a view that Churchill had held since before the war. Chiefly, Churchill believed the King George V-class to be 'gravely undergunned'. Churchill criticised this choice of calibre because 14-inch was smaller than the calibre being fitted to American and Japanese battleships, which were 16-inch and 18-inch respectively. Even the Queen Elizabeth-class (which Churchill had helped to develop as first lord of the Admiralty before the First World War) packed the punch of 15-inch guns. Churchill overcame his initial reservations when he learned that the King George V-class were to be equipped with twelve 14-inch guns, which he believed gave the ships a weighty punch and offset their smaller calibre. However, the ships were redesigned to mount only ten 14-inch guns. In August 1936, Churchill wrote to the then First Lord of the Admiralty, Sir Samuel Hoare, and stated, 'It is terrible deliberately to build British battleships costing £7,000,000 apiece that are not the strongest in the world'. The Admiralty, meanwhile, maintained that even if the punch packed was not as weighty as 15- or even 16-inch guns, ten 14-inch guns, more numerous than eight 15- or nine 16-inch guns, had a faster rate of fire and that their superior velocity and range would give them a longer reach and greater penetrative power. Churchill was still not convinced.[5]

Despite being described as a happy ship by her crew, the *Prince of Wales*, fresh out of the shipyard, had a reputation as an unlucky ship and was not ready for action. Built by Cammell Laird and Company Ltd at Birkenhead on the River Mersey, a dockyard worker had been killed on the slipway when she was launched and the ship had suffered a near miss during a Luftwaffe raid on the dockyard. Firing trials had highlighted issues with the ship's main battery. Her commanding officer, Captain John Leach, was aware that further malfunctions were possible, and that the current issues had not been fully rectified. Her hydraulic systems leaked so badly that some of her gun crews were forced to dress in oilskins. So it was that the *Prince of Wales* put to sea alongside the *Hood* with technicians from Vickers-Armstrong still aboard.

While various ships of the Home Fleet were mobilising, Tovey decided that it would be best if he and his flagship, HMS *King George V*, remained at Scapa Flow until the situation became clearer lest he be forced to put into a friendly port to refuel at a critical moment. Remaining there with the *King George V* were the light cruisers *Aurora*, *Galatea*, *Kenya*, and *Neptune*, plus the destroyers *Active*, *Nestor*, and *Punjabi*.

So it was that at 11.56 p.m. on 21 May 1941 that the *Hood*, flying the flag of Vice-Admiral Holland, and the *Prince of Wales* weighed anchor before departing Scapa Flow at midnight. Scapa Flow's Hoxa Gate was cleared at 12.50 a.m. on 22 May, and shortly thereafter, the six accompanying destroyers were divided into their divisions to screen the two capital ships.

At 4.20 a.m. on 22 May, the destroyers escorting the *Bismarck* and the *Prinz Eugen* were detached and set a course towards the port of Trondheim while the *Bismarck* and the *Prinz Eugen* continued on their northerly course at a steady 24 knots. At 12.37 p.m., alarms rang out aboard both German ships following reports of a submarine sighting and then again shortly afterwards following reports of aircraft sightings. These sightings caused the German ships to zig-zag for around half an hour before the alarms were cancelled and a reduced state of alert was resumed. When the alarms ended, the tops of both the main and secondary battery turrets on both the *Bismarck* and the *Prinz Eugen* were painted over while the swastikas (located on their decks fore and aft) were covered over with canvas in order to make it more difficult for the ships to be identified by hostile aircraft. Meanwhile, the weather remained favourable to the German battle group, cloaking them from prying eyes. Such was the thickness of the fog that enveloped the ships that at times they were forced to use their searchlights in order to maintain contact with one another and to maintain position.[6]

While the *Bismarck* and the *Prinz Eugen* had left Norway and were sailing through thick fog on their way to the Denmark Strait, the *Hood* and *the Prince of Wales* had commenced zig-zagging for anti-submarine purposes before resuming a heading that would take them to Iceland. During the course of the morning of 22 May, Holland informed Captain Ralph Kerr of the *Hood*, Captain Leach of the *Prince of Wales*, and the commanding officers of the destroyers of the gunnery policy that he wanted should they come into contact with the German ships: 'If the enemy is encountered and concentration of fire is required, the policy will be G.I.C. (Individual Ship Control); if ships are spread when enemy is met they are to be prepared to flank mark as described in H.W.C.O.'

Due to the implementation of radio silence, this order was never transmitted to the *Norfolk*, the *Suffolk*, nor to any of the other cruisers that were on patrol. Range and inclination exercises were carried out aboard the British ships until 1.07 p.m., when they commenced zig-zagging once again. The *Prince of Wales* and the *Hood* would continue to zig-zag until 6.55 p.m., when they resumed a more direct course.

During the course of 22 May, at the request of Tovey and the Admiralty, the RAF undertook extensive reconnaissance sorties of the Norwegian coast from Trondheim to Kristiansand while aircraft of Bomber Command flew to Bergen in an attempt to bomb the *Bismarck* and the *Prinz Eugen* as they lay at anchor. Due to the poor weather, only two of the eighteen aircraft dispatched by Bomber Command succeeded in locating Grimstadfjord. With no additional information forthcoming from the RAF, Tovey was forced to assume the worst-case scenario—that the German vessels had weighed anchor and put to sea towards the Atlantic.

Not knowing whether or not the German ships had put to sea, at 11 p.m., flying his flag in the *King George V*, Tovey departed Scapa Flow accompanied by HMS *Victorious*, five cruisers, and six destroyers. At the same time, HMS *Repulse* was ordered to raise steam and to sail from the Clyde to join Tovey's force. With the departure of Tovey and the bulk of the Home Fleet from Scapa Flow, two groups of Royal Navy capital ships were converging on the seas around Iceland with the ships under the command of Holland a day's sailing ahead of those under Tovey's command. Beyond the Arctic Circle, as the *Bismarck* and the *Prinz Eugen* continued on towards the Denmark Strait, owing to a lack of updated intelligence, Lütjens remained under the illusion that the Home Fleet was still at anchor.[7]

At midnight, 23 May, the *Bismarck* and the *Prinz Eugen* executed a south-west turn that would take them through the Denmark Strait. At around this time, an increase in speed was ordered aboard the German ships from 24 to 27 knots in an attempt to ensure that the transit through the Denmark Strait and break-out into the Atlantic was achieved before the favourable weather changed. Unfortunately for the German commanders, the weather was changing; by the afternoon of 23 May, the fog that had cloaked the German ships and had served to shield them from the prying eyes of RAF patrols was beginning to lift and visibility increased to approximately 10 miles. The Germans were aware from intelligence sources that the British had laid minefields off the north-west coast of Greenland, making the somewhat already tricky navigation of the Denmark Strait more difficult. During the afternoon of 23 May, the two ships continued to transit the strait. Meanwhile, HMS *Suffolk* had returned to the Denmark Strait where she made contact with HMS *Norfolk*. Wake-Walker could now put the ships immediately under his command to effective use in a patrol of the strait. The role of the cruisers was to locate the two German ships and to maintain contact with them while guiding in the heavier elements of the Home Fleet. There was no question of Wake-Walker engaging the German ships for his cruisers were unquestionably outgunned. The *Norfolk* and the *Suffolk* would patrol down the Denmark Strait in a south-east direction and would then reverse their course to the north-west. This patrol would continue until either the German ships were sighted or enough time had elapsed to ensure that the German vessels were not making a breakout attempt into the Atlantic via this route.

Both cruisers were fitted with radar equipment, but that which equipped the *Suffolk* was far superior to that which equipped HMS *Norfolk*. While the *Norfolk* was equipped with a radar system that allowed her to see ahead, the *Suffolk* was equipped with multi-directional radar, which had a range of 13 miles. The *Suffolk*'s radar allowed her to sweep all directions with the exception of a blind spot at her stern. It was for this reason that it was decided that the *Suffolk* would patrol the Greenland side of the Strait while the *Norfolk* patrolled from the Icelandic side. The *Suffolk* would keep the pack ice at the limit of her radar, which would allow her room for manoeuvre should the *Bismarck* and the *Prinz Eugen* be sighted. Protection was further enhanced by the foggy conditions. The weather was clear over Greenland and the pack ice, but a bank of fog was clinging to the Icelandic coast. This fog would provide a blanket of protection into which the British cruisers could slip should the German ships be sighted.

At 6.11 p.m., the radar on the *Bismarck* picked up two objects to starboard. Alarms were sounded, causing the crews of the German vessels to rush to their respective action stations. It was soon realised that the objects that had been picked up on radar were far from enemy ships, but icebergs. In the meantime, the Germans had reached the limit of the ice pack and had set a course that would take them through the Strait.

Meanwhile, the *Suffolk* completed the north-east leg of her patrol up the strait and, following hugging the icecap on the way up, reversed course at 7 p.m., and began the south-west leg of her patrol close to the edge of the fog bank. At 7.22 p.m., Able Seaman Alfred Newell, who was on duty at the starboard lookout position in order to cover the blind spot not covered by the *Suffolk*'s radar, was scanning the horizon when out of the mist, at a range of 7 miles, approached the *Bismarck* and the *Prinz Eugen*. A sighting report was swiftly called out. The reaction aboard the *Suffolk* was swift as the ship heeled over in order to seek the cover of the fog bank.

Those aboard the *Suffolk* were encouraged by the fact that the neither the *Bismarck* nor the *Prinz Eugen* had opened fire. In fact, the radar and hydrophones of the German vessels had detected the presence of a vessel off the port bow before the *Suffolk* sighted the German squadron. A brief glimpse of a ship was had by lookouts stationed aboard the German ships, it being noted that the vessel had three funnels and a large superstructure meaning that it was likely a British cruiser.

An initial signal was transmitted from the *Suffolk* stating that contact with the German vessels had been established. The wireless equipment on the *Suffolk* was, however, suffering from damp and the contact report got no further than HMS *Norfolk* which was 15 miles further down the Denmark Strait. The sighting report was also picked up aboard the *Bismarck*, which prompted Lütjens to transmit a brief signal to Group North advising them that his ships had been sighted and reported by a British cruiser.

Upon picking up the report, the *Norfolk* steered to take up a position on the edge of the fog bank to assist in the maintaining of contact with the

German vessels. Meanwhile, as the *Norfolk* sailed northwards to assist with the shadowing operation that would now commence, the *Suffolk* sought the cover of the fog bank and waited for the *Bismarck* and the *Prinz Eugen* to pass before leaving the fog shield to take up a shadowing position behind the German ships. The initial sighting report from the *Suffolk* was followed by a succession of reports from the cruiser transmitted periodically detailing the speed, course, and position of the German ships.

At 8.30 p.m., the *Norfolk* strayed too close to the edge of the fog bank, which resulted in a loss over cover, albeit briefly. The *Norfolk* was sighted aboard the *Bismarck*, which opened fire immediately. The *Bismarck* fired five salvos, three of which straddled the British cruiser throwing splinters aboard. Although not hit by a direct impact, the *Norfolk* launched a smokescreen and hastily retired into the fog. This was the first time that the new, mighty German battleship had fired her guns in anger, and it served as a deadly warning to the British of the accuracy of the *Bismarck*'s guns.[8] Following retreating into the fog, HMS *Norfolk* transmitted her own contact report. Like the *Suffolk* before her, the *Norfolk* sought the cover provided by the fog bank until the German ships had passed before sailing out of the bank and taking up a shadowing position. With the *Suffolk* off the starboard quarter of the German formation, the *Norfolk* took up a position off the port quarter. As the pack ice precluded the Germans from turning to starboard, the position of the British cruisers was ideal for shadowing the enemy vessels.

Aboard the *Bismarck*, there was a problem. The firing of the forward turrets during the one-sided engagement with the *Norfolk* had disabled the forward radar. As a result, the *Bismarck* was blind to what lay ahead of her. The *Prinz Eugen*'s radar was functioning effectively, so Lütjens ordered that the *Prinz Eugen* and the *Bismarck* exchange positions so that the heavy cruiser with her fully functioning radar could take the lead. The powerful guns of the *Bismarck* at the rear of the battle group would serve to prevent the British from sailing any closer. This change of position would later cause great confusion for the British.[9]

Aboard Tovey's and Holland's ships, tensions were high. The tension was further heightened by the report from the *Norfolk* at 8.30 p.m., which stated: 'One battleship, one cruiser in sight'. This was the first signal to reach Tovey of the position of the *Bismarck* following receiving the reconnaissance photographs showing the German vessels at anchor in Norway, and confirmed that the German ships had put to sea.[10] HMS *Hood* and the *Prince of Wales* were under 300 miles away from the German ships.

Aboard the *Hood*, when Vice-Admiral Holland received the sighting report from the *Norfolk*, he worked out the position of the two opposing forces on a chart. Looking at the chart, Holland realised that he was in a favourable position to bring about an engagement that evening. With the German ships sailing in a south-westerly direction, Holland's ships were sailing a north-westerly course on an interception course. Furthermore, Holland's ships were ahead of the German squadron and would reach an interception point around 2 a.m. Holland knew that despite their individual handicaps, the aged *Hood* and the untried *Prince of Wales* could take on the *Bismarck*, and that Vice-Admiral Wake-Walker's *Norfolk* and *Suffolk* were more than capable of engaging the *Prinz Eugen*. On paper, at least, it looked as though Holland would enjoy a superiority of both firepower and numbers over his German opponent.[11]

With that, Holland intended to intercept the German squadron and to cross their 'T', a manoeuvre that would have seen the *Hood* and the *Prince of Wales* in front of the German squadron and able to open fire with full broadsides while the *Bismarck* and the *Prinz Eugen*, sailing towards the British capital ships, would have been restricted to firing their forward armament only. Such a manoeuvre would have given the Holland a four to one advantage over the *Bismarck*. If the *Bismarck* altered course to bring her aft turrets to bear, the advantage would decrease to two to one, but at the same time, the Royal Navy would have the advantage of being able to concentrating their fire on one vessel while the German fire would be divided. It is worth noting here that Holland did not have to sink the *Bismarck*. There was every possibility that with the appearance of his ships, Holland could have caused Lütjens to reverse course back through the Denmark Strait to try again another day. If this occurred, the British would have achieved their objective of preventing the *Bismarck* from breaking out into the Atlantic.

By now, the weather was becoming worse. Holland's ships began to bump around in the rough seas as snow flurries began to whip into the ships. Those aboard the destroyers felt the worsening weather the most. The plight of the destroyers became apparent when the destroyer screen's senior officer, Commander Cecil Wakeford May of HMS *Electra*, sent a signal to Holland stating: 'Do not consider destroyers can maintain present speed without danger'.

At 8.55 p.m., Holland replied: 'If you are unable to maintain this speed I will have to go on without you. You should follow at your best speed'. The determination of the British destroyers was tremendous and for the next few hours their commanding officers attempted to keep up with the *Hood* and the *Prince of Wales*. The destroyers did well to keep up with the *Hood* and the *Prince of Wales* but took a tremendous battering in doing so.[12]

Meanwhile, Lütjens knew that British cruisers would have reported his position and it was likely that the bulk of the British Home Fleet would now leave Scapa Flow. Lütjens could have decided to reverse course and head further north where he could have replenished fuel from a German tanker on station in the Arctic Circle, forcing the British fleet to waste fuel as he had done when he commanded the *Scharnhorst* and the *Gneisenau* a year earlier. This time, however, Lütjens planned to take a different course of action.

Lütjens planned to continue on towards the Atlantic with the hope of shaking off the British cruisers during the night. Lütjens was blissfully unaware of the approach of Holland's force.

At 10.30 p.m., the crews of the *Hood*, the *Prince of Wales*, and the destroyers, which had now dropped astern, were given the order to 'darken ship'. By 12.15 a.m. on 24 May, the crews of the British ships had been ordered to action stations and the battle ensigns had been hoisted.[13] Around this time, in an attempt to drive off the shadowing *Norfolk* and *Suffolk*, Lütjens used the cover of a rain squall to order the *Bismarck* to reverse course in an effort to catch the cruisers by surprise. The *Suffolk* detected the manoeuvre with her radar and merely withdrew in good time into the shelter provided by a fog bank as the German battleship approached before she resumed her original heading. The *Suffolk*'s commanding officer, Captain Robert M. Ellis, had been fully justified in ordering the course of the *Suffolk* to be altered so as to stay out of range of the *Bismarck*'s guns, but a problem befell the British. By the time they realised that the *Bismarck* had resumed her original course, and the *Suffolk* had returned to her original bearing, the German battle group had disappeared into a snowstorm. Attempts were made aboard the *Suffolk* to maintain contact with the German ships using radar, but in the circumstances, maintaining contact proved to be impossible. As it was, it was shortly after midnight on 24 May when a signal was transmitted from the *Suffolk* reporting that she had lost contact with the German ships.

Aboard the *Hood*, Holland received the news of the loss of contact in his usual reserved, calm fashion; he knew that the worst possible scenario, as far as the British were concerned, was for the *Bismarck* and the *Prinz Eugen* to successfully break out into the Atlantic. To Holland, the best course of action seemed to be to close the distance between his ships and the last known position of the German battle group as quickly as possible. As such, he ordered changes of course northwards in order to close the distance to the last reported position of the German ships. Fortunately for the British, at 2.47 a.m., the *Suffolk* regained radar contact with the German ships. Her subsequent reports placed the *Prinz Eugen* and the *Bismarck* approximately 35 miles to the north-west of the *Hood* and the *Prince of Wales*.

While they had been out of radar contact, the *Prinz Eugen* and the *Bismarck* had actually maintained their original course. Holland's change of course had, therefore, been for nothing. It would appear that Lütjens wanted to keep a wide berth between his ships and any additional British warships that might approach his squadron from the east. Therefore, as a counter against the appearance of additional British ships, Lütjens maintained a course of 22 degrees parallel to the coast of Greenland as this provided him with a limited space to manoeuvre to the west if heavy units of the Royal Navy appeared.

3

'She's Blowing Up!'

The loss of contact with the German squadron had left Holland's plans for the engagement in ruins. The turn that was made to the north to close with the expected position of the German ships had cost precious time and had caused the opportunity of being able to cross the 'T' of the German vessels to be lost. At the same time, however, Holland did still hold a slight advantage over the Germans, and he still held the element of surprise.

With contact having been regained, Holland did not want to engage in the darkest part of the arctic night. As such, at 3.21 a.m., Holland ordered the *Hood* and the *Prince of Wales* to take up a course of 240 degrees, which would permit an engagement at dawn. In order to help ensure that a dawn engagement occurred, at 3.53 a.m., speed was increased from 27 to 28 knots.

One of the most remarkable facts surrounding the Battle of the Denmark Strait is how in the dark Lütjens actually was with regards intelligence. While he was aware that the sighting of his ships in the Kattegat by the *Gotland* would likely have been leaked to the British; that the shadowing *Norfolk* and *Suffolk* would be keeping the Admiralty in London updated on his position; and that, subsequently, the ships of the Home Fleet would be mustered against his ships, Lütjens was not aware of how little a head start he actually had. He was not aware that his ships had been photographed as they lay at anchor near Bergen by RAF Coastal Command and that the departure of his ships had been noted. Further to this, Lütjens—while he knew that the Home Fleet would be mustered against his ships—did not know the whereabouts of the Home Fleet. The last intelligence report that he had received stated that it was still sitting idle at Scapa Flow.

Aboard the *Prinz Eugen*, at 4.07 a.m., the crew members manning the ship's hydrophones picked up the distinct sound of propellers on the port side. The detection of the propellers was immediately relayed to Admiral Lütjens aboard the *Bismarck*.[1] At 4.50 a.m., the *Prince of Wales* took guide of the squadron, positioning herself ahead of the *Hood* before the flagship retook the guide at 5.05 a.m.

Meanwhile, the *Prinz Eugen* and the *Bismarck* continued to make steady progress through the Denmark Strait. Aboard the *Hood* and the *Prince of Wales*, the crews were ordered to a heightened state of readiness. Everyone expected contact to be made with the German ships—it was just a question of when. As the hours had slipped by, the sky had begun to brighten as dawn neared. The command crews trained their binoculars and strained their eyes to the north where they expected the German vessels to approach from.[2]

As the sky to the east began to brighten with the coming of dawn, from on board the *Bismarck* and the *Prinz Eugen*, thin plumes of smoke could be seen on the horizon. Lookouts strained, with their eyes fixated on the smoke, to see if they could identify the source. At 5.21 a.m., a turn to port was executed taking the German ships on to a new heading of 170 degrees, which was held for approximately ten minutes before the original heading of 220 degrees was taken up once more. This manoeuvre served to provide the *Prinz Eugen* and the *Bismarck*, which had been hugging the coast of Greenland additional space to manoeuvre. Shortly after the first turn was executed, the upper portions of the superstructures of the mystery vessels could be seen, identifying the unknown vessels as British warships.

At 5.37 a.m., lookouts aboard the *Hood* spotted smoke off the starboard beam on the horizon. A small black speck began to appear below the smoke. It was at once realised that it had to be the *Bismarck*. The guns of the British ships were traversed and trained on the target on the horizon while the gunnery officers worked out the range to the target. The range was 30,000 yards (17 miles), beyond the effective gunnery range of both the *Hood* and the *Prince of Wales*. It was now just a case of waiting until the range decreased sufficiently in order to open fire.[3] Vice-Admiral Holland was aware that the *Hood* was particularly vulnerable to plunging fire due to her weak deck armour. As such, Holland ordered a turn to be executed towards the German ships in order to close the range faster, and to lower the risk to his flagship of being struck by plunging fire.

Having not received any additional or new intelligence regarding the dispositions of the Home Fleet, Lütjens could only speculate as to the identity of the warships, which were still not completely in view and which therefore could not be positively identified. With the Home Fleet still believed to be at Scapa Flow, there was no reason to believe that any elements of the Fleet had weighed anchor. It was therefore difficult to conceive that either or both of the sighted vessels might be capital ships.

If the ships were capital ships, a number of possibilities existed. If they were older British battleships such as HMS *Nelson*, the *Rodney*, or those of the Queen Elizabeth-class then, owing to their slower speed, the *Bismarck* and the

Prinz Eugen could outrun them. Another possibility was that the ships were battlecruisers. The Royal Navy possessed three battlecruisers—the *Hood*, *Repulse,* and *Renown*. The *Renown* and the *Repulse* were smaller ships, displacing 26,500 tons, and were armed with six 15-inch guns. Both of these ships could cause trouble for the *Bismarck* by dividing her fire, but Lütjens believed that they could be easily put out of action by a more modern vessel like the *Bismarck*.

The third British battlecruiser was the *Hood*; widely respected by the *Kriegsmarine*, she was viewed as being of almost equivalent size to the *Bismarck* and was armed with an equivalent armament. The *Hood* in company with one of the smaller battlecruisers could pose a more formidable foe to the *Bismarck* than the two smaller battlecruiser together. All of the battlecruisers were, however, old and vulnerable.

Finally, the Royal Navy possessed two new battleships: HMS *King George V* and *Prince of Wales*. Theoretically comparable to the *Bismarck*, it was believed that the *Prince of Wales* was still undergoing her fitting-out work and that her crew were not fully trained. That left HMS *King George V* as the sole modern British battleship that was worked up and ready for service. From the point of view of Lütjens the worst-case scenario would see his ships pitted against the *King George V* and the *Hood*. The *King George V* was a modern warship with a well-trained crew. The B-Dienst team (naval monitoring service, civilian specialists who were employed by the *Kriegsmarine* and who were responsible for the interception and monitoring of enemy communications and for cracking any codes encountered) aboard the *Prinz Eugen* had also come to the erroneous conclusion that one of the shadowing vessels (HMS *Suffolk*) was HMS *King George V* as the radio call letters of the cruiser were K3G. While the *Hood* had been the largest warship in the world following the First World War, she had seen action already during the war with the result that her crew was battle-hardened and her crew should have been trained to the highest possible degree of proficiency, especially with regards gunnery, following two decades of practice.

Soon it was noticed that the British ships had altered course as if to intercept. With this apparent, the crews of the *Bismarck* and the *Prinz Eugen* were ordered to action stations. The British ships were identified as light cruisers before being reidentified as heavy cruisers, their sharp angle of approach making positive identification difficult. Correct identification of the enemy vessels was vital in order to select the correct ammunition. The first gunnery officer aboard the *Prinz Eugen, Kapitänleutnant* Paulus Jasper, believed the approaching British vessels to be heavy cruisers and, as such, ordered the loading of 8-inch high explosive shells. With the British vessels looking intent on an interception, Admiral Lütjens had no alternative but to accept battle.[4] When it became apparent that the British vessels looked set on an interception, Lütjens ordered the *Bismarck*, 3,000 yards astern of the *Prinz Eugen*, to increase speed to 30 knots. At that speed, she would overhaul the *Prinz Eugen*, which maintained a steady 27 knots.

By 5.37 a.m., the British could make out enough of the ships on the horizon to determine that they were in fact approaching the German battle group. With certainty that they were about to engage the German vessels, the *Prince of Wales* immediately began to transmit an enemy report. Translated from code, the report read:

> Emergency to Admiralty and C in C Home Fleet.
> One battleship and one heavy cruiser, bearing 335, distance 17 miles. My position 63-20 North, 31-50 West. My course 240. Speed 28 knots.[5]

While the *Prince of Wales* was transmitting her enemy report, Holland ordered both of his ships to execute a further 40-degree turn to starboard. This turn placed the *Bismarck* and the *Prinz Eugen* off their starboard bow. The British warships were sailing at 28 knots with the *Prince of Wales* around 800 yards (0.5 miles) behind the *Hood*. Rather than come out ahead of the German vessels as planned, Holland's ships had actually been on a divergent course with their enemy. This was due to a slight deviation in course the evening previous, and also due to a positional error in the regular reports from the *Suffolk* and the *Norfolk*. Realising that his original intentions were no longer viable, Holland decided to close the range to the German ships as quickly as possible, then to execute a turn at short range to open A-arcs.

In addition to this, he also decided to keep *Hood* and *Prince of Wales* in close formation for gunnery concentration purposes. This had the result of forcing both of Holland's ships to approach the German vessels at an acute angle, which masked their rear turrets. As things stood, Holland would be going into battle with only half of his main armament. In addition to this, the heavy sea spray posed a problem for the optical directors. The German ships, on the other hand, would be able to utilise their full complement of main guns, and their optical equipment, which was superior to that of the British, would suffer less from interference from sea spray as the wind would be on their disengaged sides.[6]

At 5.50 a.m., Holland ordered that both the *Hood* and the *Prince of Wales* were to concentrate their fire on the leading German ship, which he thought was the *Bismarck*. The logic behind both British ships concentrating their fire on a single enemy vessel was to avoid wasting time attempting to distinguish whose shells were falling around which target, thus enabling swifter gunnery adjustments. If both of the British ships concentrated on the *Bismarck*, they would have more or less the same corrections to make and, above all else, could concentrate on eliminating the ship that posed the biggest threat.

Unfortunately for Holland, and the British in general, the *Norfolk* and the *Suffolk*, which had continued to shadow the *Bismarck*, had not reported the switching of positions with the *Prinz Eugen*. At the range at which the British and German capital ships were converging, the *Bismarck* and the *Prinz Eugen* had very similar silhouettes. Also, the difference in size between the heavy cruiser and the battleship was negligible at such a great range. In short, the British gunnery officers and the British commanders were unable to distinguish between the two German ships.

Convention dictated that the *Bismarck* would be the lead vessel, where she was better positioned to protect the less well-armoured vessel. The range continued to close and the British gunners prepared to fire. Moments before opening fire, the gunnery officer aboard *Prince of Wales*, Lieutenant Commander Colin McMullen, noticed the mistake that was being made and identified *Bismarck* as being the second ship. The optics that equipped the modern British battleship were far superior to those which equipped the ageing battlecruiser, and so a clearer view was presented, making it easier to distinguish between the battleship and heavy cruiser, as such McMullen was able to see that the second ship was larger than the leading one. McMullen reported this revelation to Captain Leach, who subsequently faced something of a dilemma.

Leach trusted his gunnery officer, but he was under orders to engage the leading ship. It would take at least a minute for the calculations to be made that would enable the *Prince of Wales* to engage the new target. The stakes were high. Captain Leach made the decision to follow his gut instinct rather than his orders and ordered his gunnery officer to switch targets to the second German ship, the *Bismarck*. Unfortunately, this discovery was never radioed to HMS *Hood*, which continued to track the leading German vessel, the *Prinz Eugen*.[7]

Aboard the *Hood*, Vice-Admiral Holland realised his mistake and ordered that the ship switch target to the second vessel. A signal was transmitted to the *Prince of Wales* identifying the *Bismarck* as being the second German vessel. However, for reasons unknown, despite Holland's order, the *Hood* continued to track the *Prinz Eugen*.

By 5.52 a.m., the British ships were fully visible on the horizon to those aboard the *Bismarck* and the *Prinz Eugen*, but they still could not be identified owing to their angle of approach. This led to the ships to still be considered as cruisers, which it was presumed had likely been ordered to the area to assist with the shadowing operation.

Thirty seconds later, from a distance of around 25,330 yards, HMS *Hood* opened fire. Half a minute later, at 05.53, the *Prince of Wales* followed suit and fired her first salvo. The first salvo from the *Hood* landed near the *Prinz Eugen* but did not hit the heavy cruiser, while the *Prince of Wales*'s opening salvo was observed to come down around 1,500 yards over and aft of the *Bismarck*. This was down to incorrect estimates of the distance to the target during the initial sightings, and due to a misjudgement in the speed and course of the German battleship.

Aboard the *Prinz Eugen* and the *Bismarck*, having witnessed the salvos from the British vessels, the German sailors were subsequently shocked to learn that the approaching vessels were not merely cruisers, but major heavy units, capital ships—a King George V-class battleship, which they assumed to be HMS *King George V* herself as they believed that *Prince of Wales* was still being worked up, and even worse, the famed and feared battlecruiser HMS *Hood*. The legend and reputation of the *Hood* was great and she was highly respected by the *Kriegsmarine*. German sailors commented how the *Hood* was 'the terror of their war games'. When the identification of the British ships became clearer, that they were capital ships and not cruisers, Admiral Lütjens sent an urgent signal to *Kriegsmarine* headquarters, 'Am in a fight with two heavy units.'

Meanwhile, the *Hood* fired a second salvo at the *Prinz Eugen*, which, like the first, missed the target, throwing a few splinters and much water aboard the heavy cruiser.[8] Following firing her second salvo at the *Prinz Eugen*, the guns of the *Hood* were finally traversed around towards the *Bismarck*.

At the same time, following firing her first salvo at the *Bismarck*, the *Prince of Wales* began to suffer what would be the first of a number of mechanical problems. No. 1 gun of 'A' turret temporarily broke down, meaning it could no longer fire. Nevertheless, the *Prince of Wales* continued to fire at the *Bismarck*. However, her second, third and fourth salvos all overshot the *Bismarck* and landed harmlessly in the sea. While the British shells were landing close to their targets, the guns of both the *Prinz Eugen* and the *Bismarck* remained silent.

Aboard the *Bismarck*, her first gunnery officer, *Korvettenkapitän* Adalbert Schneider (who was stationed in the foretop command post), requested permission to open fire on the British ships several times. Schneider's requests went without reply from the bridge of the *Bismarck*. Following two minutes of British shelling without response, *Kapitän zur See* Lindemann had finally had enough. At 5.55 a.m., Lindemann reportedly turned to Lütjens and stated: 'I will not let my ship get shot from under my arse!' After this exchange, the order was given for the German ships to open fire. The *Bismarck* immediately opened fire and was swiftly followed by the *Prinz Eugen*. Both of the German vessels concentrated their fire on the leading British ship—the *Hood*. *Bismarck*'s first salvo landed short of the target, coming down in the sea in front and starboard of the British battlecruiser.

At 5.56 a.m., the *Prince of Wales*'s fifth salvo landed over the *Bismarck* and was swiftly followed by a sixth salvo that straddled and is likely to have hit the battleship, although no hits were observed from aboard the British battleship. In this time, the *Prinz Eugen* fired a further three salvos at the *Hood*. The *Bismarck* fired a second salvo, which landed directly between the two British capital ships. This was followed by a third salvo, which appeared to straddle the *Hood*.

At 5.57 a.m., the *Hood* was hit by a salvo of 8-inch armour-piercing shells from the *Prinz Eugen*. The *Hood* was hit near the base of the main mast on the port side of the shelter deck. The hits sustained resulted in a fire that proceeded to spread across a portion of the shelter deck to the port side main mast and aft of the superstructure. The fire did not reach the motor launches and lifeboats, but it did reach a number of ready-use ammunition lockers. There was a crazy cacophony of wild cries of 'fire' through the voice pipes and telephones to the bridge. The *Hood*'s torpedo officer rang the bridge and proclaimed, 'The four-inch ready-use ammunition is exploding'.

The shelter deck became hellish as anti-aircraft and 4-inch shells accompanied by 7-inch unrotated projectile rocket mines began to detonate. Those who could not take cover in time were either killed or wounded by the ensuing explosions. Captain Ralph Kerr ordered that while the shells and projectiles continued to explode, the gun crews were to take shelter and that the fire and damage control parties were to keep away from the area until all the ready-use ammunition had expended.[9] While the fire and exploding shells ran riot aboard the *Hood*'s shelter deck, the battle continued to rage.

The *Prince of Wales* scored a hit on the *Bismarck* just above the waterline; oil began to escape through the hole, leaving a broad trail of oil on the surface of the sea. Therefore, Lütjens ordered the *Prinz Eugen* to change targets from the *Hood* to the *Prince of Wales*. The *Prinz Eugen* would be engaging the *Prince of Wales* alongside the *Bismarck*'s secondary armament, which had just entered the battle. Aboard the *Prince of Wales*, all the guns that could be traversed were trained on the *Bismarck* while the *Hood* continued to land shells between the two German ships.

At 5.58 a.m., believing that he was likely to be out of the danger zone for plunging fire, Holland ordered that his ships execute a turn to port in an attempt to 'open A-arcs'. This turn allowed the *Prince of Wales* to open her A-arcs with her ninth salvo. The *Hood* also managed to loose off an A-arc salvo as her aft turrets were seen to fire. However, during the first moments of the turn to port, the *Bismarck* fired her fifth salvo, which straddled the *Hood*.

At least one of the *Bismarck*'s 15-inch shells penetrated the *Hood*'s weakly armoured deck around the area of the main mast. The shell smashed its way through the decks of the battlecruiser, where it reached an aft magazine before exploding. A second or two after entering the ship and exploding, a violent explosion rocked HMS *Hood*. There was a fierce upward rush of flame, and almost instantaneously, the mighty battlecruiser was enveloped from bow to stern in smoke. Large pieces of debris were thrown into the air.

Many men aboard the different ships witnessed the explosion. Burkard von Müllenheim-Rechberg recalled events as they appeared to him from his vantage point aboard *Bismarck*:

Convinced that the *Suffolk* and *Norfolk* would leave us in peace for at least a few minutes, I entrusted the temporary surveillance of the horizon astern through the starboard director to one of my petty officers and went to the port director. While I was still turning it toward the *Hood*, I heard a shout, 'She's blowing up!' 'She'—that could only be the *Hood*! The sight I then saw is something I shall never forget. At first the *Hood* was nowhere to be seen; in her place was a colossal pillar of black smoke reaching into the sky. Gradually, at the foot of the pillar, I made out the bow of the battle cruiser projecting upwards at an angle, a sure sign that she had broken in two.[10]

Aboard the *Prince of Wales*, Able Seaman William Usher witnessed the destruction of the *Hood*:

All amidships seemed to lift up into the air. After that the ship was surrounded by yellow smoke. The smoke seemed to clear away around the foc'sle a little bit and I noticed the ship seemed to be still going ahead. All along the upper deck it seemed to be bubbling up as if it was boiling. That was the foc'sle only, the deck of which seemed to be bubbling like an egg frying. Whilst this was going on the ship seemed to be slewing over to port. The smoke then covered the foc'sle. The next thing I saw was the quarter-deck come up into the air and I saw the screws. After that the quarter-deck disappeared and all I could see then was smoke.[11]

Royal Marine Sergeant Terrence Brooks of *Prince of Wales* commented:

There was an enormous flash which blinded me for a few moments. I took my eye away from the periscope. When I looked through my periscope again I was in time to see a black pall of smoke out of which I distinctly saw a 15" gun thrown through the air followed by what appeared to be the roof of a turret. Just before the *Hood* was hit the second time 'Y' turret trained on the foremost bearing starboard side and fired. I immediately depressed my periscope to look into the sea, I don't quite know why. All I could see were objects dropping into the water. When I elevated the periscope again we were slewing round what appeared to me to be part of the forecastle of the *Hood*. The remains of the *Hood* then passed out of my view.[12]

Chief Petty Officer William Westlake reported:

> The *Hood* ... became enveloped in smoke and started to heel to port because
> I saw the black paint of her bottom coming out of the water. The *Hood*
> was covered in smoke and it was impossible to pick out anything definite of
> the ship at all. Another salvo hit the waterline of the *Hood*. I saw spurts of
> smoke coming out of five or six places. After a few seconds the whole ship
> seemed to blow up in pieces. The bow from between 'A' and 'B' turrets was
> blown out of the water and then slid directly back. The plating from the
> ship's side between the foremast and mainmast was blown into the air. There
> were huge columns of smoke and that was the last I saw of her.[13]

Steward Harold Official noted:

> I started watching the *Hood* as soon as it was piped over the broadcaster
> that she was going to engage the *Bismarck*, and I was watching with the
> naked eye. After they opened fire there seemed a sort of glow just about
> abaft the after funnel. Then there were two flashes of yellowish flame abaft
> the funnel ... There was a fire but then after there were two large flashes and
> then a huge cloud of smoke arose.... There was a huge cloud of dense smoke
> went up after the two flashes I had seen, above the funnel, and that was all
> ... I do not know what they really were; they might have been guns firing or
> an explosion. Just about with the smoke there was an explosion and while
> we were watching it was piped that the *Hood* had gone.[14]

Lieutenant-Commander A. A. Havers of the *Suffolk* commented:

> After two or three salvos and also some salvos from the ships ahead of us
> and *Bismarck* and *Prinz Eugen* I saw a big red glow, a fan shaped glow,
> followed by a stalk of red flame in the middle which rose to a considerable
> height in the air, several hundred feet at least, just like a stick of rhubarb.
>   It was perfectly obvious what it was, that some big ship had blown up.
> I thought it was either *Hood* or *Norfolk* or *Prince of Wales*. I then went
> up to the after control.... About ten minutes later when it got lighter there
> were vast quantities of black smoke over the spot where the explosion
> had taken place, which remained there for a considerable time, an hour
> I should think.[15]

Leading Seaman Joseph Bartlett of HMS *Suffolk* remarked:

> We were all standing up there and looking at the firing, and I saw a ship, we
> could not distinguish which ship it was, as it was just a blur on the horizon.

I saw her open fire and then just after that I thought I saw a small flash followed just after that by a big flash which seemed to start from the bottom and rise up to the top in the form of a triangle.[16]

Ordinary Seaman Joseph Hope noted:

I saw at first the flashes from the *Hood*'s guns as they were opening up. We could just make out a dark shape. All of a sudden there was a terrific great flash of flame and after that there was a very dense cloud of black smoke, and I got a pair of binoculars to find out which ship it was, but all I could see was the smoke.[17]

Ordinary Signalman Harry Morgan reported: 'I saw was this ball of fire amidships and then a split second after that all the ship seemed to be one mass of flame and then I could not see any more'.[18]

Ordinary Seaman Fred Howarth commented:

I saw a fire break out on the quarter deck of the *Hood* and then one amidships, and then there were orange flames and black smoke. Soon after this there was a big explosion, and she blew up.[19]

After having been rocked by the initial explosion, the *Hood* began to list slowly to starboard before stopping. The helmsman reported, 'Steering gone, Sir' to which Captain Kerr, almost as if he was on an exercise, simply replied, 'Very good' before ordering a switch over to the emergency steering.

The officers and crewmen on the compass platform of the *Hood* were so transfixed on the *Bismarck* that they did not realise that the ship was imminent danger of sinking. They felt the impact as the shells landed in the vicinity of the mainmast but they had no idea that the aft section of the ship had been blown off by an explosion. The *Hood* began to right herself as Holland kept his eyes transfixed on the *Bismarck*. Within seconds, however, while righting herself, the *Hood* lurched into a list to port. At that moment, everyone on the compass platform knew that the ship was done for. No order was issued to abandon ship, but everyone simply started walking towards the starboard door of the compass platform as Holland remained in the captain's chair in total dejection while beside him Kerr attempted to remain on his feet as the *Hood*'s deck turned into a slide.[20] At this moment, some began to break rank and made for the port door while others attempted to kick out the armoured windows.

The bow swung sharply upwards as did the stern as thousands of gallons of seawater flooded inside the hull. The stern sank first quickly followed by the bow. The sinking was so rapid, taking approximately two minutes, that

British and German sailors alike were momentarily awestruck. As the ship split in two and the bow began to raise, some observers saw what appeared to be the forward turrets firing a final, aimless salvo in defiance. For a few moments, the sea appeared to boil as air trapped inside the ship bubbled to the surface while fuel oil blazed.

For those aboard the *Hood*, there was little time to abandon ship once it became apparent that her fighting days were over and that she was sinking. Out of a crew of 1,418 men, only three—Midshipman William Dundas, Able Seaman Robert Tilburn, and Ordinary Signalman Albert 'Ted' Briggs— made it into the water to be rescued over two hours later by the destroyer HMS *Electra*.

The *Prince of Wales* Fights On

As the *Hood* exploded and sank, the *Prince of Wales* had continued to execute the turn to port and now found the sinking ship directly in her path. To avoid the wreckage of the battlecruiser, Captain Leach ordered a hard turn to starboard; so severe was the turn that to some it seemed that the *Prince of Wales* would roll completely over. Fortunately, she soon steadied herself, and once clear of the *Hood*, Leach ordered the course to be straightened out again. The evasive action served to place the *Prince of Wales* directly between the wreckage of the *Hood* and the German ships. The evasive action served to close the battleship's A-arcs, preventing 'Y' turret from re-engaging. Despite this, as soon as 'A' and 'B' turrets could be retrained on the *Bismarck*, the *Prince of Wales* let loose with her eleventh salvo, which ultimately fell short.

The *Prince of Wales* then executed a turn to port to enable 'Y' turret to re-engage. Shortly after 6.01 a.m., the battleship fired her twelfth salvo at a range of 17,100 yards. By the time that this salvo was fired, A-arcs had been re-opened, however, while 'Y' turret had been brought back into the battle, the No. 3 gun of 'A' turret suffered a mechanical issue, meaning it was temporarily put out of action, thus reducing the turret to two operational guns. With two of her ten 14-inch guns out of action, the firepower of the *Prince of Wales* was reduced by 20 per cent.

Having been momentarily awestruck by the explosion and sinking of the *Hood*, the crews of the *Bismarck* and the *Prinz Eugen* quickly realised that in the *Prince of Wales*, they still faced a dangerous foe who could inflict serious damage. Fortunately for the gunnery officers of the *Bismarck*, the *Prince of Wales* was at approximately the same range as the *Hood* was when she was hit and only 2 degrees to the left, thus presenting them with an easy target correction. The gunners on the *Bismarck* did not detect the hard turn to starboard that had been executed by the British battleship to avoid the sinking *Hood* and used the same lead angle that they had when targeting the *Hood*, with the result that the first salvo fired against the new target at forty seconds after 6 a.m. landed harmlessly to the right of the target. Following making the necessary corrections, from a range of 15,700 yards, a few seconds after the clock turned 6.01 a.m., the *Bismarck* fired her second salvo at the *Prince of Wales*.

A few seconds after the *Prince of Wales* had fired her twelfth salvo, the *Bismarck*'s second salvo against the *Prince of Wales* splashed down in line with the battleship but short of the target. Despite this, one shell from the salvo struck the battleship 25 feet below the waterline amidships where it penetrated the hull plating and continued on for another 12 feet before coming to a rest beside an armoured bulkhead. The shell did not explode as it did not hit anything solid enough to set off the fuse with the result that the impact went unnoticed.

Increasing the range to compensate for the previous salvo falling short, the *Bismarck* fired a third salvo at the *Prince of Wales*, which struck the battleship at 6.02 a.m. One of the shells from the salvo tore through the compass platform from where Leach was fighting the battle. The passage of the shell killed or mortally wounded everyone on the compass platform with the exception of Captain Leach, the navigation officer and the chief yeoman of the signals. Exiting the compass platform, the shell continued on through the port searchlight control position without exploding. Meanwhile, a second shell from the same salvo struck the support structure for the forward port and starboard 5.25-inch gun directors, causing the starboard director to jam and the electrical leads to the forward port director to be severed. Having opened fire moments earlier when the range reached 18,600 yards, the ship's 5.25-inch guns now fell silent, having fired three salvos.

Having been momentarily dazed by the shell that passed through the compass platform, Captain Leach regained his composure and moved command of the ship down to the bridge. In the meantime, the *Bismarck* had fired further salvos, which scored additional hits. A 15-inch shell struck the starboard crane and exploded against the second funnel sending splinters through the boat deck. Several boats were damaged and the ship's Walrus aircraft which was on the catapult at the time was so damaged that it had to be jettisoned overboard. Control for the 5.25-inch guns was passed to the aft directors but these too were soon put out of action by another hit sustained by the battleship.

In the meantime, the *Prinz Eugen* had kept up her stream of fire against the *Prince of Wales*. The sharp turn that was executed so as to avoid the wreckage of the *Hood* momentarily threw off the gunners of the *Prinz Eugen*, but they soon regained the range and bearing of the target. Within a matter of minutes, the heavy cruiser scored hits on the *Prince of Wales* augmenting the damage caused by the *Bismarck*. Like one of *Bismarck*'s 15-inch shells before it, an

8-inch shell from the *Prinz Eugen* caused carnage around the boat deck. An 8-inch shell penetrated the boat deck near the aft funnel, destroying a boat in the process before continuing through several compartments, including that containing the ammunition hoist for the nearby 5.25-inch guns before finally coming to a rest on the port side having failed to explode. The shell was immediately thrown overboard by members of the *Prince of Wales*'s crew. The *Prinz Eugen* scored additional hits, including one that entered the hull around the waterline abaft the armoured bulkhead, which caused flooding to some of the middle deck compartments.

Despite the damage that the ship was sustaining, aboard the *Prince of Wales*, McMullen kept up a steady stream of fire against the *Bismarck*. Seconds after the shell from the *Bismarck* tore through the compass platform, the thirteenth salvo of the *Prince of Wales* splashed down straddling the *Bismarck*. Like the previous two straddles, no hits were observed on the German battleship.

When the battle had begun preparations were made on the *Prinz Eugen* to launch a torpedo attack against the British ships should they come into range. The Type G7a (T1) 21-inch torpedo that equipped the *Prinz Eugen* had a maximum range of 15,300 yards at 30 knots. At that range and speed, it would have taken one of the torpedoes approximately fifteen minutes to reach its target. When the battle had begun, the *Bismarck* had increased speed to 30 knots with the result that she began to close the range to the *Prinz Eugen* and actually overtook the heavy cruiser. With the *Bismarck* moving up the port side of the ship, it was decided by those aboard the *Prinz Eugen* not to launch a torpedo spread as the weapons would have to swim directly across the path of the oncoming flagship. In the ship's war diary, however, *Kapitän* Brinkmann neglected to record any considerations of launching a torpedo attack against the *Prince of Wales*. With the *Bismarck* moving up the port side of his ship, Brinkmann realised that salvos falling long over the *Bismarck* might serve to hit his ship. As such, at 6.03 a.m., Brinkmann ordered the helm to make a series of three hard turns to starboard, which would serve to increase the separation between the heavy cruiser and battleship. The sharp turns would also serve to put the *Prinz Eugen* on the leeward side of the *Bismarck* sooner, providing her with greater protection from fire from the *Prince of Wales*.

The fact that provisions were made aboard the *Prinz Eugen* to launch a torpedo attack, and that the heavy cruiser was in fact within torpedo range of the *Prince of Wales* at one point in the battle, combined with the turns to starboard have led some to speculate that despite having been sunk, *Hood* had an opportunity to deal a final lethal blow by having launched torpedoes. It is likely that this theory comes from the fact that Brinkmann sought to justify increasing the separation between his ship and the *Bismarck* by claiming that he was avoiding three torpedoes reportedly heard by the hydrophone operators of the *Prinz Eugen*.

The *Hood* was the only British ship engaged in the battle equipped with torpedoes. Given this fact, and given that the *Prinz Eugen* could, on paper, have struck the *Prince of Wales* with torpedoes, it is possible that the hydrophone operators on board the *Prince Eugen* heard torpedoes fired from the *Hood*. In his work *The Loss of the Bismarck*, Graham Rhys-Jones has stated that 'There is no evidence that the *Hood* fired torpedoes although the possibility cannot, perhaps, be totally discounted'.[1] Rather, Rhys-Jones has speculated that the hydrophone operators aboard the *Prinz Eugen* may have been guilty of panic and a false alarm over hearing torpedoes in the water.

It is unlikely that the *Hood* would have launched torpedoes from such an extreme range. Even more unlikely is that they would have come close to the German ships. Furthermore, the survivors from the *Hood*, principally Ted Briggs and William Dundas, did not recall hearing any orders being issued for the launch of torpedoes. Whatever the case may be, if the *Hood* did fire torpedoes at the German ships, and their detection coincided coincidentally with the manoeuvre to increase the separation ordered by Brinkmann, the torpedoes failed to find their mark. Whether or not the *Hood* managed to fire any of her torpedoes is something which shall never be known as those who would be able to answer this question with certainty were all lost with the ship. When the series of turns was completed, the *Prince of Wales* was out of torpedo range from the *Prinz Eugen*. Brinkman would later be criticised by his superiors for the failure of his ship to use its torpedo armament against the British battleship.

To Captain Leach, it was clear that the *Prince of Wales* was being outfought. The Germans continued to direct relatively accurate fire against his ship while his ship, in turn, was apparently unable to land a significant blow against the *Bismarck*. Four hits from 15-inch shells and three hits from 8-inch shells had been sustained, and difficulties were being experienced with the main battery armament. With the difficulties being experienced by the main armament, it was difficult to keep up effective fire. The damage done to the ship, which was not in itself critical, had an obvious adverse effect on the further execution of the battle by the crew. Believing that further engagement would possibly result in more serious damage being sustained, or perhaps even lead to the loss of the ship, Leach made the decision to break off the engagement.

Subsequently, between 6.02 and 6.05 a.m., Leach ordered the ship to execute a sharp turn to port on to a course of 160 degrees away from the battle area. As the ship executed her turn to break off the engagement, the *Prince of Wales* produced a smokescreen in an attempt to obscure the ship from the view of the German gunners. While turning, two salvos were fired which were ragged and landed short. With the completion of the turn, 'A' and 'B' turrets could no longer be brought to bear on the German ships and the *Bismarck* could no longer be observed. The turn had placed the *Prince of*

Wales on an almost perpendicular course with the German squadron with the result that the line of sight extending for the forward director was obscured by the support structure for the 5.25-inch directors.

Fire control was subsequently passed to the aft director, but the smokescreen being produced by the battleship served to obscure visibility from the aft director. In effect, this served to prevent the firing of any of the *Prince of Wales*'s main battery armament. The turrets were, however, capable of being fired under local control. While the German ships were not visible from the aft director, the gunnery officer in charge of 'Y' turret could see the *Bismarck* below the smokescreen and took it upon himself to fire the turret under local control. Between 6.07 and 6.08 a.m., two one-round salvos were fired from 'Y' turret.

As she began to execute the series of turns to starboard, from 6.03 a.m., the *Prinz Eugen* continued to fire at the *Prince of Wales*. As her last turn was completed at 6.07 a.m., while trained on the *Prince of Wales*, the bow of the *Bismarck* became visible in the sights of the *Prinz Eugen*'s First Gunnery Officer Paulus Jasper. With the sighting of the *Bismarck*'s bow, it became quite apparent that the battleship was passing between the *Prinz Eugen* and the *Prince of Wales*. Moments later, the order was issued on board the *Prinz Eugen* not to fire over the *Bismarck*. Almost immediately after that order was issued, at 6.09 a.m., the order to cease fire was issued aboard the heavy cruiser.

With the *Prince of Wales* partially obscured by her smokescreen, the fire from the *Bismarck* was reduced to the forward and then the aft turrets before being reduced to individual turrets. As the *Prince of Wales* increased the range, coupled with her smokescreen, she became increasingly obscured to those on board the *Bismarck*. With this, the further expenditure of ammunition became unwarranted. At 06.10, immediately after the *Bismarck* fired one final salvo from her forward turrets, Lütjens issued the order to cease fire. Having issued the order to cease fire, Lütjens ordered the *Prinz Eugen* to once again take up guide of the squadron. As such, the cruiser began to increase speed from the reduced speed of 27 knots to 32 knots, which she maintained until 6.20 a.m., when, after a comfortable margin had been gained over the *Bismarck*, she reduced speed to 30 knots.

The *Prince of Wales* continued her retreat with the gunnery officer firing a two-round salvo at the German squadron, the war diary of the *Prinz Eugen* noting: '*King George* briefly opens fire. Strikes are outboard of the ship'.[2]

As the *Prince of Wales* disengaged from the battle, it would appear that something of a heated debate erupted on board the *Bismarck* between Lütjens and Lindemann. Having managed to sink the *Hood* and damage and force the *Prince of Wales* to bid a hasty retreat, it would appear that Lindemann wanted to pursue the British battleship and to destroy her. Lütjens on the other hand was prepared to let the *Prince of Wales* make good her escape. No doubt Lütjens was mindful of his directive to not engage unnecessarily with enemy capital ships. With the *Prince of Wales* clearly disengaging, to follow and engage her would have constituted an unnecessary engagement and one that placed the *Bismarck* at risk in direct contradiction to his orders. Lütjens was also conscious of the fact that a pursuit of the wounded battleship could lead the *Bismarck* closer to additional heavy units of the Home Fleet, which it had to be assumed were undoubtedly on their way to try and intercept the squadron. Finally, with the belief that the battleship was the *King George V* with a relatively experienced crew, Lütjens must have thought that it would not be so easy to simply finish off the battleship.

No sooner had the German ships ceased fire than a warning resounded throughout the ships with the sight of a Sunderland flying boat overhead which prompted the anti-aircraft guns of the ships to open fire. The Sunderland, piloted by Flight Lieutenant Vaughn, immediately sought the shelter provided by the clouds. For the next few minutes, however, whenever the Sunderland appeared through the clouds, it was met by a volley of anti-aircraft fire before a cease fire was ordered at 6.20 a.m. when it became clear that the Sunderland was maintaining its distance astern of the squadron out of anti-aircraft range.

With the loss of the *Hood* and Admiral Holland, Rear-Admiral Wake-Walker became the senior British officer on the scene. Having witnessed the battle from on board the *Norfolk*, and with the *Prince of Wales* falling under his command following the loss of Admiral Holland, when Captain Leach informed Wake-Walker of his intention to break of the engagement, the admiral had no other option but to concur with his captain owing to the fact that he had no detailed knowledge of the construction of the *Prince of Wales* nor knowledge of any other circumstance bearing on the matter. Wake-Walker did, however, intend to find out quickly whether or not the *Prince of Wales* was in a position to support the ongoing operations against the *Bismarck*.

At 6.05 a.m., Wake-Walker was informed by the *Suffolk* that she was setting a course and speed to keep on the starboard side of the German squadron. At 6.16 a.m., the ranging radar of the cruiser was trained on the *Prinz Eugen* and indicated that the German vessel was 19,000 yards away. With this, the crew of the *Suffolk* believed that the *Prinz Eugen* had altered course and was now closing in on them. At 6.19 a.m., the *Suffolk* opened fire in the direction of the *Prinz Eugen* using the data from the radar. At 6.23 a.m., the range began to rapidly decrease and a minute later, at 6.24 a.m., it was down to 12,400 yards. It was quickly realised that something was wrong. After having fired six salvos, the *Suffolk* ceased fire. It was later deduced that the radar had not in fact been ranged on the *Prinz Eugen*, but rather on the Sunderland that had joined in the shadowing operations. When the *Suffolk* opened fire, the forward guns of the *Bismarck* were traversed towards the British cruiser, but they remained silent. At 6.21 a.m., realising that the *Suffolk* was not at risk of hitting either of the *Bismarck* or the *Prinz Eugen* as the range was not 19,000 yards but 29,540 yards, the *Bismarck*'s guns were returned to their normal fore-aft position.

HMS *Norfolk* and the *Suffolk* had maintained contact with the *Bismarck* and the *Prinz Eugen* throughout the night and during the course of the battle hitherto. Members of the respective cruisers had bore witness to the events as they unfolded. At the conclusion of the battle, the *Norfolk* transmitted a signal to Admiral Tovey aboard the *King George V* informing him of the loss of the *Hood*. The signal send to Tovey simply stated: '*Hood* has blown up'.

The *Prinz Eugen* had not sustained any hits during the course of the battle and remained undamaged despite the shells from the *Hood* landing close by. The *Bismarck* on the other hand had been struck by three shells from the *Prince of Wales*. In addition to scoring three hits on the *Bismarck*, the *Prince of Wales* had managed to straddle the German battleship with three of her eighteen salvos. The first shell that hit the *Bismarck* struck her below the waterline and passed through the outer hull just below the main belt before exploding against the 1.7-inch armoured torpedo bulkhead. Seawater flooded a number of compartments but was brought under control by the damage control parties. The second shell entered the bow section above the waterline, and passed through the ship without exploding leaving a large hole into which 1,000 tons of seawater entered. The seawater entered the forecastle, and as a consequence, 700 tons of fuel oil was blocked in the lower fuel tanks. The third shell passed through the *Bismarck* amidships without doing any appreciable damage, asides from hitting one of the ship's boats. As a result, the *Bismarck*'s maximum speed was reduced to 28 knots and the ship began to list 7 degrees to port and was 3 degrees down at the bow. A full breakdown of the damage sustained by the *Bismarck* is outlined in Chapter 15.

The news of the battle and the loss of the *Hood* soon found its way to the Admiralty in London where it was passed on to Churchill at Chequers. Major General Hastings 'Pug' Ismay was woken on the morning of 24 May by the sound of voices. Ismay climbed out of bed to see Churchill walking down the corridor. The door to Averell Harriman's bedroom was open so Ismay walked down the corridor and went inside whereupon he was told that Churchill had arrived a few minutes before, muttering, 'Hell of a battle. The *Hood* is sunk, hell of a battle'.[3]

The Battle of the Denmark Strait was a heavy blow for the Royal Navy. The pride of its fleet, 'the Mighty *Hood*', had been sunk within minutes of battle being joined while its newest battleship had been outfought. The sinking of the *Hood* and the breaking off of the engagement by the *Prince of Wales* came as a shock to the Admiralty and to the government. When it was learned that the *Prince of Wales* had suffered mechanical defects with her main battery guns but that some of these had been rectified, there was outrage in some circles. So it was that some began to call for Captain Leach to be court-martialed for breaking off the engagement while calls went out for Wake-Walker to also face a court-martial for failing to engage the *Bismarck* despite having almost a two-to-one superiority over the German battle group. The First Sea Lord Sir Dudley Pound was one strong advocate of a court-martial for Captain Leach for breaking off the engagement and for Wake-Walker for not re-engaging the *Bismarck* when the armament of the *Prince of Wales* was returned to a serviceable state.

Admiral Tovey, on the other hand, supported the action that had been taken by both Wake-Walker and Leach. As an illustration of his support for the action taken by Leach, Tovey sent a signal to the *Prince of Wales*:

> I wish to congratulate you on the very efficient and effective part you took in the recent operation against the *Bismarck*. Knowing your Captain as I do, I was always confident that he would take, as he did, exactly the action I would have wished had I been in company at the time. It is a fine start to what I am sure will be a very great commission.[4]

Indeed, such was Tovey's support for the action of his commanders that he threatened to resign from his position as the commander in chief of the Home Fleet if either were court-martialed for their actions and stated that he would appear at any court-martial hearing as 'defendant's friends' and as a defence witness.[5]

The favourable outcome with regards the sinking of the *Bismarck* without any further loss of life or damage being incurred by the ships involved, coupled with Tovey's threat served to weigh against the idea of a court-martial. Instead, Wake-Walker was made a commander of the order of the British Empire (CBE) while Leach was awarded a Distinguished Service Order for their parts in the action against the *Bismarck*. It is highly likely that had the *Bismarck* succeeded in making it to one of the ports on the French Atlantic coast that the idea to court-martial Wake-Walker and Leach would have been pursued.

The news of the loss of the *Hood* stunned the British public. The sinking of the *Hood* was front-page news, with newspapers such as the *Sunday Pictorial* running the headline: 'Nazis hit-and-run in great sea battle: *Hood* blows up after hit by freak shot'.[6] Other newspapers ran headlines surrounding the sinking such as: 'Nazis sink *Hood* near Greenland'; '1,300 dead as *Hood* sinks in battles'; 'Germans sink *Hood*, world's biggest warship, in sea battle'; '*Hood* sunk; British hunt *Bismarck*'; 'HMS *Hood* lost in North Atlantic battle'.[7, 8, 9, 10, 11] Having failed to stop the *Bismarck* in the Denmark Strait, she, along with the *Prinz Eugen*, posed a great threat to the Atlantic trade routes. The events subsequent to the Battle of the Denmark Strait have been extensively recounted elsewhere and lie beyond the scope of this book and will, therefore, not be detailed here.

Admiral Holland's Actions

Since the Battle of the Denmark Strait, many authors and historians have sought to blame Vice-Admiral Holland for the loss of the *Hood*, the damage suffered by HMS *Prince of Wales*, and the failure to sink the *Bismarck* in the Denmark Strait. Many historians have endeavoured to address the question of how far Holland was to blame for these events, and while their findings have varied, most have laid the blame squarely on Holland and his actions. Such a critique is largely unfair as, while historians have made their conclusions with the benefit of hindsight, historians have failed to address the actions from the point of view of Holland.

When one looks at the situation from Holland's point of view, with the information that he had available to him at the time, one can begin to gain a new appreciation of the tasks with which he was faced.

Lancelot Ernest Holland was born in Middleton Chaney in 1887 and entered the Royal Navy on 15 May 1902 as a midshipman at HMS *Britannia*. Passing out of HMS *Britannia* in September 1903, he was drafted to the China Station where he served aboard the protected cruiser HMS *Eclipse*. Holland would see service out in the Far East until August 1905, spending the latter half of his time there aboard the armoured cruiser HMS *Hampshire*. In 1906, Holland was promoted to sub-lieutenant before attaining the rank of lieutenant in 1907 and lieutenant-commander in 1915.

During this time, Holland's naval record records him as being of 'good judgment' and as being 'steady' and 'reliable'. During the summer of 1908, Holland saw a brief period of service aboard the Admiralty Survey Ship HMS *Research*. From 1910 until 1912, then Lieutenant Holland undertook the 'Long Course' at HMS *Excellent*, which made him a gunnery specialist. Holland would return to HMS *Excellent* between 1916 and 1918 to continue his studies as his potential with regards gunnery became clear.

Upon leaving HMS *Excellent* in 1918, Holland was appointed as the gunnery officer aboard HMS *Royal Oak*. On 31 December 1918, Holland was promoted to commander and was appointed as the experimental commander of HMS *Excellent* and to the Naval Anti-Aircraft Gun Committee. By this point in his career, Holland has established himself as being one of the Royal Navy's most proficient gunnery officers. During the Chanak Crisis of 1922–23, Holland was brought up to notice by then Commander in Chief of the Mediterranean Fleet Vice-Admiral Sir Osmond de Beauvoir Brock for good services before being promoted to captain in 1929.

From May 1929, Holland served as the flag captain of the 2nd Cruiser Squadron aboard HMS *Hawkins*, a position he was to keep until February 1931. From May 1931 until May 1933, Holland was sent to Greece as part of a British naval mission before being appointed to the battleship HMS *Revenge*. As a temporary staff officer, Holland saw service during the Abyssinian crisis of 1935–36 before, while still holding the rank of captain, he was appointed to the position of assistant chief of the naval staff from 1937 to 1938. Just prior to the outbreak of the Second World War, Holland was appointed the commander of the Third Battle Squadron before being appointed as the first naval representative to the Air Ministry. Holland followed this with a posting as chief of staff to Commander in Chief of the Home Fleet Admiral Sir Charles Forbes.

From July to October 1940, Holland commanded the 7th Cruiser Squadron. During the course of this command, Holland led his cruisers during the inconclusive engagement of the Battle of Cape Spartivento on 27 November 1940 in which he and Admiral James Somerville, the commander of Force 'H', were later criticised by an Admiralty Board of Inquiry.[1] By this point in his career, Holland had established himself as something of a gunnery specialist.

In early 1941, Holland commanded the Home Fleet's 18th Cruiser Squadron during which time he led his cruiser squadron north to the volcanic island of Jan Mayen to capture the German weather trawler *München*. In early May, the *München* was surprised and boarded by the Tribal-class destroyer HMS *Somali*. Prior to being boarded, the crew of the *München* threw the ship's Enigma machine overboard in a weighted bag, but the crew neglected to destroy documents relating to the operation of the Enigma machine, nor did they destroy the code books that remained on board, which proved crucial in the breaking of the Enigma code.

Holland was part of a clique of officers, which was eventually headed by Sir Dudley Pound, that monopolised many of the senior posts in the Royal Navy from the 1930s. On 12 May 1941, Holland was promoted to vice-admiral commanding Battlecruiser Squadron and became the second-in-command of the Home Fleet. Command of the Battlecruiser Squadron was to be his last seagoing command before he was to be posted to the Admiralty as Pound's vice chief of the Naval Staff in late 1941. Holland himself had hopes of one day attaining the position of first sea lord.[2] It was not to be as Holland, alongside 1,414 other sailors, died when HMS *Hood* was sunk at the Battle of the Denmark Strait on 24 May 1941.

In the wake of his death and the loss of the *Hood*, Holland has often been criticised for his handling of the Battlecruiser Squadron. It has only been in recent years that there have been publications vindicating his actions, and then only partially. Most criticisms of Holland have been made with the benefit of hindsight; also, they fail to take into account the constraints Holland was under to bring the *Bismarck* to battle. One such work that was highly critical of Holland was the *Bismarck Episode* by Russell Grenfell.[3] Grenfell's work was written shortly after the war in 1949 and is damning of both Holland and his tactics. Grenfell's analysis and criticism of Holland are somewhat incomplete owing to the fact that not all of the details of the battle were known at the time of publication. Furthermore, Grenfell fails to acknowledge that Holland appeared to be following contemporary fighting instructions. Grenfell also made the argument that the *Hood* and the *Prince of Wales* had roughly the same armament as the *Bismarck* and that as such, Holland should have stood off and used the range of his ship's guns to destroy her. This argument completely ignores the vulnerability of the *Hood* to plunging fire, and therefore the need to close the range to limit the *Hood*'s vulnerability. This book, nevertheless, is an apt starting point for the examining of and formulating counterarguments to criticisms of Holland.

While some works have ridiculed Holland, works such as that by Ludovic Kennedy, *Pursuit: The Chase and Sinking of the Bismarck*, have sought to vindicate Holland.[4] Indeed, Kennedy points out that Holland ordered a turn to the north, which was aimed at bringing about action between the two opposing squadrons, not as a result of losing contact with the *Bismarck* as some have claimed. Indeed, when Holland's handling of the operation that resulted in the Battle of the Denmark Strait is studied and the benefit of hindsight is removed, a very carefully and thoughtfully executed plan remains.

While Holland has all too frequently been criticised for the way in which he handled his squadron, including by Grenfell among others for his apparent reckless handling of the *Hood* and the other ships under his command, on analysis, Holland's actions do not, in fact, appear as reckless as has previously been suggested. Most historians who have been critical of Holland and his actions have made their critiques of his command with the benefit of hindsight. In this, one must be mindful because it is 'problematic to judge historical decisions with hindsight without taking into account the full extent of the information available to the decision makers and the circumstances in which the decision was made'.[5] Holland never had the luxury of hindsight and was never presented with the opportunity to defend his handling and conduct of the Battle of the Denmark Strait either at the time or with the benefit of hindsight.

Those that have sought to criticise Holland have also generally failed to fully appreciate the constraints that Holland was placed under in order to bring the *Bismarck* to battle and to prevent her from breaking out into the Atlantic. Finally, the vast majority of historiography dealing with the Battle of the Denmark Strait cover events other than the Battle of the Denmark Strait, and focus either solely on HMS *Hood* or focus on the *Bismarck* and the entire saga surrounding her breakout, the Battle of the Denmark Strait, and then the subsequent hunt for and sinking of the ship; they do not delve into the engagement on the morning of 24 May in fine detail.

This chapter is based on the papers produced by Tim Woodward and Sean Waddingham among others and will examine the actions and decisions made by Admiral Holland from the moment when contact was made with the *Bismarck* in the Denmark Strait by HMS *Suffolk* until the end of the Battle of the Denmark Strait when HMS *Prince of Wales* retired. While Admiral Holland is the subject of this chapter, some of the actions of Admiral Lütjens, where necessary and appropriate, will also be detailed an analysed. For ease and to enable the most effective analysis to be offered and presented, this chapter will be broken down into sections with each one analysing the difficult decisions made by Holland.

Literature

Before looking at the actions of Admiral Holland, it is first necessary to say a little on notable pieces of literature detailing the actions of Holland. Perhaps the most interesting insight into the battle is provided by Alan Coles and Ted Briggs in *Flagship Hood*. *Flagship Hood* is based on the memories of the longest-lived of the *Hood*'s survivors and provides an insight into the discussions that took place on the compass platform and the reactions of different individuals during the engagement with the *Bismarck*.[6] While interesting, *Flagship Hood* is also at times quite vague. When it comes to Holland, this work 'sits on the fence'.[7] On the one hand, it does not heavily criticise the actions of Admiral Holland, yet at the same time, it does not seem to vindicate him.

On the opposite side of the engagement is *Battleship Bismarck* by Baron Burkhard von Müllenheim-Rechberg. This work is indecisive about the actions of Holland on 24 May 1941 and concentrates on events from the point of view of a crewman aboard the *Bismarck*. This is perhaps the case because as fourth gunnery officer of the *Bismarck*, Müllenheim-Rechberg was not privy to the decisions that Holland had to make and did not give detailed consideration to why he made the decisions that he did.

In his work on the official history of the war at sea encompassing three volumes, Stephen Roskill also sits on the fence. Roskill points to the need to bring the *Bismarck* to battle and points to the fact that Holland was following his orders, yet he is critical of Holland's turn to the north and the fact that he did not break radio silence.

As noted, there are works that have been highly critical of Holland, such as *The Bismarck Episode* by Russell Grenfell, which was written shortly after the war and is damning of Holland. Owing to when *The Bismarck Episode* was written in relation to the end of the war, the arguments that it puts forward are limited because not all of the details of the battle were known. Grenfell does not take into account ideas such as that Holland could have wanted to bring on the action earlier than he in fact did, and fails to acknowledge that Holland appeared to be following contemporary fighting instructions. Grenfell also ignored items such as the vulnerability of the *Hood* to plunging fire and makes the assertion that the *Hood* and the *Prince of Wales* had the same armament as the *Bismarck* and therefore Holland could have stood off and destroyed her.

On the other hand, works such as Ludovic Kennedy's *Pursuit* or David Mearns and Rob White's *Hood and Bismarck* have sought to defend Holland to a certain degree. In contrast to Grenfell, Kennedy has pointed out that the turn to the north was designed to bring about an engagement between the two forces, that he achieved surprise over the German squadron, and that Holland forced Admiral Lütjens into accepting battle. Mearns and White have underlined the limitations of the situation faced by Holland while the Naval Staff History, with a foreword by Admiral Sir Nigel Essenhigh and an introduction by Dr Eric Grove, *German Capital Ships and Raiders in World War II* fully supports the actions of Holland (including his turn to the north and his decision to detach his escorting destroyers and to employ them as scouts) and offers what is likely the most detailed analysis on Holland's approach.[8] This work does fail, however, to address all of the issues that existed once battle was joined.[9]

Use of Radar

During his approach to the battle, a relatively new factor was at play—radar. The Battle of the Denmark Strait was to be the first major engagement at sea during which the two opposing forces were equipped with such technology. For both the British and the Germans, the main radar systems in use were the gunnery ranging sets that were to be found mounted on the director towers. It has been suggested by a number of different sources that the radar sets used by the *Bismarck* and the *Prinz Eugen*—the FuMo 23 and FuMo 27 Seetakt respectively—likely had a slightly longer range than the Type 284 Gunnery Radar that was fitted to HMS *Suffolk*, *Hood*, and *Prince of Wales*. It has additionally been suggested that the German sets were effective up to a range of 28,000 yards while the British sets were effective up to 24,000 yards.

Admiral Holland operated a strict policy of radar silence, even when contact with the *Bismarck* and the *Prinz Eugen* had been lost by HMS *Suffolk* and the *Norfolk*. This would appear to be a strange action to take. It has been suggested that the use of radar may have increased Holland's chances of locating the *Bismarck* during the period when the *Norfolk* and the *Suffolk* had lost contact and may have enabled Holland to manoeuvre his ships into a better position to attack.[10] Prior to sailing from Scapa Flow the radar equipment of the *Hood* and the *Prince of Wales* was in full working order; this fact is known courtesy of Stephen Roskill, who checked the radar equipment personally.[11] As such, accusations that the radar equipment used by both of Holland's ships can be discounted. It is quite possibly the case that Holland's decision to maintain radar silence was a prudent one.

In May 1941, radar was still in its infancy and was not as effective as it would be later in the war, nor indeed was it anywhere near as effective as the radar sets we know today. A number of critics have condemned Holland for not using radar when the *Suffolk* and the *Norfolk* lost contact with the German squadron and have claimed that the *Hood* and the *Prince of Wales* were sailing 'blindly' without the eyes of the shadowing cruisers. Such criticisms completely miss the point that at this stage in the war, the radar sets that equipped the British ships (while they could locate ships beyond the visual range of the naked eye) were effective only up to a range of 20 miles— much too short for detecting the *Bismarck*.[12]

One problem with radar at the time was that it could also act as a beacon with the radar waves capable of being picked up and used to identify a location. This was demonstrated in exercises conducted shortly before the outbreak of war in 1939 when HMS *Rodney* detected the radar of HMS *Sheffield* when the latter was 100 miles away and not transmitting. As such, the Royal Navy elected to concentrate on radar wavelengths of 25 mm or shorter because they offered a reduced risk of detection.[13] As a result of this, commanding officers began to treat radar-like wireless sets, with regulations governing its usage at sea with one sweep being made every so often.

As the advantages of radar became clear, individual commanders would begin to use their initiative in using the technology. Holland was in a difficult position as with the *Suffolk* and the *Norfolk* having lost contact with the German ships he needed to locate the *Bismarck*. However, he was hoping to bring about an engagement that would not have occurred if he was discovered from the radar transmissions of his ships.[14] Surprise was vital, and the use of radar had the potential to throw that surprise away. According to Alan Coles and Ted Briggs, the restrictions placed by Holland on the use of radar 'at least did obtain a degree of surprise in the early stages and, together with his signal that radar should not be used until action was imminent, was a wise enough precaution'.[15] Holland's strict limitations on the use of radar and in maintaining radio silence virtually up to the moment that battle was joined shows that he and his staff had fully grasped the nascent skills of electronic warfare.

A number of commentators have put forward the idea that the *Hood*'s Type 284 radar had become unserviceable by the early hours of 24 May because at 2.03 a.m., Holland requested that the *Prince of Wales* make a radar sweep across the sector astern of the squadron. Given that Stephen Roskill had stated that the radar sets of both British ships were in full working order, this is unlikely and it is most likely the case that Holland ordered this because the Type 284 of the *Hood* would not bear astern. Holland had presumably not realised that the *Prince of Wales* did not have Type 284 radar on her aft director, only on her forward one. Holland did distinguish between the radar sets that equipped the ships under his command as Captain Leach noted that following Holland's request for the *Prince of Wales* to sweep aft with Type 284, as the Type 284 would not bear beyond 70 degrees, permission was sought to conduct a sweep with Type 281 early warning radar but that permission was refused.[16]

In his article 'Decision in the Denmark Strait: VADM Holland—Blunderer or Blighted by Fate?' Sean Waddingham has noted that questions have been raised over the ability of the German squadron to detect incoming radar pulses. Waddingham, from an analysis of signals made by Lütjens and Group West, has suggested that the Germans were capable of detecting radar pulses at ranges at which the British could no longer detect returns. Further to this, Waddingham has suggested that this may well have reinforced Lütjens's dismay that the intelligence he had been provided with had failed to inform him that British radar was at least as advanced as his own meaning that an undetected breakout into the Atlantic through the confines of the Denmark Strait was unlikely.[17]

Against this, Holland's decision not to use radar does not appear to be so much of an error, especially once the limitations of radar are analysed. Not only did radar have the potential to give away the position of Holland's forces, but the results shown by radar were sometimes uncertain as highlighted by Admiral Tovey's report on the action against the *Bismarck* when he refers to the radar of the *Prince of Wales* 'throwing up three echoes when there were only two ships in the German squadron'.[18]

Holland's Engagement Plan

Holland was an able commander. His original plan as conceived and his course to intercept were excellent.[19] Indeed, it was only an unfortunate turn of events that served to turn the situation on its head. The German ships were sailing in a south-westerly direction while Holland and his force was sailing north-westerly, which enabled Holland to cross the path of Lütjens and to bar the progress of the German ships into the Atlantic. By sailing in such a direction and by being in such a position, Holland intended to engage the enemy force at around 2 a.m. on 24 May.[20]

With the element of surprise on his side, Holland held the advantage. Further to this, Holland's advantage over Lütjens also included the weight of heavy guns in the form of eight 15-inch guns and ten 14-inch guns plus the potential combined total of sixteen 8-inch guns aboard the *Norfolk* and the *Suffolk* against the eight 15-inch guns of the *Bismarck* and eight 8-inch guns of the *Prinz Eugen*. Intending to cross the 'T' of the German force, Holland planned to place the *Hood* and the *Prince of Wales* in a position whereby they could bring their full broadsides to bear against the German raiders while the German force would be limited to fighting the engagement with their forward guns. In addition, the *Bismarck* and her unknown consort would be silhouetted against the setting sun. At the latitude at which the battle was fought, the sun set around 2 a.m. and did not completely disappear and would thus make the German ships very visible while Holland's force would be hidden in the comparative darkness.

Holland's intention to engage the enemy at around 2 a.m. is clear and is highlighted by the screening orders he issued to his destroyers at 9.10 p.m. on 23 May.[21] Another indication is the fact that Holland ordered his crews to action stations at midnight, which serves as a clear indication that he intended to fight the engagement much earlier than it occurred.[22] Holland had planned the engagement well.

A little before 11 p.m., he ordered an alteration of course by 10 degrees, which would have enabled him to stay ahead of the German squadron and to thus keep his advantage. Up to that point, he stood a good chance of victory; he knew the location of the German forces and he held the advantages of surprise and heavy guns. One could even go so far as to say that Holland had read the situation well and was set to take advantage of his opportunity to strike.[23]

His original plan had clearly been soundly thought out, which was in itself quite an achievement when the pressures of the situation are taken into account. The main aim of Holland and the ships under his command, since the *Bismarck* had been located, was to close the range undetected and to achieve tactical surprise. Even though he was likely tempted to break radio silence once the *Norfolk* and the *Suffolk* lost contact, Holland did not and succeeded in engaging the *Bismarck* and the *Prinz Eugen* with the element of surprise intact.[24] The first gunnery officer on board the *Bismarck* initially thought the approaching *Hood* and *Prince of Wales* to be another pair of cruisers sent to bolster the shadowing the *Suffolk* and the *Norfolk*.[25]

It is likely that the thought flashed through Holland's mind that the impending engagement had the potential to be the only time that the Royal Navy might bring the *Bismarck* to battle, especially given that we now know that the *Tirpitz* spent the vast majority of her operational life lurking as a fleet in being in the fjords of Norway.[26] Holland would also have been acutely aware that if he failed to engage the *Bismarck*, to damage or sink her, or if an error was made on his part, then the *Bismarck* would evade the British forces sent out to contain the threat that she posed and whereupon she would pass into the Atlantic where she could sink merchant vessels almost at will. If this occurred, Holland would have known that he would face a great difficulty in regaining and maintaining contact since the *Hood* and the *Prince of Wales* would be short of fuel (the King George V-class had a short range).[27] Also, both the *Prince of Wales* and Tovey's *King George V* were slower than the *Bismarck*, which was capable of 30 knots against 28 knots. Yet, at the same time, Holland must have been aware that the pending battle was to be the largest engagement fought between the Royal Navy and the German Navy since Jutland a quarter of a century earlier.

All commanding officers are subjected to pressure, and it is all too easy to let these pressures impair judgement, which allows mistakes to appear. Despite the pressures that he was under, Holland's decisions were shrewd and calculated.

The Turn to the North

What perhaps amounts to the biggest criticism of Holland surrounding the Battle of the Denmark Strait concerns his turn to the north—whether the turn was executed in order to search for the *Bismarck* or to bring about the engagement sooner. The latter would seem to provide a sensible explanation for Holland's decision as it is likely that he recognised that he needed to bring about an engagement sooner due to the uncertainty surrounding the situation with the shadowing *Suffolk* and *Norfolk*. As such, it was the need to bring about an engagement that led Holland to order and execute the turn to the north.[28]

Two turns were executed before the shadowing cruisers lost contact. The first turn was made at 12.12 a.m., by which time a reduction in speed to 25 knots had been ordered, and was the result of a report from the *Suffolk* at 11.59 p.m. reporting that the *Bismarck* had altered course from south-west to south, from 230 degrees to 200 degrees. As such, Holland ordered an alteration of course from 285 degrees to 340 degrees designed to bring about an engagement when the Germans would have been in the narrows of the Denmark Strait, silhouetting the *Bismarck* against the sky and limiting the

Germans' freedom of movement. This course change would have served to bring forward an engagement between the opposing forces from 2 a.m. to 1.40 a.m., which adds further support to the idea that Holland wanted to bring on an engagement as soon as possible.[29]

Had Holland continued on his course of 285 degrees, the *Hood* and the *Prince of Wales* would have cut across the track of the *Bismarck* some 60 miles ahead of the Germans at the time Holland wanted to engage, which would not have helped bring about an early engagement. The only option open to Holland was to have his ships sail a reciprocal course to that of the enemy.

The second turn ordered by Holland saw his ships sail due north. It was executed at 12.17 a.m. and would appear to be in response to the signal from the *Suffolk* at 12.09 a.m. confirming that *Bismarck* was in a snowstorm. Given that this signal was sent three minutes before Holland ordered the execution of the first turn, it is likely that he was unaware of the message's contents. Holland's second turn was a counter to the German ship's entering the snowstorm under the cover of which they could alter course further south.

It should be noted that at this time Holland was not to know that the *Bismarck* would not be sighted by the *Suffolk* for a significant period of time. Indeed, this did not become apparent until 12.28 a.m. Even if Holland did have knowledge of the 12.09 a.m. signal earlier than 12.17 a.m., then there was no cause for alarm; every possibility existed that the *Bismarck* might soon emerge from the snowstorm, so any hasty reactions would be unwise. Also, hitherto throughout the course of the night, there had been small lapses of contact between the *Suffolk* and the *Bismarck*, but the battleship had always been located again on a similar course to that of her last known bearing.[30]

Based on the last report received by Holland from the *Suffolk*, it was possible that the *Bismarck* would have continued to alter course southwards, meaning that Holland's turn north at 12.17 a.m. would have enable him to execute his plan of bringing on an early action. There is evidence that suggests Holland wanted to bring about an early engagement: those aboard the *Hood* were ordered to change into clean underwear, a measure intended to help reduce the risk of infection in the event of becoming wounded and went to action stations at midnight.[31] In his narrative of events, Captain Leach wrote that 'At 0015 ships assumed first degree of readiness, final preparations for action were made, and battle ensign hoisted. It was expected that contact with the enemy would be made at any time after 0140'.[32] Leach goes on to note how shortly after 2 a.m., with the *Norfolk* and the *Suffolk* having failed to regain contact with the *Bismarck* and the *Prinz Eugen*, the crew of the *Prince of Wales* were ordered to relaxed action stations.[33] Therefore, one may assume the crew of the *Hood* had received the same order. Holland's actions up to this point had been geared towards an engagement with the German squadron at around 1.40 a.m., which might well have occurred had the shadowing cruisers succeeded in maintaining contact. Holland was not to know that they would not.[34]

With the signal from the *Suffolk* at 12.28 a.m. confirming that she had lost contact with the German squadron, Holland faced the additional task of covering all German movements when their exact location was uncertain, and of not causing the Germans to bid a hasty retreat before he brought them to action. Holland made a sensible assessment of the situation and decided almost immediately that he would continue north until 2 a.m., by which time, in accordance with his plan, he should have engaged the enemy. If the German ships had not been located by that point, then he would order an alteration of course 180 degrees to the west. This was a sensible course of action because if the German squadron had stayed on the same course, or one very similar, the two sides would have met more or less in accordance with Holland's preconceived plan. The German ships had not radically altered course during four hours of shadowing by the British cruisers, meaning that the likelihood of them radically altering course now was slight. Furthermore, if Holland had made the rash decision and altered course radically and the Germans did not, he would miss the enemy altogether. The fact that Holland had decided on a course of action quickly after he had received notification that contact had been lost shows that he had made preparations for such an eventuality and had considered a subsequent course of action to ensure that the *Bismarck* was located again and to ensure that all possible eventualities were covered.[35]

With contact not having been regained at 2 a.m., Holland stuck to his preconceived plan and executed a turn of 180 degrees to the west. It was clear by this point that the German squadron had not done as he intended. The decision to turn west has been described by some as a brave decision as the German squadron could have passed Holland's force to the south or south-east. The turn to the west allowed Holland to maintain a bearing on the *Bismarck* if she had indeed turned south.[36] Although he was not to know it at the time, it was this turn that put Holland back on a reciprocal course with the Germans.

When contact was regained by the cruisers at 2.47 a.m., Holland became aware that he had lost his bearing on the German ships. With the resuming of contact, it became apparent that the original plan of crossing the 'T' of the German squadron was impossible, but all was not lost.[37] An engagement was still possible. Holland still enjoyed a heavy gun advantage, and he still held the element of surprise.

Holland had accomplished two of his objectives. Owing to the presence of ice to the west, his own ships to the east, and the shadowing cruisers to the north, Holland had backed Lütjens into a corner, meaning that, at least until she made good an escape, the *Bismarck* would be forced to fight. The biggest problem faced by Holland at this point was the weather. The *Prince of Wales* and the *Hood* would be sailing into the weather that would upset the gunnery of his ships while the Germans would have the benefit of having the weather on their disengaged sides.

Bernard Ash has written that 'although *Bismarck* knew she was being shadowed she was completely unaware of the presence of the Battle-Cruiser Squadron, so would not be trying to avoid it' and that the '*Bismarck* had superior fire power and speed to fight her way out, therefore she stayed on the same course—Holland's turn lost him bearing putting his gunners and ship in peril'.[38] This is an unfair criticism and an assessment that fails to take in to account that the turn to the north was executed with the intention of achieving the exact opposite of what Ash accuses. Holland was under pressure to bring about an engagement as he knew that he was presented with an opportunity to sink a major enemy warship and that if he did not bring about an engagement, such an opportunity, at least for him, might not come again.[39] Furthermore, if the *Bismarck* succeeded in reaching the Atlantic, she could make good her escape and wreak havoc among merchant shipping.

In the long run, the turn to the north weakened Holland's position, but at the same time, it was a sensible assessment of the situation with the best knowledge available at that time designed to bring about an engagement. The 180-degree turn at around 2 a.m. rectified the situation somewhat and ultimately enabled Holland to bring the *Bismarck* to battle.

Escorting Destroyers

Another criticism that has been levelled against Holland concerned his use of the destroyers escorting the *Hood* and the *Prince of Wales*. As he ordered the *Hood* and the *Prince of Wales* westwards, Holland ordered the destroyers north with the result that they were unable to take part in the battle and use their most potent weapons—their torpedoes. Bernard Ash, among others, has claimed that this was an oversight on Holland's part.[40]

It is correct that by sending the destroyers north while he took the capital ships west that the destroyers were unable to participate in the battle in which they could have proved useful assets to Holland. Nevertheless, this assessment does not represent the situation. In fact, one could argue that the decision to send the destroyers north at the time was a prudent move as when he did this, Holland had no idea where the *Bismarck* and the *Prinz Eugen* were; Holland had to contend with the possibility that the German squadron may have radically altered course. If the German ships had altered course, then by dispatching the destroyers north, Holland was able to search a wider area with the possibility that the destroyers may have relocated the German ships and shadowed before guiding in either the *Hood* and the *Prince of Wales* or other heavy elements of the Home Fleet under Tovey's command.[41] Two years later, at the Battle of North Cape, Admiral Erich Bey executed a similar manoeuvre by using his destroyers to search one area for convoy JW-55B while he took the *Scharnhorst* in another direction.[42]

Holland's main priority at the time was to relocate the *Bismarck*, so to dispatch the destroyers north to enable a wider area to be searched makes sense. In fact, the destroyers would pass within 16 miles of the German ships, but owing to poor visibility, the *Bismarck* would remain hidden from them. The decision to search a wider area with the destroyers is even more of a sensible decision when it is considered that poor visibility meant that the Walrus aircraft carried by the *Prince of Wales* could not be launched and used for reconnaissance.[43] Also, the use of radar would have either simply not picked up the *Bismarck* or would have given away the presence of Holland's ships, meaning Lütjens could have taken steps to avoid an engagement.

Having failed to engage the *Bismarck* between 1.40 and 2 a.m., Holland was not preparing for an engagement until daybreak as an engagement in the darkest period of the artic night would have been, from Holland's point of view, disadvantageous. For all that Holland knew, therefore, the destroyers may have been able to rejoin the capital ships.

Finally, the weather played a major part. At 8.55 p.m. on 23 May, owing to the destroyers finding it tough going in the heavy seas, in response to a signal from Commander May of HMS *Electra* stating, 'Do not consider destroyers can maintain present speed without danger', Holland ordered the signal 'If you are unable to maintain this speed I will have to go on without you. You should follow at your best speed' be made to the destroyers, after which they attempted to keep pace with the *Hood* and the *Prince of Wales*.[44] Given that Commander May had informed Holland that it was possible that the destroyers would not be able to keep up, to a degree, serves to nullify criticisms of Holland's use of destroyers. Every possibility exists that Holland could have continued on with the destroyers in tow. The destroyers may have reduced speed to better cope with the heavy seas and, as such, would have dropped astern of the *Hood* and the *Prince of Wales*. Owing to the distance that would open up between the capital ships and the destroyers while following behind the *Hood* and *Prince of Wales*, the destroyers may still not have been able to play a part in the battle. Of course, in such a scenario, Holland could have ordered the *Hood* and the *Prince of Wales* to reduce speed to allow the destroyers to maintain station, but if that occurred, there was a high probability that the *Bismarck* and the *Prinz Eugen* would have overtaken Holland's force, meaning an engagement would not have been possible. Given the severity of the weather, even if the destroyers had participated in the battle, the weather would likely have made it difficult for them to get into a position to launch a torpedo attack in any case. This difficulty would be highlighted by the destroyers under the command of Captain Philip Vian during their attempts to launch torpedo attacks against the *Bismarck* on the night of 26–27 May.

End-On Approach

Here we come to the vexed question of the 'end-on approach' and its relevance to gunnery factors during the course of the Battle of the Denmark Strait. It is quite possible that it is on this subject that more mistaken opinion has been expended than on almost all other features of the battle. Even Ernle Bradford in *The Mighty Hood* discussed Holland exposing the *Hood* and the *Prince of Wales* to additional danger as they were 30 degrees off from pointing directly at the German ships. A number of commentators have debated whether or not it is easier to hit a target end-on or side-on and have speculated whether or not the shape of a salvo on landing makes a difference. In the case of the Battle of the Denmark Strait, it would appear that the application of apparent common sense to the problems of relevant vessel positions and gunnery matters have led to conclusions being formed that ignore a number of fundamental factors.

Having regained contact, Holland waited until the sun began to rise before engaging the *Bismarck*. Having waited to commence the engagement, it was at 5.37 a.m. that HMS *Prince of Wales* made a contact report. Holland's plan was to employ an end-on approach with a turn to 280 degrees, which has been denounced as foolhardy.[45] Indeed, it would actually appear that Holland adopted a tactic that was within Admiralty regulations and made the best that he could out of what had turned into an unfavourable situation.

Criticisms of the end-on approach centre around the fact that Holland hurried to close in on the German ships. Baron Burkard von Müllenheim-Rechberg would comment on the subject, 'To approach nearly bow-on, as they were doing, appeared to me absolutely foolhardy; it reminded me of an enraged bull charging without knowing what he's up against'.[46] By approaching in this manner, Holland could only engage the *Bismarck* with the forward turrets of his ships while the German squadron could engage the British ships with their full complement of main battery guns, thus 'British superiority was thrown away'.[47]

The end-on approach that was employed meant that Holland's ships were sailing into the weather, which affected the accuracy of the British gunnery as spray covered the rangefinders while the German ships had the advantage of having the weather on their disengaged sides.[48] Given that Holland was a gunnery expert, he must have known that the *Hood*'s Dreyer control table (an early mechanical computer used to process data to permit a ship to engage a distant target with its main armament) would not give very accurate results to a target directly ahead, meaning that the chances of scoring a hit on the *Bismarck* were significantly reduced.[49] As such, on the face of things, it would appear that Holland had made a tactical error. There is, however, more to this approach than meets the eye.

The two opposing squadrons were on slowly converging courses with Holland's turn from 240 degrees to 280 degrees executed at 5.37 a.m., causing the range to be closed quickly. Holland had reason to close the range between the two squadrons quickly. In the first instance, there is the most often cited reason behind the need to close the range to lower the vulnerability of the *Hood* to plunging fire. In a select number of places, the *Hood*'s deck armour was 3 inches thick at its maximum and 1 inch thick at its thinnest, but by and large, on average, the *Hood*'s deck armour was 2 inches thick.[50]

By closing the range quickly, Holland could ensure that his flagship was less vulnerable to plunging fire and the end-on approach would serve to achieve this. Owing to advances in gunnery (meaning that engagements could be fought at longer ranges), shells would fall at a steeper angle. By the standards of the day, the *Hood*'s horizontal protection was weak. Indeed, one Admiralty document produced in 1939 indicated that the *Hood*—and the Royal Navy's other battlecruisers—had no immune zone against 15-inch German shells (See Appendix I).[51] It must be assumed that Holland was aware of this vulnerability and needed to close the range to ensure that the German shells were fired on a flatter trajectory in the hope that any incoming shells would strike the *Hood*'s thicker side armour, which could better withstand the impact of a shell and was more likely to protect the vitals of the ship.

There are also other reasons behind the need to close the range. If not engaged, Lütjens could have used the slight speed advantage of the *Bismarck* and the *Prinz Eugen* to pull ahead and away from Holland's ships, making good their escape into the Atlantic or to a friendly port.

On paper, the *Hood* was the fastest capital ship in the engagement with a speed of 32 knots while the *Bismarck* was capable of 30 knots. The *Hood*'s speed had, however, been achieved during sea trials in 1920. By 1941, owing to her age, build-ups on the underside of her hull, and the fact that she was in dire need of a refit, her maximum speed had been reduced to somewhere in the region of 26.5 knots.[52]

Second, it is likely that a slight navigational error was working against Holland. As a number of individuals, including Sean Waddington, Graeme Rhys-Jones, and Tim Woodward, and even the charts and records of the pursuit of the *Bismarck* from HMS *Suffolk* have pointed out, it was thought the *Bismarck* and the *Prinz Eugen* were 14 miles further east on a bearing of 110 degrees than they in fact were.[53] When sighted at 5.37 a.m., the German squadron was marginally abaft the beam of Holland's force and further west than expected, meaning that the German squadron was actually closer to escaping into the Atlantic than previously thought. As such, Holland needed to take the initiative and act both quickly and decisively.

In *The Royal Navy's Home Fleet in World War II*, James Levy has pointed out that Holland had another two options open to him neither of which were particularly satisfactory, points which have been echoed by Tim Woodward. The first option open to Holland was to avoid action and to continue using the *Suffolk* and the *Norfolk* to shadow the *Bismarck*, an action which was contrary to the traditions of the Royal Navy and was an action that would allow the German ships to reach the vastness of the North Atlantic unmolested. Such a move would also lessen the chance of bringing the *Bismarck* to battle again in the future.[54] Furthermore, such an action would evoke memories of the embarrassment following Ernest Troubridge allowing the German battlecruiser *Goeben* to escape the Mediterranean Fleet, pass through the Dardanelles, and reach Constantinople in 1914. Indeed, Churchill would go on to describe the *Prince of Wales* retiring from the engagement with the *Bismarck* following the loss of the *Hood* as 'the worst thing since Troubridge turned away from the *Goeben* in 1914'.[55] Secondly, an engagement conducted at long range would have been ill-advised owing to the *Hood*'s vulnerability to plunging fire. As such, Holland's approach was the logical option; it may be said that the end-on approach was in this regard the best of a bad bunch of options.

Closing the range rapidly would also help the gunnery of the British squadron. In the first instance, owing to the prevailing weather conditions at the time, sea spray blanketed the rangefinders, which obscured visibility. Therefore, closing the range to the target would make it easier to hit. Related to this, the *Prince of Wales* had not been worked up properly and with problems known to exist with her main battery guns, any advantage that Holland could give to the gun crews would be beneficial.

Alan Coles and Ted Briggs have suggested that Holland should have approached the German squadron at a finer angle so that when closing the range to the enemy, all of his ship's main armaments could have been brought to bear.[56] To have approached the battle in such a manner would have served to have slowed the rate of approach between the two squadrons and would have left the *Hood* in a vulnerable position for longer. Such an approach may have even permitted the German squadron to use its superior speed to escape.

Further vindicating Holland's use of the end-on approach is the fact that the approach was advocated by Admiral Tovey, who is said to have recommended the end-on approach to all of his commanding officers.[57] One of those to whom this approach was recommended by Tovey was the man that Holland succeeded as the admiral commanding the Battlecruiser Squadron, Admiral Sir William J. Whitworth. A month before the Battle of the Denmark Strait, Whitworth had planned to make a similar end-on approach if he was the admiral tasked with bringing the *Bismarck* to battle.[58] Bruce Taylor went so far as to write, 'Holland had endorsed the tactics laid down by Whitworth a month earlier in the event of an encounter with the *Bismarck*, and from these [tactics] he seems never to have strayed'.[59] The idea behind such an approach was that in approaching bow on a commander would present a smaller target to the enemy than if they were side on. This approach was also recommended in Admiralty fighting instructions. It may be noted that the fighting instructions of the day were vague with regards to battleships and battlecruisers and were tailored more to large fleet actions such as the Battle of Jutland. As such, it is unfair to blame Holland for the end-on approach to the battle.

With regards to his approach, Holland has also been criticised for not approaching the German squadron directly bow on. Rather, as opposed to being bow on, Holland's approach was 30 degrees off it. The criticism in this regard points to the fact that Tovey only recommended an approach up to 20 degrees off being bow on while Holland was 30 degrees off. This approach meant that when Holland's ships approached, they were presenting more of a target to the enemy while not being able to use their full main armament. Again, however, this particular criticism does not take into account the fact that Holland needed to close with the enemy quickly. Indeed, the fine angle of approach taken by Holland actually served to add to the German confusion as to the type of vessels that were approaching.[60] As such, owing to the constraints of the situation that he found himself in, the end-on approach was the best option open to Holland.

The decision for the end-on approach may be rooted in the Battle of Cape Spartivento, which proved to be Holland's first real test as an operational commander.[61] Commanding a group of four light cruisers known as Force 'F' (which were crowded with approximately 700 RAF and army personnel in addition to their respective ship's companies), Holland engaged the Italian fleet with his ships in loose line-abreast formation. When battle was joined, Holland elected not to order his cruisers to concentrate on a single target nor to operate in close formation because, in his opinion, the ships had too little experience in fighting as a unit.[62] A subsequent Board of Inquiry into the battle noted the 'lack of systematic practice and exercises' and singled out 'the reluctance of Vice-Admiral Holland to attempt a concentration of fire by the cruisers of his squadron'.[63] Following hearing from Holland that he elected not to give chase to the Italian fleet when it broke off and retired because his 'ships were outgunned and he did not think it was good principle', the Admiralty showed that it disagreed with the decision to break off the engagement and the manner in which it had been fought.[64] It concluded in its report:

> The Board of Inquiry suggests ... that the time chosen to give up the chase was slightly early ... The Board of the Admiralty cannot emphasis enough

that in all cases especially when dealing with an enemy who is reluctant to engage in close action, no opportunity must be allowed to pass of attaining, what is in fact, the ultimate objective of the Royal Navy—the destruction of main enemy naval forces when and whenever they are encountered. Only thus can control of the sea communications be properly secured.[65]

From the conclusion of the Admiralty report, it may be deduced that Holland was under pressure to rectify these criticisms of his command from the Admiralty, and that this was on his mind at the time of the Battle of the Denmark Strait. Therefore, it may be said that Holland was following the Admiralty's directives and thus any criticism of Holland should be placed at the Admiralty's door.[66]

Vessel Dispositions

In the years that have passed since the Battle of the Denmark Strait, many commentators have highlighted the drawbacks that existed in Holland's decision to have the *Hood* and the *Prince of Wales* fight in close order. In the first instance, this allowed the gunnery officers of the *Bismarck* to quickly switch targets to the *Prince of Wales* following the loss of the *Hood*. Indeed, Schneider did not need to significantly alter his gunnery data, which had significant repercussions for the British battleship. Many have argued that if the *Hood* and the *Prince of Wales* were not sailing in such a close order then the speed with which the *Bismarck* was able to range in on the *Prince of Wales* would have been reduced.

Second, if the *Hood* and the *Prince of Wales* were more dispersed, then it may have been possible for Holland's ships to more readily divide the German fire as the British hunting force under Commodore Henry Hardwood had done during the Battle of the River Plate on 13 December 1939.[67] In addition to this, it has been argued that both ships would have been able to report the fall of shot of the other.[68] Some have argued that by having both ships fight in close order, Holland limited the initiative of Captain Leach and thus wasted his skills as a commander.[69] Holland's decision to have his ships fight in close order in the Denmark Strait is often contrasted to the way in which Tovey decided to fight the *Bismarck* three days later. In this, a comparison is made to the way in which Tovey allowed Captain Frederick Dalrymple-Hamilton in command of HMS *Rodney* freedom of manoeuvre against the *Bismarck*. This argument does, however, fail to take into account all of the effects of the events of the past three days, the morale of those aboard the *Bismarck* on 27 May, and the *Bismarck*'s actual capabilities.

Finally, some commentators have put forward the argument that smoke from the *Hood*, sailing in close proximity ahead of the *Prince of Wales*, would have made it difficult for observers aboard the battleship to monitor the target with the result that this likely impacted on her gunnery. At the Battle of the Falkland Islands in 1914, HMS *Inflexible* had been hindered by the funnel smoke from HMS *Invincible*.[70] While these elements may be fair criticisms and highlight limitations in Holland's tactics, there were, in fact, a number of advantages in several areas to fighting the battle in this manner.

The advantage of having both the *Hood* and the *Prince of Wales* sailing and fighting in such close proximity centre around the theory of the two ships working as one unit in concentrating their fire on *Bismarck* and utilising their advantage of heavy guns. It would appear that Holland was following the instructions of the Admiralty in his choice of approach in light of the criticism that he had received following his actions at the Battle of Cape Spartivento and in view of the close-line tactics advocated by Admiralty fighting instructions, meaning that he was acting within the accepted command and fighting doctrine. Holland's decision was based on the doctrine laid down by the Admiralty and the idea that such a formation would give him greater control over the ships under his command and allow him to concentrate their firepower. Had the *Hood* been sunk with the result that the battle lasted longer than it did, then it is possible that Holland's close formation may have proved its worth.

Furthermore, by having his ships in close proximity, Holland was seeking to remove the confusion that inevitably exists in any battle. By operating as one unit, Holland sought to ensure that either ship did not mask each other's fire. Moreover, one issue that had been identified at the Battle of Jutland in 1916 was the issue of signalling. By sailing in close proximity, Holland would have no issue in signalling instructions.

The failure to involve the shadowing *Suffolk* and *Norfolk* in the battle from the beginning of the engagement has led to Holland being heavily criticised. On the face of it, it would appear that it was a missed opportunity. The *Norfolk* and the *Suffolk* were capable of duelling with the *Prinz Eugen* on more or less equal terms, and the support provided by the cruisers had they engaged the *Prinz Eugen* would undoubtedly have served to divide the German fire, meaning that in the first instance, both German ships would have been unable to concentrate their fire on the *Hood* and then the *Prince of Wales*. The *Norfolk* and the *Suffolk* were undoubtedly on Lütjens's mind as von Müllenheim-Rechberg has described how he, in his capacity of fourth gunnery officer of the *Bismarck*, had been designated to observe the movements of the British cruisers during the battle and to react if they moved to attack.[71] It is known that Holland had intended to utilise the two cruisers against the *Prinz Eugen* as this intention was signalled to Captain Leach.[72]

The decision not to communicate with the shadowing cruisers in line with the decision not to use radar was an understandable decision as Holland did not want to alert the Germans to the presence of his ships. It is not clear, however, why Holland's intention was not communicated to the *Norfolk* and the *Suffolk* once battle was joined. A number of theories exist, including the idea that Holland may have wanted to soften up the German ships first before the cruisers were deployed in case they became casualties from a German attack. It has also been suggested that Holland may have wanted to delay to see exactly how Lütjens would react to the prospect of a battle so that he could decide how best to employ the cruisers. It may also be the case that Holland felt that he did not need to issue orders to the *Norfolk* and the *Suffolk* and that he assumed that Wake-Walker would himself pre-empt Holland's thoughts and would, of his own accord, seek to engage with the *Prinz Eugen* while Holland engaged the *Bismarck*.

However Holland planned to deploy the cruisers, the battle ultimately did not last long enough for them to be effectively employed. There is one issue, however, if Holland did wish for the *Norfolk* and the *Suffolk* to play a part in the battle—the two cruisers would have had to have been notified in advance of the battle to be able to increase speed and to begin closing the range to the German squadron.

Mistaken Identities

Another element for which Holland has been criticised is in the targeting of the German ships. At the outset of the battle, Holland ordered both the *Hood* and the *Prince of Wales* to target the lead ship, which was the *Prinz Eugen*. Meanwhile, we know that Commander McMullen on board the *Prince of Wales* recognised that the *Bismarck* was the second vessel in line and engaged the correct target on Captain Leach's orders while flashing the signal 'Make IMI' to the *Hood*, requesting clarification of the engagement order.[73] There exists, however, confusion over whether or not the order was issued for the target to be switched. According to Ted Briggs, the error of incorrectly identifying the *Bismarck* was recognised by those on the *Hood*'s compass platform and the order was issued to the *Prince of Wales* to shift her gunnery to the right-hand ship (the *Bismarck*), which she was already targeting.[74] The question arises as to whether or not the order to switch targets was issued to the *Hood*'s gunners as even after the misidentification had been recognised by Holland and those on the compass platform and the order was issued to the *Prince of Wales*, the *Hood*'s gunners continued to fire at the *Prinz Eugen*.

Holland has been criticised for this as the misidentification of the *Bismarck* cost the *Hood* time to score hits on the German battleship. There is another side to this error. British gunnery systems were fairly poor and made identification difficult. The rangefinders of the *Hood* were inferior to those of the more modern *Prince of Wales*. Further to this, the *Prince of Wales* boasted two sets of rangefinders, one of which was mounted on a higher position than that of the *Hood*. Vibration on the *Hood*'s spotting top was also a hindrance to identification. Errors from the crew of the *Hood*, the distances involved, and the weather conditions also added to the challenges of positive identification and cannot be discounted from playing a part in contributing to this error.

In addition to this, even though the *Bismarck* was larger than the *Prinz Eugen*, the two ships had similar silhouettes, which served to confused Holland and his officers. Commander McMullen would later state that he thought that the misidentification of the *Bismarck* was an easy mistake to make as 'Over the horizon came these two ships, one leading the other, exactly the same silhouette, four turrets, one funnel'.[75] McMullen would go on to reflect that it was 'very cunning on the Germans' part to have these silhouettes so exactly alike. Of course the *Prinz Eugen*, although she was a cruiser, was a very big ship'.[76]

Marco Santarini, in his work *Bismarck and Hood*, has claimed that not only did the similarity of the silhouettes confuse Holland and his captains, but also that the *Hood* engaged the *Prinz Eugen* and the *Prince of Wales* engaged the *Bismarck* because 'British tactical procedure then in force prescribed that each ship in the line had to fire against the corresponding enemy ship'.[77] Therefore, saying that the *Hood* did not engage the *Bismarck* because of tactical procedure is preposterous. Holland and the ships under his command had but one goal—to stop the German ships, and most importantly the *Bismarck*, from breaking out into the vastness of the Atlantic where they could wreak havoc upon any one of the multitude of convoys then at sea. Holland issued orders to both those on the *Hood* and to the *Prince of Wales* to engage the left-hand enemy ship, which he believed to be the *Bismarck* as flagship of the squadron and because at the fore of the formation, she was better positioned to protect the less heavily armoured cruiser.

The *Prince of Wales* engaged the *Bismarck* while the *Hood* engaged the lead ship, which happened to be the *Prinz Eugen* because her gunnery officer, Lieutenant-Commander Colin McMullen, was more readily able to identify that the second vessel in the line was larger than the lead vessel and that it must therefore be the *Bismarck*. In due course, those aboard the *Hood* realised their error and communicated this to the *Prince of Wales*, which was already targeting the correct ship. As such, the *Hood*'s engagement of the *Prinz Eugen* was not the result of tactical procedure.

The sharp angle of approach made by the British ships made it difficult for Lütjens and his gunnery officers to identify the approaching British vessels with the result that they initially thought that the *Hood* and the *Prince of Wales* were light cruisers and then heavy cruisers; the sharp angle of approach also made the German ships hard to identify for the British. As such, it was a safe bet to assume that the *Bismarck*, as the flagship of the squadron, would be the lead vessel. Holland was not known that the German vessels had switched places owing to a problem with the forward radar of the *Bismarck*. The shadowing *Norfolk* and *Suffolk* had given no indication of this change of positions. The suggestion is made in *Flagship Hood* that if Holland had permitted the use of radar when the German ships were sighted and the plot showed them to be less than 20 miles distant, the mistake in identifying the German vessels would not have been made.[78] While this may be an easy assumption to make, if the shadowing cruisers (in particular the *Suffolk* with her superior radar) had failed to pick up the change in the positioning of the two German vessels, why should the radar of the *Hood* or the *Prince of Wales* have picked this up?[79]

While a mistake in the identification of the *Bismarck* was made, it was not directly Holland's fault and it is easy to see why this mistake occurred. As the opposing forces grew closer, it became clearer which ship was which, and as the battle developed, this mistake would have counted for less. Unfortunately, the battle did not last that long, and with the loss of the *Hood*, one may say the battle was as good as over as the *Prince of Wales* took avoiding action around the sinking *Hood* before breaking off the engagement as she was outnumbered and outgunned.

The *Hood* failed to hit the *Prinz Eugen*; the closest she came to hitting the cruiser was with a salvo that landed close, sending up great columns of water and splinters aboard the cruiser. Had the *Hood* managed to hit the *Prinz Eugen*, it would have created a particularly interesting situation. With belt armour ranging between 2.8 and 3.1 inches in thickness and deck armour ranging between 0.79 to 1.97 inches in thickness, the *Hood*'s shells would have caused serious damage to the cruiser and would have left Lütjens having to decide whether or not to protect the heavy cruiser or to simply order the *Bismarck* to bid a hasty retreat.

It is worth briefly looking here at the actions of Admiral Lütjens. The fact that he did not disengage is attributable to vessel misidentification much greater than the British deliberations over which of the two German ships was the *Bismarck*. Indeed, the battle only really came about because the Germans failed to identify the British vessels as capital ships until their first salvos landed, by which time the British ships were in gunnery range, meaning an engagement could not be avoided.

Cruisers were a fraction of the size of the *Hood* and the *Prince of Wales*. The *Hood* had a length of 860 feet 7 inches while the *Prince of Wales* had an overall length of 745 feet 1 inch. HMS *Suffolk* and the *Norfolk*, by contrast, were 630 and 632 feet 9 inches long respectively. While the sharp angle of approach of the British ships made identification difficult, it has to be assumed that the inaccurate and out of date intelligence from Luftwaffe reconnaissance reports that had been passed on to Lütjens along with wishful thinking served to create the illusion that the ships were heavy cruisers arriving to reinforce the shadowing operation. Whatever the reason(s) may be, Lütjens allowed Holland to succeed in closing the range dramatically so that he was able to engage. When she opened fire, the *Prinz Eugen* fired with high-explosive rounds, which were more suited for use against more lightly armoured ships like cruisers than for capital ships against which armour-piercing rounds were more effective.

While the Battle of the Denmark Strait was a German tactical victory, it would seem that Lütjens had little input at all at a tactical level. The hydrophone operators of the *Prinz Eugen* picked up the sound of approaching vessels long before smoke was first spotted on the horizon.[80] Even when the *Hood* and the *Prince of Wales* were sighted and it was clear that they were approaching the German squadron, Lütjens seems to have made the unwarranted assumption that they could be nothing more than cruisers sent as reinforcements. Even when the *Hood* appeared over the horizon, the Germans continued to see cruisers. It was only after the British ships had opened fire and permission to return fire had been requested that those aboard the *Bismarck* identified one of their adversaries as the *Hood*.[81] Even at the angle at which the British ships approached, the crews of the *Bismarck* and *Prinz Eugen* should have noted the distinctive spotting top and tripod foremast denoting the *Hood* as a Royal Navy capital ship of First World War vintage.

Conclusions

This chapter has examined a number of the actions and decisions made by Admiral Holland during the course of events just prior to and during the Battle of the Denmark Strait. Like many commanders before him, Holland was guilty of making poor decisions during his career and has been fairly and validly criticised. To a large degree, some of the major criticisms of Holland can be vindicated through looking at the ramifications of the Battle of Cape Spartivento and the influence of contemporary fighting instructions. Holland made the decision to close the range between the *Hood* and the *Bismarck*, which appears on the face of it to be a tactical error on his part, but analysis of this decision shows it to be the result of the conclusions reached by an Admiralty Board of Inquiry following the Battle of Cape Spartivento. As this criticism cannot be validated, it is unfair to ridicule Holland for this.

During the course of the night of 23–24 May, it would appear that Holland had approached the battle in what may be deemed an acceptable and justifiable manner, especially considering the pressures he was under, the constraints placed on him, and the uncertainty of the unfolding situation. Holland fully grasped the issues and the benefits of radar and ultimately decided against its use owing to the fact that it had the potential to give his position away. Furthermore, his battle plan in electing to cross the 'T' of the German ships (which would have seen him cut off the German ships, utilise the gun advantage of the *Hood* and the *Prince of Wales* and see him take full advantage of the prevailing weather conditions) was a sound operational plan.[82]

The much-criticised turn to the north was made before the loss of contact with the *Bismarck* by the shadowing *Suffolk* and *Norfolk* had been confirmed and was a turn designed to bring about an engagement sooner rather than later and to limit the opportunity for the *Bismarck* to make good an escape into the Atlantic. It was not a turn, as many have claimed, to search for the *Bismarck*. In his decisions prior to the battle, it becomes apparent that Holland displayed good judgment but that Lütjens had not acted as Holland had hoped. Furthermore, the way in which Holland deployed his destroyers, for which he has been criticised, can be fully justified.

Once battle with the German squadron was joined, Holland appears to have continued to make sensible decisions based on the developing situation caused by factors outside of his control. The end-on approach sought to limit the opportunity for the *Bismarck* to escape and to minimise the risk of the *Hood* to plunging fire while also providing his gunners with the best opportunity possible to hit their targets. While Holland has been criticised for this, it is unfair to do so as such an approach was recommended by senior officers, including Admiral Tovey and by the Admiralty. The disposition of his ships was based on a combination of sound tactical thinking, Admiralty fighting instructions, and the criticisms resulting from the Board of Inquiry held in the wake of the Battle of Cape Spartivento. By having his ships fight in close order, Holland enabled his ships to operate as one unit and made signalling easier, serving to prevent his ships from masking the fire of each other.

Holland has been criticised for his failure to engage the *Norfolk* and the *Suffolk*. While it is known that he did intend to have them engage the *Prinz Eugen*, one can only assume that the battle did not last long enough for Holland to execute his plan; given that the *Norfolk* and the *Suffolk* would have needed prior warning to increase speed to close in on the *Prinz Eugen*, one can neither fully criticise Holland in this respect nor completely absolve him of all criticism.

Holland has equally been criticised for his failure to communicate effectively with the commanding officers of his ships. This, in turn, raises a number of additional questions, such as would the engagements have turned out differently had he communicated effectively? Such questions lie beyond the scope of this chapter.

The selection of the wrong target was a mixture of human error combined with the distances involved, the angle of approach taken by the British ships, and the weather conditions, which were far from ideal. Furthermore, the radar of HMS *Suffolk* had failed to pick up the change of positions between the *Bismarck* and the *Prinz Eugen*, and the change was not noted and communicated by anyone aboard the cruisers. As such it is not wholly surprising that Holland made the error of issuing the order to engage the left-hand ship. While Holland's order was corrected, debate remains over whether or not this issue was rectified aboard the *Hood*.

Holland made educated decisions based on the situation in which he found himself. The decisions that he made were both shrewd and served to cater for all the responsibilities and limitations that he was burdened with. Holland's mission was to take the *Hood* and the *Prince of Wales* and to prevent the *Bismarck* from raiding commerce; he did succeed in bringing Admiral Lütjens and the *Bismarck* into a battle that they could not avoid and although the *Hood* was lost along with Holland, the *Prince of Wales* succeeded in scoring three hits, two of which ultimately served to curtail the commerce raiding sortie of the *Bismarck* before she broke out into the Atlantic. As such, in this respect, Holland was successful.

Many of the criticisms that have been levelled against Holland are based on the benefit of hindsight and are unfair. Holland was unlucky. With a little more luck, the battle may have ended differently. This is, however, pure speculation. While not perfect, Holland acted professionally and was justifiably Mentioned in Dispatches for the determination and skill that he demonstrated during the Battle of the Denmark Strait.

Battle Photographs

Despite the wealth of information that exists on the Battle of the Denmark Strait, the engagement has been the source of great debate owing to the confusion stemming from the official documentation and the various accounts of the battle. Some of the confusion that exists stems from the series of photographs taken from on board the *Prinz Eugen*. The photographs taken from the *Prinz Eugen* show the *Bismarck* on both sides of the heavy cruiser, apparently engaging ships on both her port and starboard sides without any supporting evidence demonstrating how this apparent cross-over took place.

One of the theories that have been advanced to explain this cross-over is the so-called 'reverse photo theory', which argues that there was no cross-over between the two German vessels and that the photographs have simply been printed in reverse. The 'reverse photo theory' has never been universally accepted in the naval community with the idea being accepted, by and large, as implausible. In his work *Pursuit*, Ludovic Kennedy has concluded that a number of the photographs illustrating the Battle of the Denmark Strait have been printed in reverse. The German naval historian Professor Jürgen Rohwer has also accepted this theory as being correct.

What, therefore, are the reasons for the disparity between the theories on the photographs showing the engagement and have the photographs simply been printed in reverse? If so, why has the theory never been universally accepted?

During Operation Rheinübung (the codename given to the raiding operation to be undertaken by the *Bismarck* and the *Prinz Eugen* of which the Battle of the Denmark Strait was a part), the *Prinz Eugen* carried a staff photographer called Lagemann, who took still photographs of the *Bismarck* with a 35-mm camera. Lagemann was accompanied on the voyage by another cameraman who took motion picture footage of the operation with a 16-mm camera. Both of these two photographers covered the Battle of the Denmark Strait, and what they captured provides vital clues as to how the overall battle was ultimately fought. In this, the motion picture footage is useful for recording events on a second-by-second basis and helps to establish the exact sequence in which all of Lagemann's still photographs were taken.

The photographs have been the source of debate among historians and enthusiasts as they appear to show the *Bismarck* on both the port and starboard sides of the *Prinz Eugen* during the engagement. This has sparked debate as to in which direction the German vessels were in fact sailing, what ships the *Bismarck* was apparently engaging, and when and how this apparent switching of sides occurred. None of the photographs show the *Bismarck* making any turns. Many of the photographs in question are held by the US Naval History and Heritage Command with the others being held by the German *Bundesarchiv*.

The first photograph in the sequence taken during the Battle of the Denmark Strait by Lagemann is NH-69722. In this photograph, the *Bismarck* is clearly seen astern of the *Prinz Eugen* firing to port at the *Hood*. The approximate time that this image was taken is 5.55 a.m. From this photograph, it can be clearly seen that Lagemann snapped this image while looking aft on the starboard side of the *Prinz Eugen*. Having taken this photograph, Lagemann walked over to the port side of the ship and took up a position beside the aft 105-mm anti-aircraft guns. It is from this position that he took the vast majority, indeed if not all, of the other photographs during the course of the battle.

NH-69729 is the next photograph in the sequence and shows the *Bismarck* coming up on the port side of the *Prinz Eugen* during the period that she was still firing at the *Hood*. The image captures the huge cloud of smoke created by *Bismarck* as she fires broadside. NH-69730 is the next photograph in the sequence and was taken at around 6.01 a.m. Taken moments after the *Hood* had blown up, the *Bismarck* is shown firing on the *Prince of Wales*. This photograph is quite possibly one of the most famous photographs taken of the *Bismarck* and is certainly one of the most famous photographs illustrating the Battle of the Denmark Strait. In the image, the *Bismarck* is silhouetted by the flash resulting from turrets 'Caesar' and 'Dora' firing. In the top right-hand corner of the photograph, the muzzle ends of one of the *Prinz Eugen*'s the twin SK C/33 anti-aircraft guns can be seen. The darkness of the image compared to other images in the sequence owes something to overexposure and does not, in fact, show the engagement occurring at night as some have sought to argue.

The final photograph in this series is held by the German *Bundesarchiv*, BA 146-1984-055-13, and shows the *Bismarck* coming up the port side of the *Prinz Eugen*. Taken at approximately 6.03 a.m., the *Bismarck* had moments earlier fired a full broadside against the *Prince of Wales*. This helps to place the photograph in sequence with regards to its timing as it was taken near the beginning of the *Bismarck*'s action against the *Prince of Wales*, when she was still firing full salvos at the British battleship.

These photographs are consistent with the other factual evidence of the battle that show the *Bismarck* moved from a position astern of *Prinz Eugen* and travelled up the port side of the cruiser until 6.02 a.m. The salvo plot of HMS *Prince of Wales* shows that *Bismarck* covered a greater distance than the *Prinz Eugen* and therefore suggests that *Bismarck* increased speed to her top speed of 30 knots while *Prinz Eugen* continued sailing at 27 knots. According to the speed chart of the *Prinz Eugen*, the ship remained at 27 knots throughout the battle. Faced with this and the fact that the *Bismarck* was likely travelling at 30 knots, the battleship would have been able to gain approximately 100 yards per minute at a speed difference of 3 knots, which is consistent with how far *Bismarck* is seen to advance in the photographs.

Beginning at 6.03 a.m., the *Prinz Eugen* made a series of three hard turns to starboard before straightening out on a course parallel to that of the *Bismarck*. As previously mentioned, these turns were ordered by Brinkmann so as to open up the distance between his ship and the flagship and to make his cruiser less vulnerable to fire from the *Prince of Wales*, which landed over the intended target. These turns prohibited the taking of any photographs for the next four minutes as not only were the turns executed rapidly, but the slope on the deck during them made it been virtually impossible to take clear photographs or steady images in general until the ship had stabilised. It was now that the second set of photographs were taken by Lagemann, which show the *Bismarck* on the starboard side of the *Prinz Eugen* firing to starboard. The images were likely taken between 6.08 and 6.10 a.m., shortly, if not immediately after the *Prinz Eugen* had executed the last of her sharp turns to starboard.

NH-69728 is the first photograph in the second series of images and would appear to be the first image on a new roll of film. The left-hand edge of the photograph is slightly clouded, which indicates that the image may be the first on a new roll of film and that the new roll of film that was installed in the camera was not turned sufficiently to take up the film leader. Given that it would have been impossible for any meaningful photographs to be taken between 6.03 and 6.08 a.m. when the *Prinz Eugen* was making her sharp turns, it is perhaps the case that Lagemann took the opportunity to reload his camera.

NH-69728 shows *Bismarck* silhouetted against the light horizon, further ahead of the *Prinz Eugen* than she appeared in BA 146-1984-055-13. If the *Bismarck* had maintained her course while the *Prinz Eugen* was executing her turns, the *Bismarck* would have ended up somewhat ahead of the *Prinz Eugen* and some distance further away laterally than she had been at 6.03 a.m. This is indicated in the photograph. In the image, there are large separate puffs of smoke, which can be seen over the stern end of the *Bismarck*, which indicate the firing of three of the ship's main battery turrets a few seconds apart. A large water column indicating the impact of a shell can be seen approximately a ship's length behind the *Bismarck*. It is likely that this was from a single shell fired by the *Prince of Wales* as she retreated from the battle.

The next images in the sequence are *Bundesarchiv* photographs BA 146-1968-015-25 and BA 146-1968-015-26. These images were taken seconds later and are almost identical to NH-69728 with the main differentiating feature between the three images being the smoke plumes from the three turrets, which are further behind the ship and have partially dissipated. BA 146-1968-015-12 was taken approximately eighteen seconds after BA146-1968-015-26 and shows another solitary shell splash, indicating another shell landing in the water from the retreating *Prince of Wales*. In the photograph, the *Bismarck* herself appears visibly smaller, indicating that she is pulling further ahead of the *Prinz Eugen*.

NH-69726 was taken twenty-nine seconds after BA 146-1968-015-12 and provides evidence that clearly establishes the direction that the *Bismarck* was sailing and the direction in which she was firing. Like the preceding photographs, NH-69726 is a silhouette view of the *Bismarck*. A huge fireball can be seen directly above the stern of the ship, brightly illuminating parts of the battleship's superstructure. In the image, all of what are apparently the portside surfaces, including those near the fireball, are in shadow, indicating that the *Bismarck* was firing to starboard when the photograph was taken. The lack of a reflection of the fireball on the surface of the water on the port side further indicates that the *Bismarck* was firing away from the *Prinz Eugen* when the image was captured.

Of note here are images NH-69725 and NH-69731. These images both show smoke from the exploding *Hood* and smoke from *Prince of Wales*. In these photographs the *Prince of Wales* is noted as being the smoke column to the left of centre while the exploding *Hood* is the mass of smoke on the right hand side of the image. The image caption for NH-69725 from the US Naval History and Heritage Comand reads:

> British battleship *Prince of Wales* (left smoke column) turns to open the range, after she was hit by German gunfire. Smoke at right marks the spot where HMS *Hood* had exploded and sunk a few minutes earlier.

Similarly, the image caption for NH-69731 states:

> British battleship *Prince of Wales* (smoke column in left centre) under fire from the German battleship *Bismarck* and heavy cruiser *Prinz Eugen*, with smoke from the sunken HMS *Hood* at right. Splashes to the right are shells from *Prince of Wales* that fell well short of the German ships.

Debate surrounds what is shown in NH-69731. According to Robert J. Winklareth, the photograph was taken thirty seconds after NH-69724, which shows the explosion of the *Hood*. Others, such as Paul Cadogan and a number of individuals in online forums, have put forward the claim that in NH-69731, the smoke column on the left is in fact smoke from the exploding *Hood* and that the large patch of smoke on the right is, in fact, the *Prince of Wales*. It is claimed that the large smoke plume is a combination of the funnel smoke from the *Prince of Wales* and the smokescreen produced during her retreat and that the photograph was taken around 6.03 a.m.

There is also a claim that in this photograph, the shell splashes are either from the *Bismarck* or the *Prince of Wales* that fell short. In his book *Power at Sea: Volume 2*, Lisle A. Rose includes a copy of NH-69731 and a caption that states:

> Battle in the Denmark Strait, May 1941. Shell splashes from the German battleship *Bismarck* fall near HMS *Prince of Wales*, while burning oil and the final, sinking remains of HMS *Hood* are to the left. Photographed from *Bismarck*'s escort, the cruiser *Prinz Eugen*, which separated from the doomed battleship and made port.[1]

Winklareth's interpretation of the photograph is based on the official image caption provided by the Naval History and Heritage Command. If Cadogan and others are correct, then the interpretations of NH-69725 are incorrect. Winklareth commented on the photograph:

> [It] shows the splashes from the *Bismarck*'s sixth salvo, fired just before the *Hood* exploded, directly in front of the smoke cloud that still hung over the sinking *Hood*. Both photographs [NH-69724 and NH-69731] show the smoke plumes from the funnel of the *Prince of Wales* still to the left of the *Hood* after the *Prince of Wales* turned toward the German squadron and before she sailed around the wreckage of the *Hood*.
>
> The latter photograph was erroneously captioned in other publications as indicating that the splashes came from shells fired by the *Prince of Wales* that fell well short of the German ships. That caption is of course completely ridiculous for a number of reasons, and yet it is accepted by some as being the truth. The *Prince of Wales* salvo plot accounted for every salvo fired by the British battleship, and after the *Prince of Wales* once got the range on the *Bismarck*, her misses were never more than about one thousand yards off. The splashes shown in the photograph are near the horizon, over 15,000 yards (8 nautical miles) away from the vantage point of the photographer. Just looking at the photograph should be sufficient to discount those other captions.[2]

The timeline of the battle states that the *Prince of Wales* took evasive action around the sinking *Hood* before beginning her retreat from the battle. It is often written that at the time of the *Hood*'s explosion, HMS *Prince of Wales* was turning and that as she did so, she found the sinking *Hood* directly in her path. In response to this, Captain Leach ordered evasive action to starboard to avoid the sinking battlecruiser and that this placed the *Prince of Wales* directly between the sinking *Hood* and the German ships.

It is possible that the interpretation put forward by Winklareth is not correct. In NH-69724, the *Prince of Wales* is just visible to the left of the exploding *Hood*. If NH-69731 was taken thirty seconds after NH-69724 as Winklareth claims, how can it be that the range between the exploding *Hood* on the right and the *Prince of Wales* on the left had increased by such a large margin? Supposing Cadogan and those who have discussed the images in online forums are correct, what evidence supports the claim that *Prince of Wales* in on the right and that the *Hood* is on the left? In the photograph, there is the large area of smoke that Winklareth claims is smoke from the *Hood* and that others have sought to claim as being a smokescreen from *Prince of Wales*. In the centre is a drifting plume of smoke that is claimed is from burning oil on the surface of the water, and then there is a mysterious dark shape to the left of centre. In online forums, it is claimed that the dark shape to the left of centre is related to the sinking *Hood*. Winklareth has claimed that the shell splashes near the patch of smoke on the right are from the sixth salvo fired by the *Bismarck*, which was fired before the *Hood* exploded. If one analyses NH-69731 carefully, between the dark shape to the left of centre and the central drifting smoke, shell splashes can be seen. While it is possible that these could be from *Bismarck*'s sixth salvo, if the photograph was taken at 6.03 a.m. as is claimed online, then the columns of water thrown up by the impact of the shells would be long gone.

Online, it is alternately claimed that the shell splashes between the *Prinz Eugen* from where the photograph has been taken and the smoke on the right are from the *Bismarck* or the *Prince of Wales*, which fell short. While it is possible that the splashes mark the impact of shells from the *Bismarck* that fell short of their target, this is unlikely because of the angle of the shell impact in relation to the speculated *Prince of Wales* and the known position of *Bismarck*. The *Bismarck* was, by this point, ahead of the *Prinz Eugen*; for the shell to have come down where it did in relation to the smoke plume, the *Bismarck* would have had to have been behind the *Prinz Eugen*. Furthermore, the shell splash is too close to the *Prinz Eugen* for it to have come from the *Bismarck*. On the other side, it is claimed that the shell came from *Prince of Wales* and that it was from a salvo that fell short. If this is the case then it is likely that the shells are from either salvo sixteen or salvo eighteen owing to their impact positions relative to the German ships.

There is another theory that may be put forward on the image. The images show shell splashes, indicating the impact of shells from the *Prince of Wales* that fell short of the German ships as she retreated. Having taken avoiding action around the sinking *Hood*, the *Prince of Wales* made good her escape by sailing south before altering course to the south-east. This put the *Prince of Wales* approximately 1.5 nautical miles to the south of the sinking *Hood*. Based on the image caption of the *Prince of Wales* being the smoke column on the left according to the caption, and discounting the mysterious dark shape, the position of the *Prince of Wales* relative to the smoke plume that denotes the *Hood*, it is possible that this image was taken between 6.08 and 6.09 a.m. shortly before the *Bismarck* ceased fire when the *Prince of Wales* would have appeared to be astern of the *Hood* once more. It is known that when she retreated, 'Y' turret fired a number of rounds under local control directed at the *Bismarck*, which were not recorded on the salvo plot. The angle of the shell impact from the central smoke plume would appear to be more or less a direct line. Given that the *Bismarck* was ahead of the *Prinz Eugen* at the time, one can assume that if a direct line was drawn from the smoke, through the shell splashes, then the line would end off the photograph in an area that corresponds with the known position of the *Bismarck*.

The final photograph that shows the *Bismarck* on the starboard side of the *Prinz Eugen* is NH-69727. This photograph shows the *Bismarck* completely silhouetted against the light sky on the horizon. A large cloud of smoke hangs directly over the stern of the ship as a result of the *Bismarck*'s forward movement during the time period that has elapsed between this image and the previous one.

When the images showing *Bismarck* on the starboard side of the *Prinz Eugen* are reversed, the *Bismarck* is seen on the port side of the heavy cruiser, which ties in with the documentary evidence of the *Bismarck*'s movements.

There are no other photographs showing the *Bismarck* on the starboard side of the *Prinz Eugen* during the course of the battle, and there are no photographs showing the *Bismarck* exchanging positions with the *Prinz Eugen*. On average, Lagemann was taking photographs at a rate of one per minute. Given this, the lack of photographic evidence makes such a move questionable. Lagemann did not take any photographs of the *Bismarck* while the *Prinz Eugen* was making her series of turns between 6.03 and 6.08 a.m.; while some may argue that it was at this moment when Lagemann was not taking photographs that the *Bismarck* transitioned over the starboard side, one must look at the viability.

In order to make the turns to place her on the starboard side of the *Prinz Eugen*, the *Bismarck* would have had to have made sharper turns than those executed by the heavy cruiser. It is known that *Prinz Eugen* fought the battle at 27 knots, and it is estimated that owing to the rate at which she overhauled the *Prinz*

Eugen, the *Bismarck* was likely sailing at 30 knots. In order to have increased the distance that she did between photographs BA 146-1984-055-3 and NH-69728, the *Bismarck* would have had to have increased her speed to well in excess of 30 knots and attain a speed that most destroyers of the time would have found hard, if not impossible, to attain. Furthermore, if the *Bismarck* had also turned with the *Prinz Eugen* and transitioned over to the starboard side, the distance between the two ships would have been much closer. One must also ask, if the *Bismarck* turned to starboard to take up a position on the starboard side of the *Prinz Eugen,* why did the cruiser also turn to starboard and not make the execution of such a manoeuvre easier by reducing speed slightly and executing a turn to port? Further to this, neither the war diary of the *Prinz Eugen* nor that of the *Bismarck* record the ships exchanging positions during the battle. The war diary of the *Bismarck* does, however, record the change of position after the battle in which the *Prinz Eugen* dropped astern the battleship to disperse the oil slick.[3] It would surely be the case that such a manoeuvre would be recorded in the war diary of at least one of the two ships if not both, most certainly the reconstructed war diary of the *Bismarck*. Also, von Müllenheim-Rechberg makes no reference to the *Bismarck* switching sides with the heavy cruiser.

In all of the photographs that show the *Bismarck* on the port side of the *Prinz Eugen,* the sky is brightest just above the horizon, which indicates that the photographs were taken towards the rising sun. Given that the sun rises in the east and sets in the west, owing to the sun just beginning to rise as the battle occurred, the sky to the west would still be predominantly dark. Coupled with this, the German squadron was sailing in a general southerly direction with the result that their port sides would have been facing east and their disengaged starboard sides west. In order for the *Bismarck* to have been on the starboard side of the *Prinz Eugen,* the photographs would have been taken facing westwards where the sky would have been at its darkest, not lightest. This serves to suggest that the photographs showing the *Bismarck* on the starboard side of the cruiser have been printed in reverse.

One must also question what the *Bismarck* was engaging on the starboard side. It is known that the *Hood* and the *Prince of Wales* were always to port of the German squadron; only HMS *Suffolk* was on the starboard side of the German squadron. It is known that the German battle group deemed that both the *Norfolk* and the *Suffolk* did not pose a serious threat during the course of the battle, and it was believed that the British cruisers would leave the German battle group alone, allowing them to concentrate their fire on the *Hood* and the *Prince of Wales*. While towards the end of the battle, as the *Prince of Wales* retreated, the *Suffolk* fired her forward turrets at the *Prinz Eugen* in the mistaken belief that she was within gunnery range, and that the forward armament of the *Bismarck* was traversed, there is no evidence to show that the *Bismarck* ever returned fire on the *Suffolk*.

It is interesting to note in this regard image Bild 146-1984-055-14, which was taken at 6.19 a.m., just after the Battle of the Denmark Strait had ended. In the image, the *Bismarck* is on the port side of the *Prinz Eugen* with her guns trained to starboard towards the *Suffolk*, ready to engage the British cruiser. It may be noted that the *Bismarck* did not open fire on the *Suffolk*. If the *Bismarck* moved on to the starboard side of the *Prinz Eugen* and engaged a target off to starboard, which could only be the *Suffolk* owing to the dispositions of the British ships, why after the battle would she return to the port side of the *Prinz Eugen* to retrain her guns on a target on the starboard side? Tactically, it would make no sense.

Moreover, in the war diary of the *Prinz Eugen*, the ship's first gunnery officer, Paulus Jasper, reported that after the series of turns made from 6.03 a.m., the *Bismarck* came into his sights. This sighting indicated that the *Bismarck* would soon be directly between the *Prinz Eugen* and the *Prince of Wales*, leading to the order being issued for the *Prinz Eugen* not to fire over the *Bismarck*. Shortly after this order was issued, the order was given for the *Prinz Eugen* to cease fire, which indicates that the *Bismarck* was already on the port side and had been for some time before the order to cease fire was given at 6.09 a.m. In addition to this, the *Prinz Eugen*'s second gunnery officer, Paul Schmalenbach, reported in the ship's war diary that during the battle, he took an occasional look at the *Bismarck*. This would not have been possible if the *Bismarck* was on the starboard side of the *Prinz Eugen* as the *Bismarck* would have been in a position away from the target area.

It is understandable that one or two photographs may be printed in reverse, accounting for the fact that *Bismarck* is seen on both the port and starboard sides of the *Bismarck* in contradiction to the documented evidence. Robert J. Winklareth has offered a 'rational' explanation for this occurrence:

> The photographs were taken with a 35mm film camera, and after a 35mm film is developed, it is usually cut into strips of four to six frames for easier handling when using an enlarger. It is therefore possible that the strip containing the six photographs in question was inadvertently turned upside down in the enlarger, causing all of the six frames on that strip to be printed in reverse.[4]

Motion picture footage was taken aboard the *Prinz Eugen* during Operation Rheinübung, of which approximately two minutes of footage covers the Battle of the Denmark Strait. By contrasting the footage against the previously mentioned photographs and the movements made during the battle, it is possible to establish that the bulk of the footage was taken between 6.08 and 6.10 a.m.

It is worth noting the editing of the footage. In the first instance, the *Bismarck* is shown ahead of the *Prinz Eugen* while her plot map shows that the *Bismarck* only attained her position ahead of the heavy cruiser at around

6.05 a.m. In the footage, not only is the *Bismarck* seen ahead of the *Prinz Eugen*, but she is shown on the port side of the *Prinz Eugen* travelling right to left across the screen, firing at a target on her starboard side. After having seen the *Bismarck* fire a salvo, the editors of the film included footage showing the explosion of the *Hood*. Here, by looking at the direction of travel in the water, the direction of travel is from left to right, contradicting the image direction shown moments earlier. At the same time, owing to the direction of travel, the exploding *Hood* is on the port side of the *Prinz Eugen*, yet the *Bismarck* is engaging a target (the *Prince of Wales*) on her starboard side. After capturing the exploding *Hood*, the footage returns to the apparent starboard side, showing the *Bismarck* once more before the switch is again made to the port side showing the smoke of the retreating *Prince of Wales* on the right and the smoke from the *Hood* on the left.

The film footage was not taken between 6.03 and 6.08 a.m. as this was when the *Prinz Eugen* began making her series of hard turns to starboard, which would have made relatively still picture taking impossible. Furthermore, the footage shows the *Bismarck* ahead of the *Prinz Eugen*, and no radical movements are made by either vessel in the footage, which when compared to the photographs discussed previously, leads to the conclusion that the footage was shot between 6.08 and 6.10 a.m. as the clarity of the film suggests that the *Prinz Eugen* was on a steady course. The first few frames of the footage are, however, slightly blurred, which would suggest that the cameraman began capturing the footage from 6.08 a.m. and began rolling the camera just as the *Prinz Eugen* settled down from the last of her hard turns, a mere thirty-five seconds before Lagemann took photograph NH-69728.

As a result of this evidence, it must be concluded that the battle film showing a port view of the *Bismarck* firing to starboard must in fact have been processed in reverse as when properly orientated, the footage showing the *Bismarck* conform to the documentary evidence relative to the battle and conforms to the footage of the exploding *Hood*. In addition to this, the film footage reinforces the concept that the battle was fought in a straight line— the *Bismarck* travelling down the port side of the *Prinz Eugen*—and supports the notion that no cross-over of the two ships took place. This, in turns, serves to render most maps depicting the movements made during the course of the battle as incorrect.

Based on this analysis, it is also possible to place all of the battle photographs in their correct order. Included in the following sequence of images, in order to illustrate every phase of the battle are some images not discussed in this chapter. These images include NH-69723 showing shells from the *Hood* landing near the *Prinz Eugen*, and NH-69724, which was also taken by Lagemann and shows the explosion of the *Hood*.

Theories on the Sinking

Since her sinking, the exact mechanism of the loss of the *Hood* has been keenly debated. For a number of reasons, the exact cause of the ship's loss will likely never be known with any degree of certainty. As William Jurens has written:

> The event occurred with remarkable suddenness, and was to most observers completely unexpected. No cameras were clearly trained on *Hood* as she exploded and no 'black box' counted down her final, fatal seconds. There were almost no survivors and there remained virtually no wreckage on which [a] post-mortem might be performed.[1]

Despite this, a number of theories as to what caused the loss of the *Hood* have been put forward. The main theories that have been advanced include the following:

1. That the *Hood* suffered a direct hit from a shell fired by the *Bismarck* that penetrated her aft magazine. Said shell could only have come from the *Bismarck* as by the point in the battle at which the *Hood* was sunk, the *Prinz Eugen* was no longer firing at the *Hood*. This theory as a version of events was almost taken for granted at the time of the sinking, in part owing to eyewitness testimony that claimed that the explosion that had destroyed the *Hood* had originated near her main mast, well forward of the aft magazine.

2. A shell from the *Bismarck* fell short and struck the *Hood* below her armoured belt where it penetrated the magazine and detonated, resulting in the explosion. During the battle, the *Prince of Wales* received a similar hit from a 15-inch shell that travelled approximately 80 feet underwater before striking the battleship 28 feet below the water line, where it penetrated several light bulkheads. While the second board discounted this theory as improbable, William Jurens has calculated that one of the *Bismarck*'s shells

Above: Silhouettes of the German ships: the *Bismarck* (top) and the *Prinz Eugen* (bottom).

Below: This image shows two copies of NH-69728 from the Naval History & Heritage Command. The top copy shows the image in its printed orientation while the bottom shows the photograph reversed.

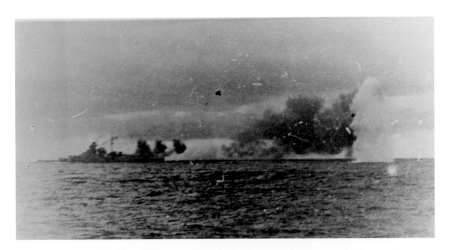

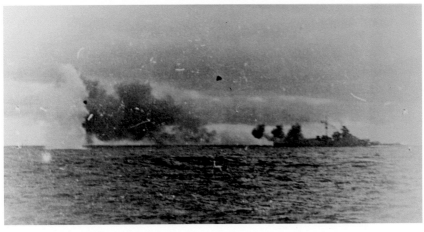

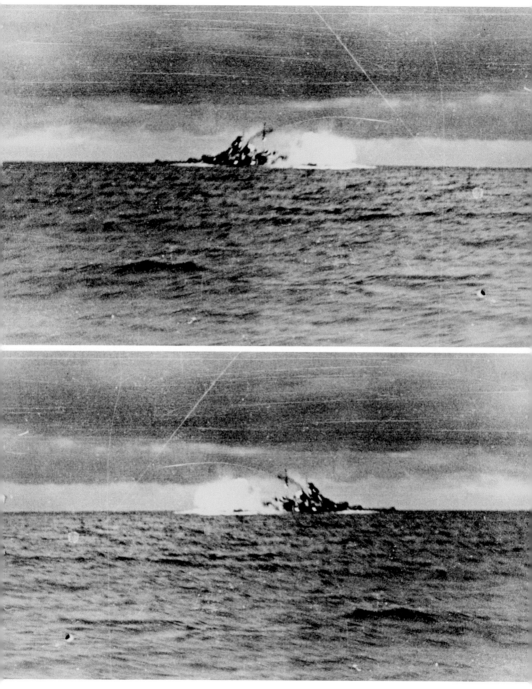

NH-69726 in its printed orientation (top) and the same photograph in what should be its correct orientation (bottom).

NH-69727. The top copy shows the image in its printed orientation while the bottom shows the photograph reversed into its correct orientation.

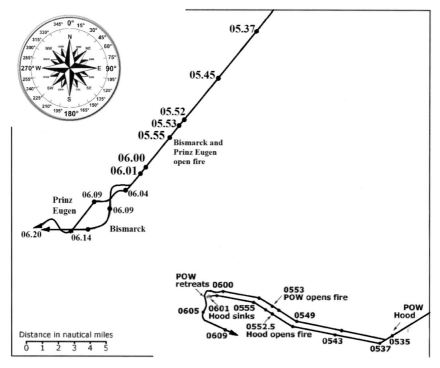

Traditional battle map showing the movements of Lütjens's and Holland's ships during the course of the battle.

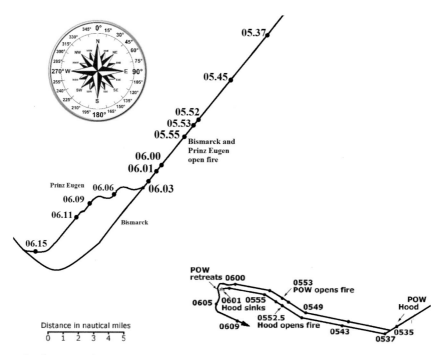

A battle map perhaps more representative of the actual dispositions and movements of the German and British ships engaged in the Battle of the Denmark Strait. (*Author's Collection*)

(NH-69722 *Naval History & Heritage Command*)

(NH-96723 *Naval History & Heritage Command*)

(NH-69729 Naval History & Heritage Command)

(NH-69724 Naval History & Heritage Command)

(NH-69728 Naval History & Heritage Command)

(NH-69726 Naval History & Heritage Command)

(NH-69725 *Naval History & Heritage Command*)

(NH-69731 *Naval History & Heritage Command*)

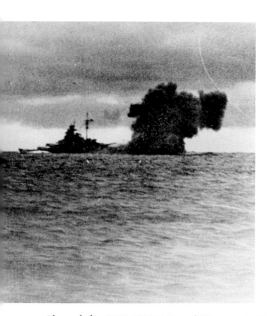

Above left: (NH-69727 *Naval History & Heritage Command*)

Above right: The explosion of HMS *Barham*, 25 November 1941.

Taken on board the *Hood* looking aft 'X' turret can be seen at the limit of its firing arc while the ship is on manoeuvres off Portland on 8 November 1926. In this image, the right-hand gun of 'X' turret is at its maximum elevation of 30 degrees. (*NH 57184, US Naval History and Heritage Command*)

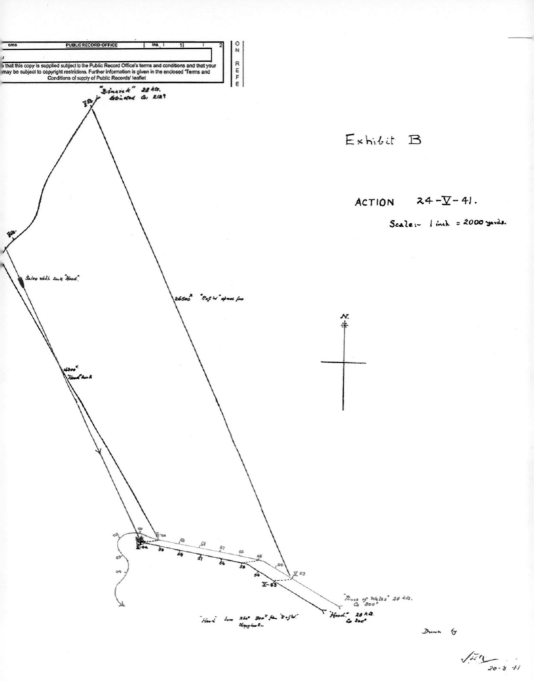

Exhibit B

ACTION   24 - V - 41.

Scale :- 1 inch = 2000 yards.

N.

Track chart of the *Prince of Wales*.

NH-69724. (*NH-69724 Naval History & Heritage Command*)

NH-69731. (*NH-69731 Naval History & Heritage Command*)

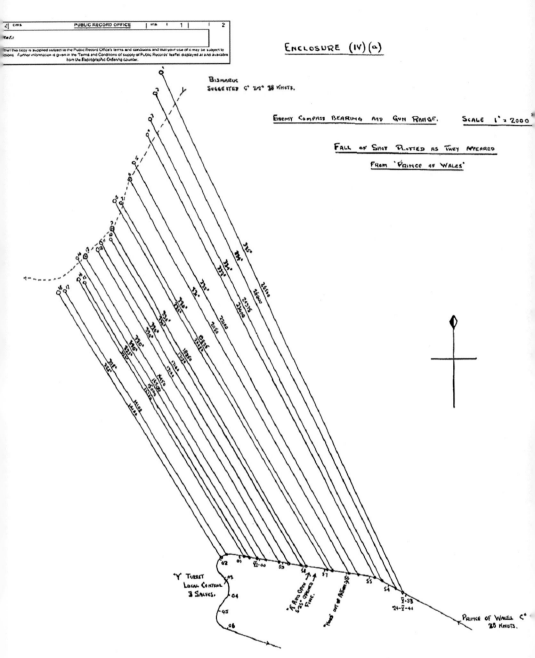

Salvo plot of HMS *Prince of Wales* during the Battle of the Denmark Strait.

NH-69724 annotated showing the position of the *Hood*'s explosion relative to the *Prince of Wales* at 6 a.m.

Annotated copy of NH-69731 showing the explosion site of the *Hood* and the position of *Prince of Wales* at 6.03 a.m.

Figure 1: A red line has been drawn on NH-69731 to indicate the course taken by the *Prince of Wales* from her position at the time of the *Hood*'s explosion. This image shows the approximate course supposedly taken by the *Prince of Wales* from the *Hood*'s explosion at 6 a.m. to her new position at 6.03 a.m.

Figure 2: How NH-69731 should look in order for the photograph to be compatible with the *Hood* exploding at 6 a.m. HMS *Prince of Wales* appears to be much closer to the site of the *Hood*'s sinking site at this time (6.03 a.m.) following the *Hood*'s sinking at 6 a.m.

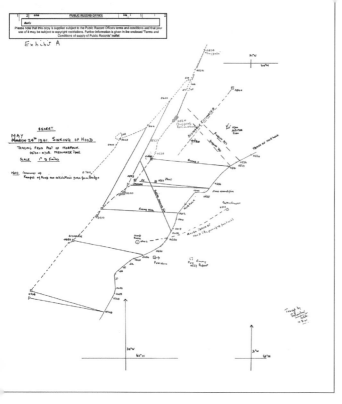

Track chart showing the
course of HMS *Norfolk*
during the battle.

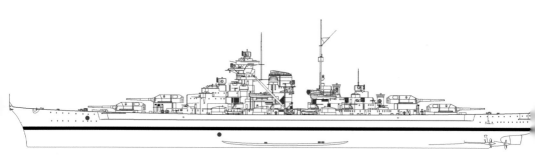

Above: Diagram of the *Bismarck* showing the location of hits sustained from the *Prince of Wales*. (*Author's Collection*)

Below: Diagram of the *Prince of Wales* showing the location of hits sustained from the combined fire of the *Prinz Eugen* and the *Bismarck*. (*Author's Collection*)

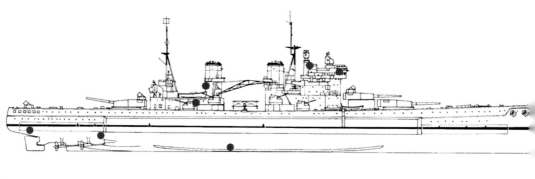

that fell approximately 20 feet short of the *Hood* could have penetrated the side of the ship beneath the armoured belt in the vicinity of the magazine and detonated it if the fuse worked correctly.

3. The ship's torpedoes were detonated by the fire on the boat deck or by a hit from the *Bismarck* that blew out the side of the ship, allowing a vast influx of water that flooded the ship and broke her back.

4. The fire on the boat deck penetrated a magazine. While the second board indicated that the 4-inch magazine doors were closed throughout the battle, some have argued that a German shell could have served to open up the magazine doors or the trunking sufficiently to admit flames into the magazine. Within this school of thought, it has also been suggested that flames reached the magazines through the ventilation shafts.

5. This final school of thought suggests that the *Hood* was blown up by the detonation of one of her own shells in one of her guns. At the second Board of Enquiry [*sic*.], some witnesses to the battle reported that unusual types of discharge were seen to be emitting from the *Hood*'s 15-inch guns. This has led to some to suggest that a shell could have detonated within one of her guns, which caused an explosion within the gun house. This suggests it is possible that within the stress and heat of the battle, the safety measures that were introduced in the wake of the Battle of Jutland to prevent gun house explosions reaching the magazines were not enacted correctly or failed.[2]

Discounting the above fifth point, the debate into the loss of the *Hood* by and large centres on whether it was her horizontal or vertical armour that was defeated. The narrative of the *Prince of Wales*'s action against the *Bismarck* reports:

During the approach *Hood* made—'G.I.C.'—followed by—'G.O.B.1'—just before opening fire at 0552 1/2. Range approx. 25,000 yards. *Prince of Wales* opened fire at 0553. *Bismarck* replied with extreme accuracy on *Hood*. 2nd or 3rd salvo straddled and fire broke out in *Hood* in the vicinity of the port after 4" gun mounting. Lighter ship engaged *Prince of Wales*. *Prince of Wales* opening salvo was observed over, 6th was seen to straddle. At this time *Prince of Wales* had five 14" guns in action. 'Y' turret would not bear. Fire in *Hood* spread rapidly to the mainmast. A turn of 2 blue at 0555 opened A-Arcs at *Prince of Wales* ninth salvo. *Hood* had a further 2 blue flying when, at 0600, just after *Bismarck*'s 5th salvo, a huge explosion occurred between *Hood*'s after funnel and mainmast and she sank in three or four minutes. *Hood* had fired five or six salvos but fall of shot was not seen, possibly because this coincided with firing of *Prince of Wales*' guns.[3]

No one aboard the *Hood* saw anything that sheds light on what caused the loss of the ship. Ted Briggs recalled that there was 'A blinding flash [that] swept around the outside of the compass platform. Again I found myself being lifted off my feet and dumped head first on the deck'.[4] Robert Tilburn recalled the explosion as thus: 'It shook the entire ship, blast and shrapnel buffeting the midships position, but the explosion did not seem any worse than the effect of *Hood* firing a salvo'.[5] William Dundas, meanwhile, got the impression that the *Bismarck* had fired a shell through the *Hood*'s spotting top, which did not explode but which caused carnage, accounting for the bodies that landed on the upper deck.

While the three survivors saw nothing of what befell their ship, hundreds of eyes watched on as *Hood* approached her end. German eyes watched through rangefinders and binoculars while aboard HMS *Prince of Wales*, the helm and commander watched the flagship in order to ensure that the correct position was maintained. In addition to this, signalmen aboard the battleship kept their eyes fixed on the *Hood* for any signals. At the same time, almost the entire complement of the *Prince of Wales*'s disengaged port side had little else to do other than watch the *Hood* in action.

The fire on the boat deck started by the *Prinz Eugen* is the first recorded hit on the *Hood*. Those who observed the hit that started the fire were left with different impressions. Petty Officer Lawrence Sutton on the Admiral's Shelter deck noted:

> [A] salvo of H.E. fell more or less in line amidships of the *Hood* also short. This was of smaller calibre than the other two ... and at the same time there was a flash just before the mainmast of the *Hood* and there was a volume of black smoke which afterwards turned into grey.[6]

Chief Petty Officer William Mockridge also witnessed the impact. In 1940, Mockridge had conducted equipment trials on the *Hood*'s 4-inch guns and had worked on supply arrangements. Sure that the fire was based in the 4-inch ready-use lockers, Mockridge 'saw a very vivid flash. It was so bright, like a magnesium flare'.[7] The shells noted by Sutton were almost certainly shells from the *Prinz Eugen*, and it may be fair to say that he, like many other British observers, accidentally confused the fall of shot from the *Bismarck* and the *Prinz Eugen*.

The fire on the boat deck would ultimately burn until the *Hood* sank. The substantial blaze began to set off the 4-inch ready-use ammunition and was so fierce that Captain Kerr ordered the damage control parties to take shelter until all of the ready use ammunition had been expended. Looking from HMS *Norfolk* some 15 miles away, Rear-Admiral Wake-Walker watched the fire 'spread forward until its length was greater than its height' before the fire began to die down.[8] Seconds later, the *Hood* exploded.

Captain Leach watched the fifth salvo from *Bismarck* from the *Prince of Wales*:

[It] appeared to cross the ship somewhere about the mainmast. In that salvo were, I think, two shots short and one over, but it may have been the other way round. But I formed the impression at the time that something had arrived on board 'Hood' in a position just before the main-mast and slightly to starboard ... I in fact wondered what the result was going to be, and between one and two seconds after I formed that impression an explosion took place in the *Hood* which appeared to me to come from very much the same position in the ship.[9]

To most who witnessed the explosion, it was an awe-inspiring event. To others, it was less spectacular. Able Seaman Richard Scott and Lieutenant Peter Slade, who were on the catapult deck of the *Prince of Wales*, recalled the explosion as a silent red glow from the surrounding bulkheads, a view held by a number of others. Almost everyone who witnessed the explosion agreed that the moment of the *Hood*'s demise was essentially noiseless, or at least sufficiently quiet so as to be drowned out by the firing of the guns of the *Prince of Wales*.

The above are the established events, yet there are a number of explanations for the *Hood*'s loss. Within the remit of what destroyed the *Hood*, it may be the case that one of the aforementioned causes is the reason or it may easily be a combination of multiple factors working together. Perhaps it was some entirely unrelated circumstance. In this particular chapter, the different theories that have been advanced concerning the loss of the *Hood* will be examined with exception of the idea that the *Hood* was destroyed by the detonation of one of her own shells in one of her guns or by accident, which will not be examined here, but will instead be examined separately in the next chapter.

When looking at the potential causes and theories behind the loss of the *Hood*, any credible explanation must conform to set criteria. In the first instance, it should be consistent with the observations of eyewitnesses. Secondly, it should have a reasonable probability of taking place. Thirdly, and linked to point two, any credible explanation must be physically plausible in as much as it is consistent with the normal laws of physics.

The Boards of Inquiry

When examining the different theories that have been put forward on the loss of the *Hood*, the first place that anyone should begin are with the findings of the Boards of Inquiry. Headed by Vice-Admiral Sir Geoffrey Blake, and with Captain Cecil Harcourt and Captain C. F. Hammill as its members, a Board of Inquiry into the loss of the *Hood* was convened on 30 May 1941. The board took testimony from a selection of different witnesses who saw the explosion of the *Hood*, including Wake-Walker, Captain Alfred Phillips, and six other officers and ratings who were on the bridge of the *Norfolk* at the time; Captain Leach, Lieutenant R. C. Beckwith, and six other officer and ratings who had been present on the bridge of the *Prince of Wales*; and William Dundas, one of the survivors of the *Hood*.[10]

On 2 June, nine days following the loss of the *Hood*, the board delivered its findings to the first sea lord. The findings were contained in a report and were classified 'Secret'. The report produced by the board stated:

> This report contains the findings of the Court, but not the evidence on which those findings are based. Hence, some of the points raised in the following remarks may have been dealt with in the evidence and the Court's conclusions reached after full consideration of such points ... It is clear ... that a 15" shell fired from *Bismarck* at the range and inclination of the fatal fifth salvo could, if lucky and possessing sufficient delay, reach the after magazines. If this shell struck 'somewhere near the mainmast' the delay would have had to be very long for the shell to reach the forward bulkhead of the upper 4" magazine. If this magazine, which contained only 467 rounds of fixed ammunition, had exploded, it is not certain that the remaining magazines would have blown up. A still more lucky shot striking the ship farther aft could actually burst in the group of 4" magazines; in that case these magazines and the adjacent 15" magazines immediately abaft would blow up, and the ship would rapidly sink stern first.
>
> DNC, however considers it premature to conclude that because the ship <u>could</u> be blown up in this way that was in fact what happened. The reason for this remark is that 'the result of the fifth salvo was a large explosion, the centre of which appeared to be at the base of the mainmast.' It is extremely difficult to associate this observed fact with the explosion of the 4" magazines, the forward bulkhead of which is 64ft. abaft the centre of the mainmast and the after bulkhead about 115ft. If the 4" magazines caused 'X' magazine to blow up, a fortiori, 'X' magazine would have caused 'Y' magazine to blow up. The after bulkhead of 'Y' magazine is about 180 ft. abaft the centre of the mainmast, so it is even more difficult to reconcile the observed position of the explosion with the blowing up of all the magazines aft.... The after group of 4" H.A. magazines comprises 6 separate watertight compartments. Over then are 7 hatches and trunks through which the explosion of the magazine contents would vent. The flame ... would then have appeared at the after end of the superstructure and forward of 'X' turret. The roof of 'X' and 'Y' magazines is the lower deck, two decks below the weather deck. If the large quantity of cordite in these magazines blew up, the pressure would be so great that the superstructure above would be

entirely destroyed and the flame from the explosion would have been seen around 'X' and 'Y' turrets. Is there any possible reason why the products of combustion from these magazines should have passed through the after engine-room and up round the mainmast over the centre engine room? No reason is indicated in the report, neither can one be imagined.

The question naturally arises, if the explosion at the base of the mainmast was not due to the after magazines, was there any other large quantity of explosives in that neighbourhood which could have caused the observed effect? The answer to that question is, 'Yes, on the upper deck abreast the mainmast there was a total quantity of about 4,000lbs of T.N.T.' If one or more shells from the fifth salvo detonated sufficiently close to one of the eight torpedo-heads confined in strong boxes on the upper deck, and if one or more of these warheads detonated, the result would be an explosion where it was actually observed.... The detonation of a torpedo-head in the open air is fairly damaging, but in a confined box in a ship would be far more devastating. In fact, such a detonation in the position of these tubes in *Hood* would probably break the ship's back and result in rapid foundering ... The foregoing alternative explanation of the occurrence appears plausible and it is considered the finding of the Court should not be accepted as final until further facts are elicited ... It is important that the doubts concerning the loss of this ship should be cleared up if possible at a very early date, as although action is being taken to implement the lessons of both explanations, it is impossible to do this quickly for all our old capital ships if the true explanation is as found by the Court. Moreover, it will never be possible to give these ships such protection to their magazines as to ensure certainty that modern shells and bombs under all circumstances that may exist in modern actions cannot reach their magazines.[11]

On 7 June, the report was passed on to First Sea Lord Admiral Sir Dudley Pound and Controller of the Navy and Third Sea Lord Admiral Bruce Fraser. Five days later, the report was forwarded on to the Director of Naval Construction Sir Stanley V. Goodall for his comments before the being distributed to various departments within the Admiralty. To the report, Goodall added the following lines:

It is important that the doubts concerning the loss of this ship should be cleared up if possible at a very early date, as although action is being taken to implement the lessons of both explanations, it is impossible to do this quickly for all our old capital ships if the true explanation is as found by the Court. Moreover, it will never be possible to give these ships such protection to their magazines as to ensure certainty that modern shells and bombs under all circumstances that may exist in modern actions cannot reach their magazines.[12]

Unsurprisingly, when the speed with which the report produced by the board was prepared is considered, it becomes apparent that the report itself is rather incomplete. While Goodall made this point clear in the introduction to the report, it was nevertheless criticised by some recipients. Admiral Fraser disagreed with the views expressed by Goodall and pointed out the reasons why he accepted the report produced by the board as written. Further to this, Fraser proposed that the findings be accepted and that Admiral Tovey be advised of its findings accordingly. On 18 July, Vice Chief of the Naval Staff Vice-Admiral Tom Philips, weighed into the debate surrounding the report with his comments. He wrote in a memorandum:

D.N.C. [Director of Naval Construction] in his minute on this paper raises a point of great importance, i.e., as he points out the report contains the findings of the Court, but not the evidence on which those findings are based. I noticed this when the report was first received in the Admiralty and discussed the matter with the President of the Court, but unfortunately it transpired that no shorthand notes of the evidence were taken. At my request, however, the Court have produced a summary of evidence which is attached in paper M.011031/41. This summary is, I understand, compiled from short notes kept by members of the Court at the time.

2. This matter of the blowing up of the *Hood* is one of the first importance to the Navy. It will be discussed for years to come and important decisions as to the design of ships must rest on the conclusions that are arrived at. This being so, it seems to me that the most searching inquiry is necessary in order to obtain every scrap of evidence we can as to the cause of the explosion. I regret to state that in my opinion the report as rendered by this Board does not give me confidence that such a searching inquiry has been carried out; in particular the failure to record the evidence of the various witnesses of the event strikes me as quite extraordinary.

3. In all normal instructions Boards of Inquiry that are issued to Commanders in Chief it is always stated quite clearly that a full record is to be kept. In this case the Board was ordered very hurriedly and the normal forms were not gone through, which perhaps accounts for the failure to appreciate the importance of this point. In may be that in years to come in the light of further action in connection with other ships our successors may wish to look back at the records of the loss of the *Hood*, and it is in the words of those who actually saw the event rather than in the conclusions drawn by any Committee that they would be likely to find matter of real value. In my view the matter is of such importance that a further Board of Enquiry should be held; that all who witnessed the blowing up should be interrogated. (I note that Lieutenant Beckwith gave hearsay evidence as the result of having interviewed a number of witnesses. I also note that of the

three survivors from the *Hood* only one was interviewed. This strikes me as quite remarkable.

4. With regard to the minutes on this paper D.N.C. gave it as his definite opinion that on the evidence at present available the blowing up of the ship was not caused by a magazine explosion but was more likely to have been caused by the detonation of torpedo war heads. Before, however, confirming this view he asks that further evidence be made available. I certainly think that action should be taken on the points he mentions.[13]

The following day, the first sea lord dispatched a memorandum to First Lord of the Admiralty A. V. Alexander regarding the report produced by the Board of Inquiry. In his memorandum, Admiral Sir Dudley Pound pointed out that the failure of the board to take a verbatim record of the evidence of the witnesses of event was a handicap to the further investigation of the matter and that it was possible that different conclusions could be drawn from those reached by the board. Pound went on to propose that a new Board of Inquiry be established to investigate the loss of the *Hood* with the assistance of a naval constructor and an expert in explosives. Alexander, for his part, agreed with Pound's suggestion for a new Board of Inquiry to be called.

So it was that a second Board of Inquiry was convened under Rear-Admiral Harold Walker, who incidentally, had been the last peacetime captain of the *Hood*. This board began by taking evidence from 176 individuals who witnessed the sinking from on board the *Prince of Wales*, HMS *Norfolk*, and the *Suffolk*. While William Dundas was unable to attend the hearing of the Board of Inquiry on this occasion, Ted Briggs and Robert Tilburn were both summoned to provide a testimony. In addition to this, technical experts were consulted along with former officers who were called upon to provide evidence and to give testimonies relating to procedures on board. Even evidence gained from interrogations of the survivors of the *Bismarck* was taken into consideration by the board. The board first convened on 12 August aboard the cruiser HMS *Devonshire* and continued the following day aboard HMS *Suffolk* before holding its final sessions in Dorland House, London, between 27 August and 5 September.

During its sessions, the board went to great lengths in an attempt to establish whether or not the fire that erupted on the boat deck or the ship's torpedoes had any bearing on the loss of the ship. During the inquiry, it was suggested by expert witnesses that what the observers from the British ships saw was a violent but not instantaneous deflagration in the 4-inch magazine and that this explosion was visible through the engine room ventilators. It was further suggested that this same deflagration would have served to separate the 4-inch and 15-inch magazines, which resulted in the catastrophic explosion that engulfed the ship. This theory was ultimately adopted by the second Board of Inquiry when it delivered its findings on 12 September 1941. The second board's findings were, however, little removed from those of the first Board of Inquiry:

(1) That the sinking of *Hood* was due to a hit from *Bismarck's* 15-inch shell in or adjacent to *Hood's* 4-inch or 15-inch magazines, causing them all to explode and wreck the after part of the ship. The probability is that the 4-inch magazines exploded first.

(2) There is no conclusive evidence that one or two torpedo warheads detonated or exploded simultaneously with the magazines, or at any other time, but the possibility cannot be entirely excluded. We consider that if they had done so their effect would not have been so disastrous as to cause the immediate destruction of the ship, and on the whole, we are of the opinion that they did not.

(3) That the fire that was seen on *Hood's* Boat Deck, and in which UP and/or 4-inch ammunition was certainly involved, was not the cause of her loss. The conclusion of the Board of Enquiry is that the after 4" magazine probably exploded first, followed by the after 15" magazine, which is only natural as it was so near.[14]

Defeat of Her Armour

One of the theories that has been put forward is that the *Hood's* armour or armoured belt was penetrated by a German shell, likely from the *Bismarck*. Both of the Boards of Inquiry carried the finding that the final turn ordered by Holland was never executed. However, in 2001, the wreck of the *Hood* was located and photographed by Blue Water Recoveries and David L. Mearns, a marine scientist and oceanographer who specialises in deep water search and recovery operations and in the discovery of historic shipwrecks. One of the standout images from the expedition to the wreck is that of the stern, which shows the rudder set in a turn to port; controlled through a worm gear mechanism, when the steering linkage was severed, the rudder would have remained frozen in place, which confirms that the *Hood* did begin making her final turn, contrary to what the Boards of Inquiry concluded and what eyewitnesses claimed.

This is an important factor to establish because a perforation of the *Hood's* belt armour would have increased in likelihood the further the *Hood* passed into the turn. The analysis conducted by Jurens showed that the *Hood's* 305-mm armoured belt could have been penetrated if she completed more than half of her planned 20-degree turn to port. However, unless the turn had been virtually completed, which this author believes is unlikely owing to eyewitness testimony even though the rudder is locked in the turn to port, it is not considered likely that a projectile that penetrated the ship's main belt armour would have been able to maintain sufficient velocity to penetrate one of the ship's magazines. While the *Hood* may indeed have been destroyed by a shell penetrating her belt armour, a shell need not necessarily have penetrated the belt in order to cause the loss of the ship.

Indeed, both of the Boards of Inquiry considered the idea that the *Hood* was destroyed by a shell that may have penetrated above or below her armour belts. It was noted by the Boards of Inquiry that it was possible that the *Hood* was destroyed by a projectile that fell slightly short of the target, penetrating the hull and detonating well below the waterline after having travelled some distance underwater. The basis of this hypothesis has its grounding in a similar underwater hit, which was sustained by the *Prince of Wales* during the engagement. During the battle, a solitary 15-inch shell from the *Bismarck* fell short of the target and landed in the water before continuing on and penetrating the *Prince of Wales* below the waterline.

After the battle in the Denmark Strait, the *Prince of Wales* retreated from the battle zone before doubling back to link up with the *Norfolk* and the *Suffolk*. The *Prince of Wales* would continue to follow the *Bismarck* until 25 May when she set a course for Iceland, where she was refuelled before sailing on to Rosyth where she was to have the damage that she sustained in the engagement repaired. As the ship entered dry dock, a shell hole was discovered 27 feet below the waterline on the starboard side. Indeed, when the dry dock was drained, a large hole was to be found just above the bilge keel. The damage control officer of the *Prince of Wales*, Lieutenant Richard Wildish, accompanied by a senior rating climbed into the hole and followed a path of twisted metal and jagged holes that marked the path of the shell. The trail of destruction ended at the armoured bulkhead. After probing around in the compartment where the trail of destruction ended, Wildish discovered an unexploded 15-inch shell from the *Bismarck*. It was concluded that the shell had landed in the sea short of the ship whereupon it had continued on with enough velocity to penetrate the ship before coming to rest beside the armoured torpedo bulkhead.[15] In the immediate vicinity of where the shell landed were the main engineering spaces. The shell, had it exploded, had the potential to blow out a sizable portion of the ship, if not destroy the ship, and could have destroyed her if it struck adjacent to the magazines.

The exact range at which the hit was sustained is uncertain, although, owing to the angle at which the shell penetrated the hull, it is highly probable that the shell struck the *Prince of Wales* shortly after the *Hood* was destroyed as prior to that time the *Prince of Wales* was not under 15-inch fire, and shortly after the destruction of the *Hood*, she began her retreat, during which time her stern was presented towards the enemy.

Jurens has pointed out, however, that even had such an event occurred in the case of the *Hood*, doubt remains over the action of the projectile fuse. Standard German projectiles had a fuse delay of 0.035 seconds. Investigators examined the fuse of the projectile that had struck the *Prince of Wales* and failed to detonate and found that it had been actuated, probably upon impact with the water, but that shortly thereafter the power train was extinguished. As Jurens has stated, this is not a great surprise given that German shells were not specially designed for stable water entry:

> It is in fact possible (though improbable) that the projectile which struck *Prince of Wales* penetrated the water normally, rotated nearly 180° shortly after impact, and stabilized base first for the remainder of its journey. Such violent rotation would almost certainly have rendered the fuze inoperative, though after it was completed the flat base might have acted like a suichi dan nose. The fact that the projectile was recovered nose forward in the bilges tends to support this somewhat unusual hypothesis.[16]

The belt armour of the *Hood* projected only 960 mm below the waterline. As such, even a projectile with a 'normal' trajectory could have easily struck the ship beneath the belt and penetrated well inside the ship before exploding. The second Board of Inquiry considered a penetrating underwater hit as being a distinct and dangerous possibility and went so far as to prepare a special drawing of the *Hood*, which showed the wave profile along the side of the ship when travelling at 28 knots. At the stern of the ship, the drawing showed that the draft of the ship at any point along the side might have ranged between 10.5 m forward of the mainmast and 9.5 m just forward of 'X' turret. The drawing also illustrated that the armoured belt would normally be covered with between 1.75 and 2.75 m of water, meaning that this was obviously a point of great vulnerability for the *Hood*.

Providing that the fuse operated correctly, an underwater hit represents one of the most plausible explanations for the loss of the *Hood*. One of *Bismarck*'s 15-inch shells that fell approximately 6 m short had the potential to penetrate the hull just below the belt armour and to penetrate the insides of the ship more or less unimpeded until it was in the area of the aft magazines.

The Boards of Inquiry noted that above the *Hood*'s probable waterline was a band of potential weakness approximately 450 mm wide abreast the aft engine room. In this area, the boards considered, it would have been possible for a projectile to reach the area of the magazines bypassing over the 305-mm belt, penetrating the 178-mm belt and by passing under the protective main deck by striking the portion of the deck that sloped down to meet the side. While such a penetration is not impossible and would rely on a projectile falling and penetrating at particular angles relative to the target, this may be deemed improbable.

While it is not impossible that the projectile that led to the demise of one of the most iconic ships of Royal Navy may have reached the magazines by passing over the armoured belt, an attractive by-product of this hypothesis is that it more readily lends itself to an explanation of the observations of eyewitnesses who claimed that the explosion that tore the *Hood* apart appeared to originate in the vicinity of the mainmast.

One possible route for a shell heading towards the aft magazines by passing over the belt armour would have been in the vicinity of the starboard torpedo tube nest. Due to the presence of the mantlet armour, a shell would not have been able to detonate a torpedo but still would have caused collateral damage. Given that there was a significant fire on the boat deck, if a shell or shrapnel from the passage of a shell perforated a charged torpedo air flask, the result would have been a spectacular burst of flame in the vicinity of the main mast followed almost immediately by the detonation of the aft magazines. In his notes, Jurens recorded that Captain William Weilcose Davies, who had served aboard the *Hood* in 1940, testified that the torpedoes would have been stowed with pistols installed if they had been shipped in the torpedo tubes and that spare torpedoes without their pistols fitted but with their warheads in place would have been stored, with the nose section of the weapons run into the protective mantlets, above the ready-use torpedoes. Despite this his hypothesis lending itself to an explanation of the observations of witnesses, penetration by a shell via this route is considered unlikely.

It has also been suggested that a projectile could have transitioned over the engineering spaces and reached the forward bulkhead of the magazines by penetrating both the forecastle and main decks before detonating between the main and lower decks.

Magazine and Torpedo Detonation

Assuming that a penetration of one of the *Hood*'s magazines occurred, in the wake of the ship's sinking, the Admiralty undertook a number of tests in order to try and understand what occurred and to try and resolve the issue.

A comprehensive British survey that was undertaken by the Boards of Inquiry and covered twenty-two cases of war damage involving a ship's magazine found only one case where the magazines were principally known to have exploded—the case was that of the *Hood* herself—six cases where a ship's magazines were suspected to have exploded, and fifteen cases where, in spite of severe damage, magazines had not detonated. These cases, alongside the experiences of the United States, indicated that catastrophic propellant explosions were rare, even in cases where shells or bombs had penetrated and detonated directly inside a magazine space. It is worth noting, however, that British double-based propellants that contained a significant amount of nitroglycerine in their make-up, were significantly more susceptible to ignition than the single-base propellants used by the United States.

In its conclusions, the second Board of Inquiry stated:

As regards the 4-inch and 15-inch magazines the following questions arise:

(1) Is it likely that enemy gunfire during this action would 'blow up' any or all of the magazines?

(2) Would the blowing up of magazines produce the effects seen and heard by witnesses?

(3) Would the blowing up of any or all of the magazines cause the rapid destruction of the ship?

Here again, expert advisers were consulted, and lead us to the following conclusions:

As regards (1). Expert evidence shows that this is quite possible if the muzzle velocity of *Bismarck's* shell was between 2721 and 3050 fps. If the muzzle velocity was over 3050 fps, the probability, bearing in mind the evidence as to the fall of shot, is considerable.

As regards (2). We consider that what was seen and heard was in accordance with what might be expected if the after group of 4-inch and/or 15-inch magazines of *Hood* had blown up. There is one important point which needed careful consideration and which was remarked on by DNC [Director of Naval Construction] in his minute NL 9821/41 (Report of previous Board of Enquiry) and by C in C Home Fleet, on NL 11131/41; namely that the position of the explosion as observed by some competent witnesses was much further forward than would, at first sight, have been expected had the 4-inch or 15-inch magazines blown up. This is partially explained ... where we reached the conclusion that not only was a tremendous pillar of flame observed just before the mainmast, but that, in addition, a very heavy explosion was seen practically simultaneously further aft.

Commander Maton and Commander Knight agreed that if the 4-inch magazines went off first, followed instantaneously by the 15-inch, the first visible sign might well be a large sheet of flame directly above or just before the 4-inch magazines. Finally, it must be remembered that our peace time knowledge and practical experience of the results of cordite explosion has been based on experiments with a maximum of about half a ton of cordite. *Hood's* after magazine contained about 112 tons, over two hundred times as much. The course of the explosion following on the terrific pressures likely to be produced in this case must be difficult to predict. From the last was there are three examples of the effects on battle cruisers of cordite explosions— explosions which both in appearance and effect gave very similar results to those experienced in the loss of *Hood*. As regards (3), there is little room for doubt that the immediate destruction of the after end of the ship followed by the rapid sinking of the remainder would result from the blowing up of the 4-inch or 15-inch magazines—in the case of the former because their explosion would cause the 15-inch also to blow up.

The peace time knowledge of cordite explosions referred to by the board was a series of trials conducted in 1936. The initial trials conducted using a 4.7-inch quick-firing shell concluded that the ignition of cordite charges from shell splinters and fragments would not blow up a magazine. This trial also concluded that when one shell detonated in contact with another, the result would not be a catastrophic explosion. When a 6-inch shell filled with shellite was used, however, the results were different. During the first trial, a 6-inch shell filled with shellite was fired into a rack containing ninety-eight rounds. A short pause followed before the magazine disintegrated. A second trial, which saw the same shell type fired into ninety-four rounds that had been 'box stowed', sparked a cordite fire that, over a period of almost fifty minutes, destroyed the magazine. Based on this, the board concluded that, in a confined space, an explosion would have been probable.

A number of commentators on the loss of the *Hood*, including some who were members of the original Boards of Inquiry, have speculated that an explosion of the torpedo warheads either directly or indirectly caused the loss of the ship. The second Board of Inquiry went so far as to conclude that such an event was possible, although it did state that the explosion of torpedo warheads was not a likely factor. On this matter, the second Board of Inquiry stated:

Evidence of eye witnesses, *Repulse* and an Officer who had recently served in *Hood* leaves little room for doubt that the mantlet doors were closed. A warhead could still, however, have been detonated or exploded by a direct hit from *Bismarck*'s shell. There is no direct evidence that such a hit occurred, but it may have done so on either side of the ship. If a single warhead had gone off one other, but probably not more than one, the other warhead would also have gone off.... Expert opinion suggested that the explosion of two warheads would produce an all round almost instantaneous flash. It would not have produced the very high column of flame of appreciable duration, which was seen by so many witnesses. Nor was the noise, reported as being heard, compatible with that of a T.N.T. detonation or explosion. The consensus of expert opinion was definitely against the characteristics of the explosion as given in evidence by eyewitnesses being that of T.N.T. ... Mr. Offord, our advisor in construction, was of the opinion that this could be the case.[17]

Director of Naval Construction Sir Stanley Goodall was one of those who agreed with Dudley Offord and held what would ultimately be a dissenting view; he stated:

> The question naturally arises, if the explosion at the base of the mainmast was not due to the after magazines, was there any other large quantity of explosives in that neighbourhood which could have caused the observed effect? The answer to that question is, 'Yes, on the upper deck abreast the mainmast there was a total quantity of about 4,000lbs of T.N.T.' If one or more shells from the fifth salvo detonated sufficiently close to one of the eight torpedo-heads confined in strong boxes on the upper deck, and if one or more of these warheads detonated, the result would be an explosion where it was actually observed.
>
> ... There is a difference between the flame and smoke from the rapid burning of a large quantity of cordite and from the detonation of T.N.T., and it would be interesting to have the views of officers with experience of both phenomena on the sketches enclosed with the report. The picture of the explosion drawn by Captain Phillips gives the impression of T.N.T. detonation rather than cordite explosion.
>
> ... The detonation of a torpedo-head in the open air is fairly damaging, but in a confined box in a ship would be far more devastating. In fact, such a detonation in the position of these tubes in *Hood* would probably break the ship's back and result in rapid foundering.
>
> ... The foregoing alternative explanation of the occurrence appears plausible and it is considered the finding of the Court should not be accepted as final until further facts are elicited.[18]

Others, however, were not so convinced, something which was also acknowledged by the board:

> Other witnesses, experts in explosives but not in construction, were of the opposite view, and the Board are not convinced that such a very rapid sinking would follow from the damage which Mr. Offord considered would result from the explosion of two warheads. Further, there is strong evidence that the widespread and immediate damage actually caused to the after part of the ship was considerably greater than that which Mr. Offord considered would result from two warheads exploding.[19]

Goodall was probably wrong in his assessment. While no formal calculations were ever carried out, the board did, nevertheless, look hard into the issue of the detonation of torpedo warheads causing the loss of the ship and received testimony from a number of expert witnesses. Typical of the witnesses who presented evidence to the board was Captain John Carslake, who stated he was not an expert on cordite explosions but that he knew 'a fair amount about these' and that there were questions on which 'I would not trust my own judgement'.[20] Nevertheless, the board subjected him to a detailed examination.

When he was asked what the probable effects would be if a torpedo warhead detonated, Carslake replied:

> I would expect the mantlet, the ship's side, and the forecastle deck to be nearly demolished, but that the major venting would have been as I suggested horizontal. Immediately after the explosion it is anticipated that the observer would have seen a gap in the ship's side, probably some 15 or 20 ft. radius down to the top of the 12" belt.... I would expect the boat deck above the tubes also to be blown away.[21]

The board proceeded to ask Carslake what the effect upon the structure of the *Hood* would be if one or more torpedo warheads had detonated:

> I would expect that not more than 2 warheads would be involved in the detonation and that they would blow away the 5" belt and the ship's side above to be blown away for the distance of perhaps 15 ft. each side, also the forecastle and boat deck to be blown away for a distance of perhaps 20–30 ft. each side. I should also expect the decks below to be blown in down to the level of the armoured deck. I would anticipate that the armoured deck might be bent but not fractured.[22]

In a memo dated 7 July 1941, Third Sea Lord and Controller of the Navy Admiral Bruce Fraser voiced his particular objections to the theory that a torpedo detonation destroyed the *Hood*:

> D.N.C. has raised the question of whether the above water torpedoes in *Hood* were responsible for the destruction of the ship.
>
> 2. [*sic.*] I disagree with his view and accept the report of the Board of Enquiry [*sic.*] for the following reasons:
>
> 1. For trials, a 15" shell burst outside a torpedo tube protected by a mantlet will not detonate the torpedo.
>
> 2. Although a direct hit may detonate one torpedo it is extremely unlikely that others will be countermined. In *Khartoum* a torpedo was fixed into the after galley by an air vessel bursting. The head did not detonate but it burnt to detonation in the fire after a considerable period, about 20 minutes, and in *Hood* the interval between the first hit and the destruction of the ship seems to have been under 3 minutes.

3. The angle from which observers saw the *Hood* i.e. on the *Hood*'s quarter, makes it doubtful whether they can accurately place the position. Lieutenant Commander Terry of *Prince of Wales* who had a good view, considers the explosion occurred between the main mast and 'X' turret.

4. Many observers saw the bow disappearing into the water. The stern appears to have disintegrated as nothing was seen after the explosion.

5. The absence of survivors tends to confirm a magazine explosion.

6. It is known that 1 15" shell can penetrate the magazines.[23]

An examination of the wreck of the *Hood* following her discovery in 2001 revealed that the aft magazines did indeed explode, although what caused the explosion remained a mystery.

Related to the idea that the *Hood* was sunk by a magazine explosion is the idea that she suffered another explosion, one in her forward magazines just forward of 'A' turret. It may be noted here that this theory does not put forward an argument that the *Hood* was sunk by an explosion in her forward magazines, but it argues that the explosion of the magazine that sunk the ship precipitated an explosion in the ship's forward magazines. An examination of the wreck of the *Hood* was conducted by David L. Mearns and Professor Eric Grove who concluded that either just before or just after leaving the surface the bow suffered significant damage from an internal explosion. What exactly was it about the wreck that has led both Grove and Mearns to form this conclusion?

When the wreck of the *Hood* was located in 2001 by David Mearns and Blue Water Recoveries, it was found to by lying at a depth of approximately 9,000 feet. The remains of the ship were spread over three distinct debris fields. There were the bow and stern sections at approximately 165 and 125 feet long respectively and, somewhat removed, an upturned section of hull some 350 feet long. Examination of the wreckage revealed that some 225 feet of ship, corresponding to the area between 'Y' turret and the middle engine room, were missing. The stern had been seen to break away from the bow section, but it came as something of a surprise when the bow was found to be severed from the rest of the ship and lying on its port side wrapped in anchor cable. According to Bruce Taylor, 'It seems probable that the break was owed first to structural weakening when the bow rose out of the water and then to implosion damage once the ship left the surface'.[24] David Mearns and Rob White have put forward the case for an explosion in the ship's forward magazines, which would account for the severed bow, who noted:

> ... the breaks near the forward turrets support this. The implosion damage we documented was very limited in scale and could not account for the massive destruction and outward-splaying of shell plating, whereas a second magazine explosion could.

A final piece of wreckage adds fuel to the fire. The conning tower—all 650 tons of it—was found over one kilometre away from the majority of the debris and two kilometres away from the upturned mid-ships section. While it appears that the mid-ships section planed away from the surface position where the ship sank, it is hard to imagine the extremely, heavy cylindrical conning tower going anywhere but straight down to the seabed once it separated from the hull. Could the conning tower have been blown free by the explosion of the forward 4-inch and 15-inch magazines and propelled away from the rest of the ship? Several eyewitnesses had noticed one particularly large piece high in the air. Was this the conning tower, or had the explosion taken place largely underwater?[25]

To reach the conclusion they have drawn, Mearns and White looked at testimony given by Chief Petty Officer William Westlake and Chief Petty Officer Frederick French of the *Prince of Wales*. From his position on the *Prince of Wales*, Westlake saw:

> The *Hood* was covered in smoke and it was impossible to pick out anything definite of the ship at all. Another salvo hit the waterline of the *Hood*. I saw spurts of smoke coming out of five or six places. After a few seconds the whole ship seemed to blow up in pieces. The bow from between 'A' and 'B' turrets was blown out of the water and then slid directly back. The plating from the ship's side between the foremast and mainmast was blown into the air. There were huge columns of smoke and that was the last I saw of her.[26]

French, meanwhile, testified at the Board of Inquiry:

> I saw pieces flying on the port side of the boat deck just before the mainmast. In a matter of seconds, a cordite fire in my opinion, occurred there. The reason I saw it was a cordite fire was because the flame was very bright, the edge of the flame was black and that coming away from it was the brown cordite fumes which you see come from the muzzle of the guns as they fire. It was similar to the burning of cordite which I have seen before. Meanwhile I saw the *Hood* fire another two salvos all from 'A' and 'B'. At the fourth salvo I saw *Hood* fire, the boat-deck appeared to raise in the middle. Before I saw any more of the boat-deck all what I term cordite fumes came from underneath the ship from aft and about abreast the after funnel. This spread right along the water line to the bows. That stopped me from seeing any more of the boat-deck. The fumes then rose very high and came up to an apex, like the apex of a pyramid, which I should judge to be between 400 and 500 feet.... From the sore part of the fumes the bows of the *Hood* were

broken off abaft number one breakwater and came up to an angle of about 40 deg. and then slid straight back into the water.[27]

It is important to note here that French stated that he saw cordite fumes spread along the waterline to the bow. This is important because for this theory to have any validity, as is acknowledged by Mearns and White, there would have had to have been a pathway of fire from the explosion aft towards the bow. In his account of his time aboard the *Hood* and of his experience of the ship's loss, Ted Briggs recalled 'A blinding flash swept around the outside of the compass platform' before he was thrown to the floor.[28]

In their book on the sinking of the *Hood* and the *Bismarck* and the discovery of their wrecks Mearns and White note testimony that was given by Robert Tilburn at the second Board of Inquiry. Having been asked about the main explosion, he stated that he could see past the foremast breakwater; when asked if he could see the bow, Tilburn was also asked if he had any reason to suppose that there was a fire below the boat deck to which he answered: 'No, Sir, except when I was going into the water there was just one flash of flame came round between the control tower and "B" turret—it came just above the forecastle deck'.[29] From his position in the aft gunnery director of the *Bismarck*, von Müllenheim-Rechberg recalled in *Battleship Bismarck* that when the *Hood* exploded, a huge column of smoke appeared before:

> Gradually, at the foot of the pillar, I made out the bow of the battle cruiser projecting upwards at an angle, a sure sign that she had broken in two. Then I saw something I could hardly believe: a flash of orange from her forward guns! Although her fighting days had ended, the *Hood* was firing a last salvo.[30]

What can account for the blinding flash reported by Ted Briggs that surrounded the compass platform and the flash of flame between the control tower and 'B' turret reported by Tilburn? Could it be the case that fire, or at least flash from the explosion of the aft magazines, travelled through the ship and detonated the forward magazines, and that Müllenheim-Rechberg did not see the *Hood*'s forward turrets fire one last salvo in defiance at all, but rather witnessed the explosion of the forward magazines? Therefore, based on this, Mearns and White concluded:

> There can be no doubt, however, that *Hood*'s loss was due to a catastrophic explosion of her aft ammunition magazines, which had been ignited following a 15-inch shell hit from *Bismarck*. *Hood*'s back had been broke immediately: the obliteration of a 70-metre section of her hull is a testament to the violence of the original explosion. Precisely where that shell hit and

how *Hood*'s armour was penetrated will probably never be known. The massive damage to *Hood*'s forward section points to a similar explosion in her forward magazines, occurring just before the bow slipped beneath the waves.[31]

The idea that the *Hood* suffered from an explosion in her forward magazines is, however, countered by William Jurens et. al. in their work *A Marine Forensic Analysis of HMS Hood and DKM Bismarck*, who stated:

The area forward of 'A' turret, though dry, was probably subjected to very considerable and unusual stresses as it was lifted bodily from the water during this transition. This forward section, which in the vertical position would have had relatively little water plane area, appears to have been rapidly pulled down by the by then more or less completely flooded stern. During this rapid descent, the hull, already subjected to considerable stress at the 'hard point' just forward of 'A' turret where the forward armor belt wrapped athwart ships, and perhaps heavily loaded from flooded chain lockers forward as well, apparently imploded at a point slightly forward of 'A' turret. This implosion, which probably took place at a depth of about 30 meters, effectively destroyed the hull girder, permitting the now separated bow to proceed essentially independently to the bottom. The authors regret that they cannot at this time support the supposition raised in recent media reports and television programs that the separation of the bow was due to a secondary explosion in the forward magazines. These conclusions, apparently based upon a very selective misreading of isolated eyewitness testimony and local observations of some outwardly-bent plating near the margin of the forward hull break, are believed to be erroneous. The forward magazine group, in fact, lies entirely aft of the point of separation. (Although drawings of the ship often locate a set of forward underwater torpedo rooms at the break point, these torpedo tubes and the associated warheads had been removed during modifications made in 1938. Although this modification was accompanied by increased internal subdivision which should have strengthened the hull in this area, there remains some possibility that structural discontinuities created during these modifications may have actually weakened some of the surrounding structure, exacerbating the high loads placed on this area during the vertical rotation.) Considering the extreme violence which must have accompanied the total separation of the bow, the local configuration of plate boundaries at the separation point—which reflects the direction in which the plates last moved, and not necessarily the direction in which they first moved—cannot be considered as highly indicative of an explosion-induced origin.[32]

Boat Deck Fire

When considering the different theories on the loss of the *Hood*, one has to look at the natural possibility that the fire on the boat deck spread and in turn led to the detonation of one or more of the magazines. If a flammable liquid such as petrol or diesel was involved, then it is possible that burning fuel could have wound its way into a magazine through a vent, shaft, or hoist. Few of those who witnessed the demise of the *Hood* seemed to think that something such as petrol was involved in the fire on the boat deck. In addition to this, as the engagement began it is almost certain that the ammunition hoists would have been shut, meaning that this is likely one route that any flammable substance did not take to reach the magazines.

As highlighted in his paper on the destruction of the *Hood* entitled 'The Loss of HMS Hood: A Re-Examination', Jurens cites the testimony of Captain William Wellcose Davis, who served as the executive officer aboard the *Hood* until he left on 20 September 1940, given at the second Board of Inquiry. When asked about petrol storage, Davis stated:

> [T]he petrol stowage was as follows: When the ship proceeded to sea, all petrol, except approximately 2 gals., was left in the drifter. This was kept behind to enable the power boats to be started up on return to harbour. There was a special organisation for landing a number of 50 gallon drums which were kept on the boat deck adjacent to the sea lifebuoy abreast the mainmast. The quick-release drums originally supplied to the ship were released into the sea and not recovered or replaced, on the first occasion of the ship being attacked by aircraft, about 3 weeks after the outbreak of war.[33]

Continuing the line of questioning on the storage of petrol, Davis was asked whether or not he thought the stowage of petrol drums had caused the deck to become impregnated with petrol to which he answered, 'I don't think so; the drums were stowed on trays and the stoker who looked after the stowage was so proud of his care that he told me he could not fill a petrol lighter'.[34] Davis was also asked questions relating to the hoists for the 4-inch ammunition and the storage of U.P. ammunition.

> The 4" ammunition supply doors in the ship were closed until the Captain passed the order 'supply 4" ammunition'. This organisation resulted from an incident when the ship was bombed at the end of September or beginning of October 1939, as it was found that 4" ammunition was being replenished before any order had been given. I can visually confirm that this procedure was rigidly adhered to as I was on the boat deck during subsequent bombings of the ship during the action off Oran … a considerable number of the protected type 4" ready use lockers on the upper deck had been replaced by a lighter but more

waterproof type.... The water-tight door organisation was extremely thorough and efficient and was practiced every day at sea.... The U.P. ammunition and the stowage arrangements were viewed with considerable concern owing to their unprotected positions and the likelihood of their causing fires on the boat deck and the forecastle deck. This view had been expressed whilst the ship was being equipped with this armament, but it was decided to place the ammunition in these exposed places as no other stowage was available.[35]

From the testimony given by Davis, it may, therefore, be assumed that while the fire on the boat deck no doubt proved spectacular, it is likely that the fire played no direct part in the loss of the ship.

8-Inch Shell

One school of thought has speculated that the fatal explosion of the *Hood* was caused by an 8-inch shell from the *Prinz Eugen*, which owing to its plunging trajectory may have penetrated the thinly armoured decks and detonated in the aft magazines. This school of thought does, however, acknowledge that the shells fired by the *Prinz Eugen* would have had little or no chance of penetrating the belt armour of the *Hood*.

Owing to the range at which the *Hood* was engaged by the *Bismarck* and the *Prinz Eugen*, the shells from the *Prinz Eugen* fell at an angle of between 13 and 19 degrees, which cannot be deemed to be plunging fire in any meaningful sense. Assuming that a shell from the *Prinz Eugen* impacted on the spot that would have seen it crash through the decks to the magazine, the shell could have penetrated between 40 mm and 60 mm of homogenous armour at best.

Although a hit from the *Prinz Eugen* could have started a fire in the aft superstructure, it would have been almost impossible for such a hit to have penetrated the aft magazines. At best, the *Prinz Eugen* would have been able to wound the *Hood*, not sink her. Paul Schmalenbach, the ship's second gunnery officer, himself discounted the possibility of one of the *Prinz Eugen*'s 8-inch shells causing the explosion that tore the *Hood* apart. Schmalenbach witnessed the heavy cruiser's 8-inch shells strike the boat deck of the *Hood* and start the fire there but quashed any assertions that the *Prinz Eugen* sank the *Hood* by stating that 'such assertions have no basis in evidence'.[36]

Multiple Hits

Most observers to the loss of the *Hood* were confident that the explosion that sank the ship originated in the vicinity of the mainmast in a position well forward of the aft magazines. It should be noted that it is entirely possible that the *Hood* was hit by more than one shell from a salvo. If the *Hood* did sustain hits from more than one shell from a salvo, a shell detonating in the vicinity of the main mast a split second before another penetrated further aft could easily explain the impression held by most observers that the explosion began further forward than it actually did. In fact, the chances of such a thing occurring are not high. Jurens noted:

> Up to the time *Hood* exploded, *Bismarck* fired five, four-gun salvos, and achieved between one and three hits, giving her a raw hit percentage of about 2/20 or 10%. In viewing this figure, however, we must remember that the five salvos she fired included at least two and possibly three to find the range, and also that *Hood* and *Prince of Wales* were making rather frequent course changes during the action, so that her hit percentage in aimed, well-ranged fire would probably have been somewhat higher.
>
> Taking this and other factors into account, once *Bismarck* had found the range it would appear reasonable to grant *Bismarck* about a 10%–15% hit probability during the final salvos she fired at *Hood*. A statistical analysis of four-gun salvos with a 10% single shot hit probability shows that about 64% of such salvos would result in no hits, 31% would result in one hit, 5% would result in two hits, and only about 0.27% would result in three. For a 15% hit probability, the figures are about 5%, 40%, 9%, and 0.8% respectively. Thus the chance of two simultaneous or near simultaneous hits on *Hood* leading to the visible effects accompanying the blast seem only to be about one in fifteen or twenty. The probability of more than two simultaneous hits causing the blast is negligible.[37]

Despite what has been advanced in this chapter, there is another theory, which will be analysed in greater detail in the following chapter.

Accidental Sinking?

It is often written that the *Hood*'s destruction was the result of her deck armour being penetrated by a 15-inch shell from the *Bismarck*, which served to detonate the aft magazines. Indeed, this was even the conclusion of the Boards of Inquiry, with the second board concluding, 'That the sinking of *Hood* was due to a hit from *Bismarck's* 15-inch shell in or adjacent to *Hood's* 4-inch or 15-inch magazines, causing them all to explode and wreck the after part of the ship. The probability is that the 4-inch magazines exploded first'.[1] There is, however, another theory.

In some circles, the idea has been put forward that the *Hood* may not have been destroyed by enemy action at all but was, in fact, destroyed by accident. While this may sound like something that is farfetched, and is admittedly of a low probability, there is a little circumstantial evidence which lends credence to this school of thought. In his paper published in *Warship International*, William Jurens allowed for the possibility that the *Hood* suffered from a magazine or turret handling problem that resulted in the spontaneous combustion of the propellants in the ship's aft magazine.

Jurens observed that a significant number of witnesses to the loss of the *Hood* considered that the explosion did not closely coincide with a fall of shot from the *Bismarck*. In this, apparent anomalies with the operation of 'X' turret during the final moments of the *Hood*'s participation in the battle were also identified, namely that 'X' turret did not fire when 'A', 'B', and 'Y' turrets did and that flames were seen from the turret.

It is interesting to note that more than one-third of those who were aboard the *Prince of Wales* and witnessed the sinking of the *Hood* actually missed the explosion itself. In addition to these, of the approximately forty-five individuals aboard the *Prince of Wales* who observed the explosion itself, less than a quarter associated the explosion with a specific fall of shot from the *Bismarck*. A further 20 per cent associated the explosion of the *Hood* with the firing of one of her aft turrets while over half of the observers did not associate the explosion with anything; to them, the *Hood* simply blew up. As such, there exists the very small possibility that the final explosion that sank the *Hood* had anything at all to do with either the *Bismarck* or the *Prinz Eugen*.

Several eyewitnesses to the explosion noticed and elected to mention what to them appeared to be unusual events aboard the *Hood* during the engagement. Petty Officer George Goff, who was a layer-rating in the port battery by the port-after director of the *Prince of Wales* told the Board of Inquiry that he saw the third salvo of the *Bismarck*:

> ... on the starboard side of the *Hood*, very close. The next thing I remember was seeing flames from 'X' turret. 'A', 'B', and 'Y' were firing at the time and I noticed that 'X' turret was not firing.... The next thing I noticed was that the 'B' turret was firing but belching out flames. After that 'Y' turret fired on its own and *Hood* went up.[2]

The board dismissed the testimony given by Goff with the statement, 'This witness is rather inclined to be imaginative'. When he had been questioned in detail about the flames he apparently saw belching from the guns of 'X' turret, he replied that 'When a gun fires the flash licks slowly round the muzzle of the gun. But there was no straight flash and the flames licked slowly round'.[3]

Goff may not have been as 'imaginative' as the board branded him for others noticed a similar phenomenon. Petty Officer James Crowley was manning a periscope in the P.4 turret of the *Prince of Wales* when the *Hood* exploded. When questioned about the loss of the *Hood*, Crowley stated, 'when I looked through the periscope again I saw a flame come from 'B' turret through one of the guns. Not many moments after that she blew up'.[4] Through the periscope of turret P.3, Petty Officer Edgar Holt saw the same sight:

> A fire broke out abreast 'X' turret on *Hood* port side About two minutes later I saw a flame about 10 feet long shoot out of 'B' turret muzzle and about half to one minute later 'Y' turret on *Hood* fired her first salvo. About a second later *Hood* blew up.[5]

Some onlookers observed something that they deemed unusual with regards 'Y' turret. From the port side of the Admiral's shelter deck of the *Prince of Wales*, Petty Officer Lawrence Sutton recalled:

> H.E. shells burst on the other side of the *Hood* which gave me the impression that *Hood* had been hit by one of the salvos which had been fired. The *Hood* was firing with her foremost turrets. 'Y' turret had been trained fore and aft

during this time. 'Y' turret then trained towards the enemy and before firing there was a flash abaft the mainmast of the *Hood* which appeared to be a fire on the boat-deck. 'Y' turret then fired and at the same time a huge flash came up all around 'Y' turret. The flash rose to well above the mainmast of the ship and all I heard was a tremendous roar and I could not see anything until the smoke had cleared away. That was all I saw of the *Hood*.[6]

Having listened to Sutton's testimony, the board stated 'This witness's evidence as regards the flash around "Y" turret would be important if it could be relied upon, but we consider his memory of what he saw very confused'.[7] What the board did not consider, however, was that a number of other witnesses confirmed the observations that were made by Sutton. At least one other witness clearly saw 'Y' turret traverse around towards the German ships then return to its regular fore-aft position before being trained once more on the enemy.

Based on this, what can be ascribed to this unusual performance? It could be the case that the *Hood* was encountering internal difficulties with regards the supply of her shells and powder. Perhaps some failure within the turret or the barbette may have disrupted the complex system of anti-flash mechanisms that had been built into the design of the ship as a result of the experience and lessons learned following the loss of the battlecruisers HMS *Indefatigable*, *Queen Mary* and *Invincible* at Jutland. It may be noted that Peter Hodges has noted that there were no fewer than thirty-seven safety interlocks controlling the operations of the BL 15-inch Mk I naval gun.[8] The 15-inch twin mount that equipped the *Hood* and other Royal Navy capital ships was recorded in an American report produced after the Second World War as being the most reliable and accurate battleship main armament of the war, although other guns and mountings had superior individual features.[9] Caught up in the heat of battle, could it be the case that someone in 'Y' turret had overridden the anti-flash interlocks in order to bring the turret back into service? May there have been something wrong with the propellant used by the *Hood*? Related to this, it could be the case that there may have been a failure in her gas ejector systems which caused a flare back into 'Y' turret which thereafter blew up the ship. Such scenarios may sound like wild speculation. Nevertheless, they are possibilities that, no matter how unlikely they are to have occurred, cannot be positively and completely excluded.

As has previously been observed by Jurens, we do not possess close-range photographs of the *Hood*'s final moments, nor do we have a 'black box' recording of her last few minutes like we have for airliners. We do, however, have footage of HMS *Barham* suffering a magazine explosion. HMS *Barham* was a Queen Elizabeth-class battleship that was built, like the *Hood*, at John Brown and Co., Clydebank. Laid down in 1913, she was launched in

1914 and commissioned in 1915. The original note from Controller of the Navy Admiral Sir Frederick Tudor to Director of Naval Construction Sir Eustace Tennyson d'Eyncourt in 1915, which resulted in the *Hood*, was for a ship design that was to 'take the armament, armour and engine power of *Queen Elizabeth* as the standard and build around them in a hull which would draw as little water as was considered practicable and safe, and which should embody all the latest protection and improvements against underwater attack'.[10] In light of this, HMS *Barham* may be deemed a suitable comparable vessel.

During the afternoon of 25 November 1941, the 1st Battle Squadron comprised of the battleships HMS *Queen Elizabeth*, *Valiant*, and *Barham* with an escort of eight destroyers departed Alexandria to cover the ships of the 7th and 15th Cruiser Squadrons as they hunted Italian convoys in the central Mediterranean. The ships were detected by *U-331* commanded by *Oberleutnant zur See* Hans-Diedrich von Tiesenhausen, which moved to intercept. At 4.18 p.m., an ASDIC operator aboard the destroyer HMS *Jervis* detected *U-331* at a range of approximately 1,000 yards, but the contact was disregarded. *U-331* subsequently passed through the destroyer screen unmolested. At 4.25 p.m., at a range of 410 yards, von Tiesenhausen ordered all four bow torpedo tubes to be fired.

With no time to take evasive action, three of the four torpedoes struck HMS *Barham* amidships. The torpedoes all struck the battleship close together and threw up a single large water column. The *Barham* capsized to port and was lying on her port side when, four minutes after she had been torpedoed, a large magazine explosion tore the ship to pieces. The sinking was captured on film by a cameraman from Pathé news aboard HMS *Valiant*. Owing to the speed with which the ship sank, 862 officers and ratings out of a complement of 1,016 were killed.[11] The subsequent Board of Inquiry into the loss of the *Barham*, like that of the *Hood*, ascribed the magazine explosion to a fire in the 4-inch magazines that spread and served to detonate the contents of the 15-inch magazines.[12]

At first, the cause of the *Barham*'s explosion seems obvious—the explosion of the magazines set off by torpedo flash. However, the waters become somewhat murky when one considers that similar vessels have received similar damage without such violent explosions. Some smaller vessels (such as destroyers, where the magazines and handling rooms were closer to the hull plating) suffered near-instantaneous explosions, resulting from torpedo strikes if hit near a magazine, while on other vessels fires have raged for a respectable amount of time before the magazines exploded. A prime example of this is the American destroyer USS *Shaw*, which was in dry dock on the morning of 7 December 1941 when the Japanese launched their surprise attack on Pearl Harbor. The *Shaw* was struck by three bombs—two through the forward machine gun platform and one through the port wing of the bridge. Fires raged inside the destroyer, and at 9.25 a.m., all firefighting facilities aboard the ship were exhausted and the order given to abandon ship. Five minutes later, before the dry dock could be sufficiently flooded, the fires finally succeeded in detonating the forward magazine.

The flooding of the *Barham* with water as she capsized would appear to have been unable to quench the fires if they were the cause of the explosion. At the same time, the case of the USS *Shaw* would suggest that fire could have detonated the magazines of both the *Hood* and the *Barham*, but after a respectable amount of time, not instantaneously.

Descriptions of the sound of the *Barham*'s explosion, as quoted by Peter Smith, vary as they do in the testimony at the Boards of Inquiry into the loss of the *Hood*. What is interesting, however, is that several witnesses mention the lack of a shockwave. The relatively limited blast effect and the way in which the ship lost way as she capsized most likely accounts for the comparatively large number of survivors when compared to the *Hood*. The footage taken from HMS *Valiant* shows little apparent evidence of fires raging on the port side of the *Barham* as the ship began to list, and there are no indications of any smaller explosions inside the hull prior to the main one, which tore the ship apart.

These factors combined lead one to speculate that it may have been the case that the explosion inside the magazine of the *Barham* was more likely a result of the capsize than flash. Some, such as Sean Waddingham, have suggested that the explosion was more likely caused by the collapse of shell or cordite stowage. Given that it would be surprising if the shocks produced in a vessel capsize would trigger a shell detonation, one cannot help but look to see if there are any grounds for such a claim.

A number of different sources have commented on the loss of the battlecruisers *Indefatigable*, *Queen Mary*, and *Invincible* at the Battle of Jutland on 31 May 1916. In my own work on the battlecruiser HMS *Hood* in which I first looked at the battlecruiser concept and the deployment of HMS *Invincible*, it was noted that shell hoists in First World War-era British vessels were slower than those in their German counterparts and that in an effort to increase the rate of fire, charges were left at various points between the magazine and the turret. In addition to this, it was noted that magazine doors were often left open in combat and propped open by sacks of cordite with the result that the combination of poor charge handling practices along with the highly flammable cordite used in British shells exposed the Royal Navy's battlecruisers.[13] It was also noted that at Jutland, the Royal Navy's battlecruisers exploded and sank without being exposed to a tremendous barrage of fire, yet, a year and a half earlier at the Battle of the Falkland Islands in 1914, the German battlecruisers *Scharnhorst* and *Gneisenau* were subjected to a tremendous barrage of fire and finally sank without a hint of a magazine explosion.

Part of the reason for this lay in the type of power charge that was used and the brass cartridges in which it was housed. One of the key differences that existed between German and British powder was that the former tended to burn when set alight while the latter exploded. German charge cases were made out of brass whereas British charge cases were made out of silk. This serves to explain why an impact such as that which contributed to the sinking of HMS *Invincible* at Jutland did not prove fatal in the case of the *Scharnhorst* or the *Gneisenau* at the Falkland Islands.

An additional example is that of the *Seydlitz* at the Battle of Dogger Bank. The *Seydlitz* was hit by British shell fragments that penetrated a magazine and ignited a fire, killing everyone inside. Crucially, the cordite charges did not explode. This is significant because a similar hit on a British vessel would almost certainly have resulted in the loss of the ship.[14]

A Board of Inquiry was convened into the loss of the three battlecruisers at Jutland and recommended a number of changes be enacted in order to prevent similar incidents in the future. During the interwar years, considerable modifications were made to the constituents of British cordite, but it remains likely that it was still more delicate than German cordite by the time of the Second World War.

In the case of the *Hood*, it is therefore at least a possibility that a cordite handling accident, potentially as a result of frustration that 'X' and 'Y' turrets were unable to be rotated sufficiently to participate from the beginning of the battle, began the chain of events that led to the detonation of the magazines.

Nevertheless, as Jurens has concluded, it remains the case that *Hood* was unlucky if one of the shells fired by the *Bismarck* penetrated her thinly armoured decks to detonate a magazine. While the possibility that the *Hood* was destroyed by accident has been put forward here, along with the basis for such a theory, this author believes that a cordite handling accident resulting in flash or an explosion that detonated the magazines and tore the ship apart to be highly unlikely and that the most likely cause for the *Hood*'s loss is that which is most widely accepted—that a 15-inch shell from the *Bismarck* struck the *Hood* in or adjacent to one of her 4-inch or 15-inch magazines, which caused them to explode, tearing the ship apart and causing her to sink.

Likely Cause of the *Hood*'s Loss

In his article *The Loss of HMS Hood: A Re-Examination*, Bill Jurens wrote, 'The exact origin of the explosion is now, and shall probably always remain, somewhat in doubt'.[1] An examination of the testimony that was given at the Boards of Inquiry shows that while the majority of those who witnessed the destruction of the *Hood* felt that the explosion originated forward of the mainmast, this opinion was by no means universal. Some witnesses have associated the explosion with a fall of shot from the *Bismarck* while others did not.

Given that conflicting and confusing evidence exists and, indeed, has been presented, there exists what may be deemed a 'most probable' or 'most likely' explanation for the loss of the *Hood*, one which reconciles the observations of eyewitnesses with the ship's movements and actions.

Most witnesses recalled that the explosion was essentially noiseless or could not be heard over the roar of the guns of the *Prince of Wales*, for instance. The sound we hear when an object explodes is a vibration that travels as a wave. The sound waves travel by forcing the particles of air to vibrate back and forth and to collide with each other in the same direction as the wave is travelling. When burning occurs, however, the vibrations that we hear are necessarily absent, even if the burning is rapid. The noiselessness of the explosion, combined with other circumstantial evidence, therefore, would suggest that the fatal explosion was not caused by the detonation of the *Hood*'s shells or torpedoes but by the rapid combustion of her propellants. It may be noted that on 7 December 1941, during the Japanese attack on Pearl Harbor, a similar noiseless explosion was associated with the explosion of the propellant magazines of the USS *Arizona*. The explosion of the *Arizona* was marked by an obvious vertical venting of gasses through the engineering spaces while the decks located directly above the magazines remained substantially intact. A survey of the wreck of the *Arizona* was undertaken shortly after the ship's loss and provided an insight into the explosion:

The divers found the interior of the *Arizona* had been severely damaged by the explosion of the forward magazines. Evidence of its power had shown that the explosion had vented through the deck forward of turret No. 1 causing a separation of the bow and the rest of the ship. Divers found further that the sides of the bow had been blown outward almost to a horizontal position. Closer examination of the exterior hull was assisted by jetting away mud with high-pressure hoses. When divers attempted to move forward into the interior of the vessel, they found that the main and second decks were blocked with wreckage forward of frame 76. The furthest divers could move toward the bow of the ship was on the third deck to frame 66, where the second deck sloped into the third deck. Hatches that had once led to the interior of the ship from various decks were now twisted and distorted. Captain Homer Wallin and his staff found that gun turrets No. 1 and 2, the conning tower and uptakes had fallen 20–28 feet indication a collapse of the supporting structure.[2]

The conclusion that the *Hood*'s loss was the result of the rapid combustion of her propellants is in accordance with the findings of the Boards of Inquiry. Assuming that one or multiple shells from the *Bismarck* precipitated the disaster by being the root cause of the ignition, this would also explain the short delay that eyewitnesses noted between the arrival of the *Bismarck*'s fifth salvo and the explosion.

As has previously been shown, determining where the fatal hit arrived aboard the *Hood* is problematic as it could have been via one of a number of routes. Nevertheless, this author is inclined to believe that it was likely that one shell from the *Bismarck*'s fifth salvo set in motion the chain of events that sent the *Hood* to the bottom of the Denmark Strait. As stated at the beginning of this chapter, the majority of witnesses believed that the explosion originated in the vicinity of the mainmast, some way forward of the aft magazines. It is possible that a shell could have penetrated the *Hood* and passed through the aft engine room and detonated in or near the magazines, which were located immediately adjacent. According to the analysis conducted by Jurens:

> If this occurred, and ignition of the propellant followed from it, then a large part of the rapidly expanding gas bubble would have taken the path of least resistance and vented into the engineering spaces immediately forward of this area. For a time the sheer inertia of *Hood*'s structure would have slowed expansion in any other direction. Once the expanding gasses had reached the engine rooms, the quickest exits to the outside would have been the series of massive exhaust vents located on the centreline immediately forward of and aft of the mainmast. These huge ducts, changing in size and shape as they rose through the ship, ended in roughly square vents 1.8 metres [each] side

on the boat deck. It was as spectacular, near-vertical columns of flame from these vents near the mainmast, foreshortened to observers on surrounding ships, that the explosion first became visible.

Shortly thereafter, the entire stern of the ship exploded. At the time of the blast, the Board of Enquiry [*sic.*] calculated the 'X' 15-in magazine contained about 49 tons of cordite, 'Y' magazine contained 45 tons, and the 4-in magazines contained about 18.5 tons. The uncontrolled burning of this quantity of propellant in the after magazines might have slowed briefly as the volume of the engineering spaces served as a space into which the gasses could expand, and as the vents directed much of the combustion products outboard. But although this expansion and venting could temporarily relieve the pressure, it could never be enough to prevent an explosion from eventually tearing the ship apart.[3]

It is this that is the likely cause of the loss of HMS *Hood*.

10

Loss of Life on the *Hood*

The loss of 1,415 men aboard the *Hood* on 24 May 1941 was the single greatest loss of life sustained by the Royal Navy during the course of the Second World War. When HMS *Electra* arrived at the reported position of the *Hood*'s sinking, her crew at first believed that the *Hood* had been lost with all hands; there were no traces of her 1,418 crewmen living or dead, save William Dundas, Robert Tilburn, and Ted Briggs.

There are four main factors behind why so many men died and why there was such an obvious lack of bodies: the battle; the explosion that tore the ship apart; the sinking; and the suction. Each of these factors will be analysed in turn in order to offer an insight into why so many died and how Tilburn, Briggs, and Dundas managed to survive.

Early on during the engagement, the *Hood* was struck by an 8-inch shell from the *Prinz Eugen*, which caused the fire on the boat deck. The fire spread rapidly and was fed by the 4-inch ready-use ammunition, which exploded in every conceivable direction and turned the deck into a holocaust. A number of men were killed in this area when the shells from the *Prinz Eugen* found their mark. Robert Tilburn and two other sailors were ordered by a gunner's mate to tackle the fire on the boat deck. Faced with the blaze (which was 'pinkish in colour, with not much smoke') and the exploding ammunition, Tilburn and the other sailors decided they would tackle the fire once the ready-use ammunition had finished exploding. The gunner's mate went to inform the gunnery officer, but at that moment, the recreation space in which the gunners were taking shelter was hit by a German shell, which, according to Tilburn, killed everyone inside, approximately 200 men.[1] In addition to this, the exploding ready-use ammunition turned the positions above the platform deck, such as the flag deck, into a charnel house.

Additional crewmen were likely killed when a 15-inch shell from the *Bismarck* passed through the spotting top of the *Hood*. Whether or not the *Hood* sustained a hit on her spotting top is debated, but it is likely that *Hood* did sustain such a hit because in the wake of the explosion that rocked the *Hood*, Robert Tilburn recalled seeing bodies and parts of bodies fall from that area. Further evidence in support of this is the fact that William Dundas developed the impression that one of the *Bismarck*'s shells had passed through the spotting top and caused carnage without exploding because of the number of bodies that landed on the ship's upper deck. Dundas recalled being asked by Captain Kerr to identify one body that had fallen close by the compass platform. Dundas reported that he could not identify the individual as the body had no head or hands, but could say that from his uniform that the body was that of a lieutenant.

When it comes to the sinking of the *Hood*, one fact is certain—something caused her aft 15-inch magazines to detonate or to burn so violently that the area between 'Y' turret and the second funnel was devastated and that the keel of the ship was weakened to such an extent that it broke immediately. Whatever occurred, be it an explosion, flash, or a fierce blaze, it almost certainly caused the deaths of the majority of the crewmen who were in the affected areas of the hull and in the aft stations. After the main explosion in the 15-inch magazines, it is highly likely that the interior of the ship was engulfed by a rapidly spreading fire that resulted in another explosion in the forward areas of the ship. It should be noted that this scenario of a fire rapidly ravaging the interior of the ship before causing a second explosion forward is based on the findings, observations, and analysis of the wreck by David L. Mearns and Bluewater Recoveries in 2001. If this occurred, then this alone would account for the vast majority of the 1,415 casualties. It is likely that many of those within the blast radius were vaporised in the explosion while others were burned so badly in the fire that raged inside the hull that little remained.

Following the explosion of her aft magazines, the *Hood* initially broke into two and sank stern and bow up with her midsection pointed down in a 'V' shape. Though the very end of the stern section was intact, from 'X' turret forwards was a mass of twisted framework and blasted-out plating. The damage caused to the stern caused it to point skywards and to sink almost immediately. Indeed, so quick was the sinking that anyone who had somehow survived the explosion and the conflagration would have had no time to escape and would have been drowned by the inrush of water. The forward section remained afloat approximately two minutes longer than the stern. Between the damage that was caused by the explosion that caused the split between the bow and stern sections, the ensuing fires, the possible explosion forward, power failures, and the splitting and collapse of the ship combined with the rapid sinking meant that for those in the forward section of the *Hood*, there was very little time in which to react, let alone escape. Those in the bow section who survived the conflagration were trapped inside the dark, inverting, and rapidly sinking hull.

Based on the testimonies that have been given by Tilburn, Dundas, and Briggs, when she sank, the *Hood* generated a lot of suction. The suction that was generated as the ship sank was likely the cause of many deaths among the ship's company in the forward portion of the ship. It is believed that a sizeable number of crewmen made it out of the forward section of the hull but that once they ended up in the water the sea overtook them. Others were likely trapped under deck heads or pinned to the twisted and rapidly sinking ship by the suction. More members of the crew were likely trapped by elements of the ship as she was torn apart.

The lack of survivors was due not only to the enormity of the explosion but also to the speed of the sinking. It must be assumed that a few were to be found sealed in compartments, which went untouched by the explosion and that the first of the men inside these compartments knew of anything out of the ordinary occurring was when the hull began to rise up out of the water.

Ted Briggs recalled that at around midnight, Commander Cross spoke to the ship's company about the impending engagement and encouraged them all to change into clean underwear to lower their risk of infection if wounded; he dressed with his life jacket beneath his Burberry. If Briggs did this, then it may be assumed that many other members of the ship's company did the same. By wearing their life jackets beneath their coats, jumpers, anti-flash gear, and other articles of clothing, the buoyancy of those who tried to swim to the surface would have been drastically reduced. This would, therefore, explain why they were less able to escape the suction of the ship as it rapidly sank. It must also be noted that Briggs and Tilburn found themselves being sucked down before being rapidly propelled upwards. It is likely that they were within pockets that helped them to survive as suddenly they found themselves being propelled to the surface among air bubbles, possibly as a result of the boilers exploding.

The real question when considering the loss of the *Hood* is not why so many men died but, rather, how anyone survived. The fact that Biggs, Dundas, and Tilburn survived the sinking is down to nothing more than pure chance. They were propelled to the surface as a result of the ship's boilers exploding or by air escaping the rapidly imploding hull. Had they been in other positions and not entered the water where each of them did, it is highly likely that they would also have been dragged down to the dark depths of the Atlantic with the other members of the crew. It was their good fortune that they managed to land in air bubbles, propelling them to the surface where they located floats that had managed to break away from the ship, meaning that they did not have to remain in the freezing water.

Even though they were wet, the wind chill factor would have made their experiences excruciating, but had they remained in the water, it is likely they would have succumbed to hypothermia. They were also fortunate that HMS *Electra* rescued them when she did as Briggs and Tilburn were beginning to slowly succumb to the urge to sleep, from which it is likely they would never have regained consciousness as Dundas sat singing 'Roll Out the Barrel' in an effort to keep them alert.

11

Time

When the different accounts that have been given of the battle and the different maps and charts produced by both the Germans and the British are studied, one thing that becomes apparent is that they appear to be using the same time. For example, both sides state that the battle began at around 5.53 a.m. and ended at 6.09 a.m. Given that the time in the United Kingdom is traditionally behind that in Europe (with Greenwich Meant Time (GMT) and British Summer Time seeing Britain an hour behind continental Europe), the question arises as to how and why conformity existed between the two sides during the battle.

The answer to this question is a time zone called British Double Summer Time. During the Second World War, British Double Summer Time was invented as an energy-saving device and served to put the United Kingdom on the same time zone as mainland Europe—GMT +1 in the winter months and GMT +2 in the summer.

In order to bring about Double British Summer Time, at the end of the summer of 1940, British clocks remained on British Summer Time (GMT +1) as opposed to being turned back to Greenwich Mean Time. In the spring of 1941, British clocks were put forward by one hour as normal, thus bringing about Double Summer Time. This served to put Britain on the same time footing as Europe. During the winter months, the clocks would be turned back from GMT +2 to GMT +1 to keep Britain aligned with Europe.

There was also an operational advantage to this. Operational coherence requires all units in a command to work on the same clock as immense confusion would result if each command, or in the case of the Battle of the Denmark Strait, each ship, adjusted its time according to its longitude. As such, during the battle, HMS *Norfolk*, *Suffolk*, *Hood*, *Prince of Wales*, the *Bismarck*, and the *Prinz Eugen* were all operating on the same time. Of note here, therefore, is that the local time was GMT +1, or an hour behind the time used on the ships meaning that while the *Hood* and the *Prince of Wales* opened fire at 5.52 a.m., according to British Double Summer Time; in Reykjavik where the distant rumblings of the battle could be heard, the time was 4.52 a.m. Britain would revert back to its normal time standards in 1947.

Battle Conditions

Depending on the time of year and one's global location, the length of night and day vary. For most, day and night are two distinct periods of time. In the extreme latitudes, this is not the case. The Battle of the Denmark Strait occurred in northern waters. The location is such that during May, the days are long while the period of night is brief. The night of 23–24 May was brief indeed; the sun set at 11 p.m. and rose again at 3.45 a.m. with a few hours of murky twilight both before and after.

At the time of the battle, the sun had risen, yet it was not high in the sky, but it has been estimated that the sun was a mere 4 degrees high in the sky at the time of the battle with the result that the sky was reasonably bright behind the *Hood* and the *Prince of Wales* and somewhat dimmer behind the *Bismarck* and the *Prinz Eugen*. This should not be mistaken, however, for the classic image of the German ships emerging out of the darkness as both Holland's and Lütjens's ships were sufficiently illuminated to visually detect one another at a range of approximately 23 miles.

The war diary of the *Prinz Eugen* described the weather conditions in the Denmark Strait on the morning of 24 May as being overcast with Force 3 (7–10-knot) winds. The exact cloud ceiling is unknown, but it is known that a Sunderland that flew overhead during the battle took cover in clouds at 2,500 feet.

Severe weather had been encountered during the night of 23 May by Holland's ships, but by the time of the battle, the seas were less violent. Ted Briggs noted that there was a heavy swell from the north-east in the hours preceding the battle and that some water was splashed up on to the ship. The conditions have been described as a 'steely blend of sky and sea' and 'grey sky on grey sea'.

The weather on the morning of 24 May was bleak and grey, but the battle area was amply lit by the rising sun. There would have been little colour in the Denmark Strait save the white spray of the impacting shells that sent up towering columns of water, the purplish coloured smoke of the British ships, the colourful signal flags and battle ensigns, and the reddish brown cordite smoke.

Timing of the Fatal Hit

This chapter leans on the theories that have been put forward by Dr Paul Cadogan in his article 'The Sinking of H.M.S. Hood: An Examination of the Timing of her Fatal Hit', which was produced in May 2004 and puts forward an argument that the so-called 'fatal hit' that caused the *Hood* to sink was sustained earlier than has previously been thought.

This chapter will examine the documented evidence in an effort to demonstrate that the officially accepted time of the fatal hit that detonated *Hood*'s magazines and caused her to sink may not be accurate. It is fitting to emphasise here that this chapter is not an attempt to change the history of the battle but rather to put forward what amounts to a rational possibility for which it is up to the reader to decide for themselves whether or not there is merit. The events that led to the Battle of the Denmark Strait have already been detailed, therefore it is not necessary to recap them here.

In the decades following the loss of the *Hood*, the documented evidence has been examined more closely and has had the effect of altering the timeline of the events that occurred on the morning of 24 May 1941. Errors in the recording of times by personnel during the heat of the battle or after the event, combined with the fallibility of memory of those who witnessed events, have led to some confusion and a misinterpretation over what happened in the Denmark Strait. As highlighted by Paul Cadogan, one prime example of this would be the time at which HMS *Prince of Wales* disengaged from the battle following the loss of the *Hood*. The commander in chief of the Home Fleet Admiral Sir John Tovey issued a dispatch recording the *Prince of Wales*'s disengagement as being 6.13 a.m. In the wake of the battle, this was found to be erroneous with a later Admiralty document 'correcting' the time to show that *Prince of Wales* broke off the engagement at 6.23 a.m., a time that more closely aligned with the plot of the action that was drawn up by the ship's navigating officer, Lieutenant-Commander G. W. Rowell.[1]

An example of the accepted, 'traditional' timeline can be found in Angus Konstam's *The Bismarck 1941* and Bruce Taylor's *The Battlecruiser HMS Hood: An Illustrated Biography 1916–1941*.[2] This timeline has been outlined below:

05.37   Smoke from funnels of German vessels sighted by *Prince of Wales*. Admiral Holland orders a 40-degree turn to starboard to close with the enemy.

05.49   Holland orders '2 Blue', a 20-degree turn to starboard onto a course of 300-degrees. The turns serves to prevent the opening of A-arcs of both *Hood* and *Prince of Wales*.

05.52:30 *Hood* opens fire on the lead vessel which it is believed is the *Bismarck* but which is in fact the *Prinz Eugen*.

05.53   *Prince of Wales* opens fire on the *Bismarck*.

05.55   *Bismarck* and *Prinz Eugen* open fire, targeting the lead vessel which is the *Hood*.

05.56   *Hood* hit by shells from the second salvo fired by the *Prinz Eugen* which starts a fire near the base of the main mast among the 4-inch ready-use ammunition.

05.56:30 *Bismarck* straddles *Hood* with her third salvo.

05.57   Admiral Holland orders '2 Blue' a turn of 20-degrees to port to open A-arcs. *Prince of Wales* opens A-arcs shortly after the turn begins.

05.58   *Prinz Eugen* begins targeting *Prince of Wales*.

06.00   Another '2 Blue' flag is seen to be flying from the *Hood*. The fifth salvo from the *Bismarck* strikes the *Hood*. A sheet of flame is seen to rise skywards as the ship is engulfed in smoke. *Prince of Wales* takes evasive action to starboard around the *Hood*.

06.01   *Hood* sinks. *Bismarck* switches targets to *Prince of Wales*.

06.02   Captain Leach makes the decision to disengage.

06.02   *Prince of Wales* retreats behind a smokescreen.

06.09   *Bismarck* and *Prinz Eugen* cease fire.

An analysis of the timeline of the battle raises a number of questions. The first question that arises concerns the salvo count of the *Bismarck*. It is traditionally claimed that the *Hood* was struck by the *Bismarck*'s fifth salvo. Between 5.55 and 5.57 a.m., the *Bismarck* fired three salvos at the *Hood*. It therefore seems strange that in the subsequent three minutes, only an additional two salvos were fired at the *Hood*. The *Bismarck* was armed with eight SK C/34 15-inch guns arranged in four turrets. Each turret was electrically trained and hydraulically elevated. They were capable of being elevated to 30 degrees, which gave the *Bismarck* a maximum firing range of 22 miles. For loading, each gun was required to return 2.5-degrees elevation. Despite this, under optimal conditions, three salvos per minute were capable of being fired.[3]

In the first instance, it is important to point out that conditions in the Denmark Strait on the morning of 24 May 1941 were not ideal. In order to fire three salvoes in two minutes, the *Bismarck* was firing one salvo approximately every forty seconds following opening fire. At such a rate, in the subsequent three minutes, the *Bismarck* could have fired another four salvos, as opposed to the generally accepted two. Even when shell flight times, fall of shot observations, and gunnery corrections are taken into account, the number of salvoes fired appears unusually low.

Baron Burkhard von Müllenheim-Rechberg, the fourth gunnery officer on board the *Bismarck* provides an insight that further examines how this can be explained:

> I heard [Adalbert] Schneider [the *Bismarck*'s First Gunnery Officer] order the first salvo and heard his observation on the fall of shot, 'short'. He corrected their range and deflection, then ordered a 400-meter bracket. The long salvo was described as 'over', the base salvo as 'straddling', and immediately ordered, 'Full salvos good rapid'.[4]

The account given by Burkhard Müllenheim-Rechberg is consistent with the accepted British account of the first salvo from the *Bismarck* landing short ahead of the *Hood*, the second salvo falling between the *Hood* and the *Prince of Wales* before the third salvo straddled the *Hood*. Given that with the firing of the third salvo, Schneider had the range to the *Hood* and that he ordered 'Full salvos good rapid', why were apparently only two salvos fired at the *Hood* between 5.57 and 6 a.m.?

Another question concerns the time taken for the *Hood* to open A-arcs and to fire the first salvo from her 'X' and 'Y' turrets, which is noted as having occurred seconds before her demise. At approximately 5.55 a.m., Admiral Holland order '2 Blue', a 20-degree turn to port in an effort to open A-arcs. This turn was executed at 5.57 a.m. At this point, the *Prince of Wales* is recorded as having her A-arcs open.[5] If the *Prince of Wales* opened A-arcs at 5.57 a.m., the *Hood*, being ahead, should have also opened A-arcs. Capable of rotating each of her 15-inch turrets 300 degrees, the *Hood* possessed a greater forward-bearing capacity for her aft turrets than the *Prince of Wales* did. It may be noted, however, that traversing the gun turrets to such an angle would likely not have been practical given the blast damage to the ship's structure that would result. That is not to say, however, that the guns were never fired at an angle close to 300 degrees as can be seen in the photograph in the plate section.

Allowing time for the turrets to be trained and for the guns to be elevated in preparation to fire, the fact that the *Hood*'s aft turrets did not open fire for three minutes after the *Prince of Wales* had opened A-arcs seems peculiar. Given that the *Hood* was under accurate and damaging fire from both the

Prinz Eugen and the *Bismarck*, one cannot help but question why the full force of her gunnery would be withheld for so long.

The final alteration of course is another point of debate. One order of '2 Blue' was definitely executed, but the second order has remained controversial. In his report of the battle given at the second Board of Inquiry into the *Hood*'s loss, Captain Leach of the *Prince of Wales* stated that the *Hood* had the second signal flag for '2 Blue' flying when she was hit.[6] The order to execute the command would have been signalled by the hauling down of the flag at which point the two ships would have begun the turn simultaneously. An examination of the wreck of the *Hood* by David Mearns showed the *Hood*'s rudder to be locked at 20 degrees. The discovery of the rudder at such an angle brought to an end the debate on whether or not the *Hood* began to execute her final turn, which many (like Roger Chesneau) claim would have allowed the *Hood* to open A-arcs, and which would also have served the purpose of reducing the *Hood*'s risk to plunging fire.[7]

Forensic experts who have examined the images from David Mearns's expedition have claimed the rudder position is as it would have been when the *Hood* was on the surface as a fighting entity. This, therefore, begs the question of why the *Hood* was turning when the *Prince of Wales*, based on Captain Leach's testimony, was not. Additional confusion is posed by testimony given by some on board the *Prince of Wales*, who claimed that the battleship was indeed turning in tandem with the *Hood* when the latter was hit.[8]

According to the track chart of the *Prince of Wales*, she began to take avoiding action around the sinking *Hood* between 6.01 and 6.02 a.m.[9] In addition to this, it would appear that this turn took place after Captain Leach ordered the action to be broken off due to his ship being hopelessly outgunned and damaged, plus owing to the ship's defective armament. Apparently, Captain Leach ordered this turn after one of the *Bismarck*'s shells tore through the bridge, killing everyone aside from himself, the chief yeoman of the signals, and the navigating officer. According to Geoffrey Brooke in his work *Alarm Starboard*, Leach himself was temporarily knocked unconscious and left dazed by the carnage wrought by the 15-inch shell on the bridge.[10] This hit has been timed as occurring as the *Prince of Wales* passed between the wreck of the *Hood* and the German ships, around one minute after the *Hood* exploded.

If the *Hood* was hit at 6 a.m., the hit that devastated the bridge of the *Prince of Wales* would have occurred close to 6.01 a.m. According to the track chart, with the *Prince of Wales* beginning her swing away to break off the action thirty seconds later, Leach would have had fewer than forty-five seconds to recover from the effects of the shell passing through the bridge, move to a position to place the order to turn away (it is reported that Leach descended to the conning tower), and issue the order at which point the helmsman had to respond before the ship responded to her rudder. How can it be that this whole sequence occurred in so short a time frame?

Photographs taken from on board the *Prinz Eugen,* which are held by the US Naval History and Heritage Command, namely NH-69724 and NH-69731, also pose questions.

NH-69724 shows the moment that the *Hood* exploded. In the photograph, the *Prince of Wales* can be seen a short distance behind the exploding *Hood* on the left of the image. NH-69731, on the other hand, shows the *Prince of Wales* at some point during her retreat from the battle (See Chapter 4). It should be noted that the theory put forward by Paul Cadogan that is put forward here is based on the idea that the smoke column on the left is the *Prince of Wales* with the dark trail of smoke in the centre of the image denoting the sinking *Hood.* When these two images are compared against the track charts drawn up after the battle showing the course taken by the *Prince of Wales* around the sinking *Hood,* it appears that the *Prince of Wales* proceeded much further to starboard around the *Hood* than the supposedly tight turn made by the ship as shown on the chart. The slight change in perspective of those viewing events from the *Prinz Eugen* that occurred around 8 nautical miles away does not, on the surface, appear to count for the distance travelled by the *Prince of Wales.* The question therefore arises of how the *Prince of Wales* managed to proceed so far beyond the sinking *Hood* before turning away.

The final question that arises concerns the time it took the *Hood* to sink, which is generally accepted to be within a period of one to two minutes. It becomes apparent from reading the witness testimony given at the Boards of Inquiry, and the accounts that have been given by the survivors from the *Hood,* in particular Ted Briggs, that the sinking was rapid. If a stopwatch is taken and used to measure a period of two minutes as one pictures the unfolding events that morning as described by Ted Briggs, it becomes clear that such a period appears too short a time from the point of explosion to the moment the ship finally slipped beneath the waves.

In his narrative dated 4 June 1941 (which was included in the second Board of Inquiry), Captain Leach claimed that 'a huge explosion occurred between *Hood*'s after funnel and mainmast and she sank in three or four minutes'.[11] Was Captain Leach in fact correct with his analysis of the *Hood* sinking within three or four minutes as opposed to two?

Having raised the above questions, we may ask where the designation of 6 a.m. as the time of the fatal hit comes from. Crewmen on five ships—HMS *Prince of Wales, Norfolk, Suffolk, Bismarck,* and *Prinz Eugen*—witnessed the destruction of the *Hood.* Some of the crewmen who witnessed the *Hood*'s destruction made a note of the time personally, while other times were derived from reports. Unsurprisingly, there is something of a significant inconsistency in these times.

Captain Leach stated that the *Hood* was hit at 6 a.m.[12] This is also noted by Lieutenant-Commander Anthony Hunter Terry, who witnessed events from the Port-After High-Angle Director.[13] The ship's log of the *Prince of Wales* was destroyed by the shell that tore through the compass platform. Subsequently, a reconstructed log was produced, noting the time of the *Hood*'s sinking as being 6.05 a.m.[14] In the war diary of the *Prinz Eugen*, the time noted by *Kapitän* Brinkmann is 6.01 and twenty seconds, while *Korvettenkapitän* Fritz Otto Busch provides two alternate times.[15]

Busch wrote an account of the *Prinz Eugen*'s first operation entitled *Prinz Eugen im Ersten Gefecht*. Translated into English, the title is 'The First Battle of the *Prinz Eugen*'. This book details Operation Rheinübung from aboard the *Prinz Eugen* and covers events of the operation including the Battle of the Denmark Strait. In a battle map in *Prinz Eugen im Ersten Gefecht*, the time of 5.59 a.m. is noted as the timing of the fatal hit, but the *Hood* is shown as sinking at 6.01 a.m.[16] In his book on the *Bismarck*, Baron Burkard von Müllenheim-Rechberg notes the time as 6.01 a.m.[17] According to the narrative that was produced detailing the involvement of the *Suffolk* from 23 May to 26 May 1941, the *Hood* was observed to blow up at 5.59 a.m.[18]

It would appear that the Boards of Inquiry accepted the timing of events as put forward by Captain Leach, which is depicted on the salvo plot of the *Prince of Wales*, and with that, 6 a.m. became the official British time for the loss of the *Hood*.

Given that the times for the events were recorded by individuals that all had different vantage points of events and who were likely preoccupied with numerous things during the course of the battle, determining the accuracy of the time recordings can be challenging. When looking at an event such as the sinking of the *Hood*, one has to consider a range of factors.

1. The accuracy of the timepieces used by the different witnesses to record time must be questioned because it is almost impossible to conceive that all of the timepieces used during the battle were perfectly synchronised.

2. The shock factor is also relevant as eyewitnesses would have been awestruck by what they were witnessing. In *Battleship Bismarck*, Baron Burkard von Müllenheim-Rechberg conveys what may be interpreted as the sense of excitement, shock, and nerves when the *Hood* was first sighted:

On the telephone I heard Albrecht shout, 'The *Hood*—it's the *Hood*!' It was an unforgettable moment. There she was, the famous warship, once the largest in the world, that had been the 'terror' of so many of our war games.[19]

This is followed by his awestruck description of watching the *Hood* explode:

I heard a shout, 'She's blowing up!' 'She'—that could only be the *Hood*! The sight I then saw is something I shall never forget. At first the *Hood* was nowhere to be seen; in her place was a colossal pillar of black smoke reaching into the sky. Gradually, at the foot of the pillar, I made out the bow of the battle cruiser projecting upwards at an angle, a sure sign that she had broken in two. Then I saw something I could hardly believe: a flash of orange from her forward guns! Although her fighting days had ended, the *Hood* was firing a last salvo. I felt great respect for those men over there.[20]

Those whose responsibility it was for noting the timing of events were also likely awestruck at the sight of the *Hood* exploding, meaning that it is likely that the noting of times would have also been affected as the time may not have necessarily been noted at the very moment that the event was initiated with some events being recorded after the fact. As such, it is therefore impossible to pinpoint an event such as this to a particular second as some may try, and indeed have tried to do. Rather, it is far better to designate a time window for an event. Therefore, it is possible to examine more carefully the points in favour of an earlier time for the fatal hit, which resulted in the destruction of the pride of the Royal Navy.

It is generally accepted in British documents and by historians that it was the fifth salvo from the *Bismarck* that resulted in the loss of the *Hood*.[21] It has been concluded that the *Hood* was the first ship of the two opposing squadrons to open fire. However, with regards who opened fire next, the history has changed. It was the belief that after the *Hood* opened fire, the *Bismarck* responded immediately before the *Prince of Wales* let loose with her first salvo. This fact was later corrected when it was shown that the *Bismarck* and the *Prinz Eugen* did not open fire until 5.55 a.m., by which time the *Hood* and the *Prince of Wales* had fired at least four salvos, having opened fire at 5.53 a.m.[22]

The account from aboard the *Bismarck* written by Baron Burkhard von Müllenheim-Rechberg, the senior surviving officer from the *Bismarck*, described the *Bismarck*'s first salvo as falling short and the second as being over with the base salvo straddling before Schneider then ordered, 'Full salvos good rapid'. The implication of this order is that having established the range to the *Hood*, the *Bismarck* began firing for effect, firing her salvos as rapidly as was practical. The first and second gunnery officers aboard the *Prinz Eugen*, Pailus Jasper and Paul Schmalenbach, observed that the *Prinz Eugen*'s second salvo struck the *Hood* and started a fire. The war diary of the *Prinz Eugen* recorded the observation as 'a rapidly spreading fire at the level of the aft mast was observed, apparently involving the aircraft hangar or petrol storage'.[23] British observers incorrectly attributed the hit to the third salvo fired by the *Bismarck*. The time quoted in the *Prinz Eugen*'s war diary for this observation is 5.55 a.m. Given that the German squadron opened fire at 5.55 a.m., this time would not be too far wide of the actual time, which was likely 5.56 a.m. Based on this, therefore, if the *Hood* was sunk by a shell from the *Bismarck*'s fifth salvo, and that this occurred at 6 a.m., the *Bismarck* took over three minutes to fire two salvos. Given that Schneider issued the order 'Full salvos good rapid' after the third salvo, in a period of three minutes to fire the fifth salvo, the firing solution would have been long lost.[24]

If the third salvo from the *Bismarck* landed between 5.56 and 5.57 a.m. and she started firing salvos at intervals in order to allow spotting of her fall of shot, then the fifth salvo would have landed in the region of 5.58 a.m.

A large proportion of the evidence as to the timing of the fatal hit aboard the *Hood* and the ship's subsequent loss is derived from the Gunnery Aspects Report of the *Prince of Wales*, which was prepared by the ship's chief gunnery officer, Colin McMullen. The Gunnery Aspects Report provides precise information on the salvos fired from the main and secondary armament batteries of the *Prince of Wales* as each salvo was timed and recorded on the salvo plot. Events have been reported in relation to these salvos, pinning down the timing of events to a reasonable extent.

Prior to the battle, Admiral Holland ordered that both the *Hood* and the *Prince of Wales* would concentrate their fire on the *Bismarck* in G.I.C. or individual ship control, in which each ship would fire in alternating time sectors in order for their respective falls of shot to be determined.[25] It is known that when the *Bismarck* and the *Prinz Eugen* were sighted, the order was forthcoming from the *Hood* to concentrate fire on the lead ship, which it was believed was the *Bismarck* but that on board the *Prince of Wales* McMullen was able to determine that the trailing vessel was in fact larger and therefore had to be the *Bismarck* leading Captain Leach to order that the right-hand ship be ranged by the *Prince of Wales*. As the *Prince of Wales* fired at the *Bismarck*, the *Hood* incorrectly engaged the *Prinz Eugen*. When the mistake was realised aboard the *Hood* the order was given to the *Prince of Wales* to switch targets to the right-hand ship (which she was already targeting). When exactly the *Hood* trained her guns on the *Bismarck* is unknown, and it is widely accepted that the gunners on the *Hood* did not switch targets immediately. Nevertheless, even with the *Hood* firing initially at the *Prinz Eugen*, the two ships would have been following the firing plan stipulated by Admiral Holland, in which case the *Prince of Wales*'s salvo plot could be used as a guide to extrapolate the salvos that were fired by the *Hood*.

According to the Gunnery Aspects Report, the *Prince of Wales* opened fire at 5.53 a.m. and over a period of eight minutes and fifty-eight seconds, she fired eighteen centrally controlled salvos with her main armament. Firing under central control ended at 6.02 a.m. as the ship retreated from the scene of the battle, during which three additional salvos were fired from 'Y' turret operating under local control between 6.03 and 6.05 a.m. In addition to these salvos, three salvos were fired from the ship's eight starboard 5.25-inch batteries. Opening fire at a range of 18,600 yards (which corresponds with shortly before the clock turned 5.58 a.m.), these secondary armament guns ceased fire when their directors were temporarily disabled by two separate hits.

The Gunnery Aspects Report shows that just after salvo 8 was fired, at 5.57 a.m., the *Prince of Wales* opened A-arcs, bringing her aft turret into the battle for salvo 9. Based on the salvo plot of the ship, at 5.55 a.m., the *Bismarck* was on a course of 333 degrees while the *Prince of Wales* was on a course of 300 degrees. The *Bismarck* was therefore 33 degrees off the bow of the *Prince of Wales*. The foremost bearing of 'Y' turret was 45 degrees off the bow, meaning that the *Prince of Wales* needed only to conduct a turn of 12 degrees in order to open A-arcs. Admiral Holland had ordered a turn of 20 degrees to open A-arcs. Based on this, the *Prince of Wales* would not have needed to fully execute the turn in order to bring 'Y' turret to bear on the *Bismarck*. It is quite possible, therefore, that the *Prince of Wales* was still executing the 20-degree turn after the time that had been noted on the salvo plot for A-arcs being opened.

The key point of discussion with regards the Gunnery Aspects Report relates to salvoes 10 through to 14. Salvo 10 was fired just after 5.59 a.m. at a range of 17,150 yards and was noted as falling 'short'. Salvo 11 was fired just before 5.59 a.m. with salvo 12 following shortly after. Both of these salvos were set for a range of 17,100 yards, and both of these salvos were recorded as falling 'short'. McMullen noted that an 'unexplained' spread was noted with the shell splashes that were observed being seen to be spread over a wider area than the previous salvos. The fact that salvoes 10, 11, and 12 all fell short serves to indicate that the *Bismarck* was at a greater range than 17,100 yards.

Salvo 13, which was fired just before 6 a.m. to a range of 16,450 yards, was observed to have straddled the *Bismarck*, yet it did not merely straddle the *Bismarck*, but it scored the third and final hit that was sustained by the *Bismarck* during the engagement. Salvo 14, fired just after 6 a.m. to a range of 16,300 yards, was noted as falling 'over' the target, indicating that the range to the *Bismarck* was closing and that she was closer than 16,300 yards. Salvoes 15 through to 18 all fell short with salvoes 17 and 18 being fired at around 6.02 a.m. when the *Prince of Wales* was altering course to disengage.

So what exactly is presented here? In the first instance, we have an 'unexplained' large spread in salvoes 11 and 12. Between salvo 12, which fell short, and salvo 13, which straddled the target, the range rapidly decreased from 17,100 to 16,450 yards before decreasing still further to less than 16,300 yards by the time salvo 14 was fired, which was viewed as falling 'over'. It is known that at some point after the *Hood* exploded, the *Prince of Wales* executed a hard turn to starboard to avoid the sinking battlecruiser, smoke, and debris. This emergency turn would, purely out of necessity, have been made without a warning being issued to the ship's gunners to allow for an adjustment. Given the fact that an unexplained large spread was developed in salvoes 11 and 12, could they be an indicator of the timing of the *Prince of Wales*'s rapid turn to avoid the wreck of the *Hood*? Such a conclusion may be supported by the rapid decrease in the range to target to less than 16,300 yards as this would indicate that the *Prince of Wales* had closed on the German ships at a steeper angle than she previously had for some time. If this is indeed the case, then the timing of the emergency turn to starboard to avoid the sinking *Hood* would be in the region of 5.59 a.m. Of course, Captain Leach had to observe the explosion of the *Hood*, recognise the danger to his own ship, order the execution of the turn, and wait for the ship to respond to the helm. This would therefore place the explosion of the *Hood* to somewhere around 5.58 a.m.

Another factor that exists in the Gunnery Aspects Report is the firing of the secondary armament of the *Prince of Wales*. According to McMullen, the ship's eight starboard secondary armament guns opened fire at a range of 18,600 yards. This corresponds with a time shortly before 5.58 a.m. Three salvos were fired before the forward secondary armament directors were disabled by a shell that passed through without exploding. With the forward directors disabled, control was passed to the aft director which was itself very quickly shaken by the ship sustaining another hit, one which struck the ship's crane and exploded against the second funnel sending splinters through the boat deck. After this hit was sustained the starboard secondary armament guns did not participate further in the battle. In his narrative dated 4 June 1941 detailing events between 22 and 27 May that was presented to Admiral Tovey, Leach wrote:

> *Prince of Wales* starboard 5.25" battery was now in action. Course had to be altered to starboard to avoid remains of *Hood*; meanwhile *Bismarck* had shifted main and secondary armament fire quickly and accurately onto *Prince of Wales*. A heavy hit was felt almost immediately.[26]

Observing events from on board the *Prinz Eugen* was *Korvettenkapitän* Fritz Otto Busch. When writing about the Battle of the Denmark Strait in his book, there is one paragraph that is particularly noteworthy as it covers the firing of the secondary battery of the *Prince of Wales*:

> Now the [enemy] ship fires: The housings of the stacks light up bright pink in the reflection of the afterglow. Now his intermediate artillery also fires. Flashes came from below the superstructures and from behind the aft funnel. It is not a continuous level string live on the *Hood*: these are distinct separated shot groups from the 13.2 cm guns that are firing here.

The opponent turns now somewhat towards us, since—as it became known shortly thereafter—he had to dodge the ruins of his flagship.[27]

What is presented, therefore, are two individuals, both of whom were observers to the battle, on both sides of the engagement, Captain Leach and *Korvettenkapitän* Busch linking the turn executed by the *Prince of Wales* to avoid the sinking *Hood* to the firing of the firing of the ship's secondary armament. It is clear from the gunnery report that three salvos were fired by the secondary armament before 5.58 a.m. The QF 5.25-inch Mk I guns that were fitted to the *Prince of Wales* were quick-firing weapons. A Royal Navy pocket book published in 1945 stated:

> The 5.25 in. calibre with separate ammunition is used for dual High Angle and Low Angle Armament, since it gives the reasonable maximum weight of shell which can be loaded by the average gun's crew for sustained periods at all angles of elevation. The maximum rate of fire should be 10-12 rounds per minute.[28]

By 5.59 a.m., these guns were silenced owing to the forward director being put out of action by a hit sustained by fire from the *Prinz Eugen* at which point we also have the turning of the ship to avoid the *Hood*. This ties in with the firing of salvos 11 and 12, which developed large spreads at 5.59 a.m. from the unexpected turn. Again, this points to a time of around 5.58 a.m. for the *Hood* sustaining the fatal hit and exploding. As previously noted, the *Prince of Wales*'s secondary armament of 5.25-inch guns was silenced after sustaining two hits. The second hit around the area of the crane and second funnel knocked the control officer over, preventing him from immediately taking over control of the guns from the aft director. The hit sustained in the area of the crane and funnel was the only hits sustained on the *Prince of Wales* to result in an explosion of any consequence. In the damage report produced on the ship, it is stated that the damage was caused by a 15-inch shell. A heavy hit was felt aboard the *Prince of Wales* in the ship's transmitting station just after salvo 12 was fired. As the reader may also note, Captain Leach in his report also noted a heavy hit that was felt almost immediately and came as the ship's 5.25-inch guns were firing and the ship was turning to avoid the *Hood*. It would appear, therefore, that these hits were one and the same. Salvo 12 was fired just after 5.59 a.m. The 5.25-inch guns were silenced at the same time, which, combined, serve to place the turn to avoid the sinking *Hood* as occurring around that time.

If the so-called 'heavy hit' was in fact from the explosion of a 15-inch shell, then it could only have been fired by the *Bismarck*. At a range of 16,000 yards, the flight time of one of the *Bismarck*'s 15-inch shells would have been approximately twenty-five seconds. Based on this, taking in account the shell flight time, if the heavy hit was indeed a 15-inch shell, then it would mean that the *Bismarck* had switched targets to the *Prince of Wales* before 5.59 a.m., which in turn would add additional support to the idea that *Hood* received the fatal hit around 5.58 a.m.

One of the great uncertainties that exists with the Battle of the Denmark Strait is with regards the gunnery of the *Hood*. All of those who could report accurately on when the ship opened fire, how many salvos were fired, where the salvos landed, and when the ship switched targets from the *Prinz Eugen* to the *Bismarck* were all lost in the sinking. We do know that the *Hood* opened fire at 5.52 and thirty seconds on the leading German vessel, which was the *Prinz Eugen*. We know from evidence provided by German observers that the *Hood*'s first two salvos appear to have fallen ahead of the *Prinz Eugen*, that her third salvo landed short and slightly off the bow, that the fourth salvo was over, and that her fifth (and indeed all subsequent salvos) fell in the wake of the *Prinz Eugen*.[29] Paul Schmalenback, the second gunnery officer of the *Prinz Eugen*, estimated that the *Hood* fired approximately ten salvos before she exploded.[30]

Given that the *Hood* was firing G.I.C. with the *Prince of Wales* with each firing in alternating time sectors, if the salvo plot of the *Prince of Wales* is used as a guide to the timing of the salvos from the *Hood*, it can be seen that the *Hood* would have fired her tenth salvo at approximately 5.57 and thirty seconds.

One of the most confusing aspects of the battle surrounds rationalising the turn(s) that were made to port before the *Hood* was lost. Most the eyewitnesses from the *Prince of Wales* and, indeed the survivors from the *Hood*, describe one turn being executed to open A-arcs after which the *Hood*'s aft turrets opened fire seconds before the ship exploded. In his narrative of events, Captain Leach reported 'A turn of 2 blue at 0555 opened "A" Arcs at *Prince of Wales* ninth salvo. *Hood* had a further 2 blue flying when, at 0600, just after *Bismarck*'s 5th salvo, a huge explosion occurred between *Hood*'s after funnel and mainmast and she sank'.[31] In such a case, the execution signal for the turn is the hauling down of the flag.

Examination of the wreck of the *Hood* shows the rudder locked in a turn to port and that forensic experts have determined that the position of the rudder is the same as it would have been when the stern slipped beneath the waves. In the first instance, it could be considered that the second turn was not executed before the first turn was completed. Another possibility would be that the second turn was signalled while the first was in progress with a view to it being continued for a further 20 degrees to make a total turn of 40 degrees. On this, it would have to be assumed that the helm did not return to an amidships position after the first turn. This too is highly unlikely as it seems like too much time to be in a continuous turn without signalling its execution.

Paul Cadogan has put forward the idea that battle damage intervened and prevented the lowering of the signal flag. As evidence for this theory, Cadogan relies on observations made by Robert Tilburn when he was summoned to provide evidence at the Board of Inquiry, and the 'crazy cacophony of wild cries of "Fire" through the voice-pipes and telephones' heard by Ted Briggs on the compass platform.[32] Based on this, Cadogan has put forward the idea that the boat deck fire and the subsequent detonations of the 4-inch ready use ammunition which caused carnage making a charnel house of positions on the upper deck prevented the signalmen from hauling down the flag and that *Hood* may have begun the turn and that the helmsman of the *Prince of Wales*, duty-bound to keep station with the flagship, simply followed the *Hood*, accounting for Leach's statement that the order to execute the turn was never executed.[33]

Ted Briggs recalled the signal being run up the yard-arm:

We had been under fire for just two minutes, which already had taken on the time-scale of two hours. It was the moment for Holland to try to bring our aft turrets, X and Y, to bear, because we were being hopelessly outgunned. 'Turn twenty degrees to port together', he commanded. Chief Yeoman Carne passed the word on to the flag deck, where surprisingly someone still seemed to be capable of obeying orders, Two blue—flag 2, a blue pendant— went up the yard-arm. I remember musing: 'Not everyone on the flag deck is dead then.'

If it was the case that battle damage prevented the flag from being hauled down, it must be assumed that the damage was inflicted as soon as the flag reached the top of the yard-arm. However, it may be noted that while Briggs recalled a 2 Blue pendant being run up the yard-arm, Captain Leach wrote that at 5.55 a.m., 2 Blue was hoisted and the *Prince of Wales* opened A-arcs with her ninth salvo, which occurred at approximately 5.58 a.m. and that when she sank, the *Hood* had a further 2 Blue flag flying. In the account given by Briggs, he states that seconds after the order to open fire was given, he was aware of the helmsman repeating orders. Briggs does not record what the orders were that the helmsman was repeating, however.[34] When describing the pennant being run up the yard-arm, Briggs states that the *Hood* had been under enemy fire for two minutes. Given that the German vessels opened fire at 5.55 a.m. that places the time of the pennant being run the yard-arm at 5.57 a.m. Given that the timings of Leach and Briggs do not correlate, could it possibly be the case that a 2 Blue pendant was run up the yard-arm of the *Hood* at 5.55 a.m., which was seen by Leach and that this signal and the subsequent turn allowed the *Prince of Wales* to open A-arcs with her ninth salvo and that the flag hoisting recalled by Briggs was the second pennant?

If a pennant was hoisted at 5.55 a.m., by the time the signal was seen aboard the *Prince of Wales*, orders for a turn issued to the helm, and time enough elapsed for the ship to respond, A-arcs were opened, during which time, as the first turn was underway, a second pennant could have been ran up the yard-arm of the *Hood* at 5.57 a.m.

Though this does not point directly to 5.58 a.m. as the timing of the *Hood* receiving the fatal hit, it nevertheless shows that a scenario encompassing either one or two turns is compatible with the time frame. Whatever the case was, and indeed may be, one thing is clear—the *Hood* was executing a turn when she sank.

When the battle photographs taken from on board the *Prinz Eugen* are analysed—specifically the two images held by the US Naval History & Heritage Command NH-69724 and NH-69731—it appears that the *Prince of Wales* proceeded significant distance beyond the site of the sinking *Hood*. As previously stated, this is based on a presumption that NH-69731 was taken at 6.03 a.m. as opposed to thirty seconds after NH-69724 as Robert Winklerath has claimed or at 6.09 a.m. Indeed, it would appear that she proceeded a much more significant distance than she should have, given the tight turn the ship executed according to the battle map produced by Lieutenant-Commander Rowell.[35]

NH-69724 shows the moment that the *Hood* exploded, which, according to the traditional timeline, would place the photograph at just after 6 a.m. In the photograph, the *Prince of Wales* can be seen a short distance behind the exploding *Hood* on the left of the image. Based on the position of the ship on the battle map NH-69731, which shows the *Prince of Wales* breaking off from the engagement, would be timed somewhere around 6.03 a.m. The photographs in the plate section have been marked in order to indicate the course of the *Prince of Wales* and where she would have been relative to the site of the *Hood*'s sinking (Figure 1) and how it should perhaps be interpreted to be compatible with the battle map (Figure 2). Figure 1 shows that the *Prince of Wales* would have proceeded even further to the right before turning to port to take up her disengagement course.

According to Cadogan's theory, the *Prinz Eugen*, viewing the *Prince of Wales* from over 8 nautical miles away and sailing at 27 knots, would have moved approximately 2,600 yards in the three minutes that elapsed between the photographs. The change in perspective may not be sufficient enough to account for the difference in separation that is shown in the photographs.

When the *Hood* and the *Prince of Wales* engaged the *Bismarck* and the *Prinz Eugen*, HMS *Norfolk* increased speed to try and catch up with the unfolding battle. The *Norfolk* sailed on a parallel course to the *Bismarck*, keeping the German battleship off her starboard bow. At 5.55 a.m., when the *Hood* and the *Prince of Wales* were fully engaged and the German ships opened fire in kind, the *Norfolk* executed a starboard turn in an effort to rapidly close the range to the *Prinz Eugen* and the *Bismarck*. At 6 a.m., the *Norfolk* executed a hard turn to port and took up a course parallel to the *Bismarck* before opening up the range to the German vessels once the *Hood* had been sunk and it became clear that the *Prince of Wales* was disengaging. During the course of the engagement and the immediate aftermath of the battle, HMS *Norfolk* did not open fire.

The reader may question the relevance of the course changes made by the *Norfolk* to this discussion. The answer to the relevance is to be found in the timing and sequence of events that are required for a ship to turn.

When the *Hood* exploded, her demise was witnessed from on board the *Norfolk* by both Wake-Walker and Captain Alfred Phillips. So vivid were Wake-Walker and Phillip's observations of the *Hood*'s explosion that both were able to draw diagrams illustrating what they saw. Undoubtedly Wake-Walker recognised above all else the significance of the explosion and the sinking of the *Hood* as with the sinking of the *Hood* and the loss of Admiral Holland, Wake-Walker became the senior British officer on the scene and inherited command of the immediate British forces. Wake-Walker, having witnessed the loss of the *Hood*, would have made the decision to alter course, then informed Phillips of his decision, who, in turn, would have passed the order to the helmsman that would have altered the course of the wheel accordingly, after which the ship would have begun to respond.

Had the explosion of the *Hood* occurred at 6 a.m., the *Norfolk* could not have made the turn she executed at 6 a.m. that is shown in her track chart, especially if she was turning in response to an event. Therefore, the turn executed at 6 a.m would be in response to an event that occurred before then.

A careful examination of various pieces of eyewitness testimony suggests that the time from the first hit on the boat deck to the final explosion of the ship was not very long. Going over every piece of eyewitness testimony lies beyond the scope of this chapter, but there are pieces that are noteworthy, which may be analysed here. These pieces of eyewitness testimony come from Ted Briggs, Rear-Admiral Wake-Walker, Captain Phillips and Paul Schmalenbach.

In an interview contained within the sound archive collections of the Imperial War Museum recorded in 1989, Ted Briggs stated: 'From the time that we opened fire to the time that *Hood* was fatally hit was about five minutes and she went down in less than three'.[36]

When giving his testimony to the second Board of Inquiry, on the subject of the fire on the boat deck of the *Hood*, Wake-Walker stated:

> I watched this fire and it then spread forward until its length was greater than its height and after a time it died down, particularly at the forward end. I thought that they may be able to get this fire under. Previous to this I had been so impressed by the fire that the ship would not continue as a fighting

unit. As it died down I saw her two fore turrets fire and the thought 'they may be able to get it under', came into my mind. Almost immediately there was an enormous explosion, which was of the same colour, and appeared to have a fairly broad base, widening out as it rose and then spreading into a mushroom of flame. I particularly noticed that the mushroom was flame and not smoke, at any rate in the lower half of it.[37]

Meanwhile, when giving his testimony to the same Board of Inquiry, Captain Phillips stated:

This fire shortly afterwards died down, spread forward and pulsated rather like the appearance of a setting tropical sun and it appeared to me to get somewhat lighter in colour. I have tried to indicate this in rough sketch Phase III. *Hood* appeared to continue firing and I particularly noticed either 'X' and/or 'Y' fire at this stage and I remarked on the fact at the time. Very shortly after this there appeared to be another salvo from the *Bismarck*, 2 rounds of which I should say landed short, and she immediately blew up with an enormous explosion and was not seen again.[38]

Finally, the second gunnery officer of the *Prinz Eugen*, Paul Schmalenbach, in his account of the engagement recorded in the ship's war diary, described the fire on the boat deck of the *Hood* caused by a salvo from the *Prinz Eugen* before stating:

Shortly after the impacts of a salvo from the *Bismarck* (I cannot explain it in any other way because of the rapid sequence of impacts on the opponent to the right as well as the change in colour and height of the impacts), a salvo from *Prinz Eugen* was delivered, which, according to my observations through large binoculars, caused a conflagration in the vicinity of the aft mast. Before further hits were made, the source of fire rapidly spread to an estimated length of 15 metres. *Oberleutnant zur See* Tilleßen, who stood next to me, spontaneously uttered the same opinion. A few seconds (3-5) transpired between the salvo's impact and the absolutely instantaneous initiation of the described conflagration. I deem it as very probable, nearly certain, that the above-mentioned salvo was from the *Prinz Eugen* [and that it] caused the conflagration. A few seconds later, a salvo from *Bismarck* hit the ship aft, and that resulted in an explosion of major consequence.[39]

Petty Officer Cyril Coats and Ted Briggs tell of the *Prince of Wales* passing the wreck of the *Hood* a short time before the battleship turned away as opposed to circling the wreck as is implied by the official track charts produced by Rowell. Coats stated:

I saw the *Hood* on our port bow and I saw several salvoes fall astern, just over and ahead. Then one salvo appeared to strike right amidships. I got the impression of a shower of sparks on the boat-deck not far abaft the after funnel about mid-ships. It was followed then by one roll of flame from the after screen which enveloped the after turrets. After that I did not see very much of the subsequent explosion because we had had a hit on the starboard crane which knocked me down. As I got up the *Hood* had disappeared from sight. I do not mean she was sunk, but was obscured by our superstructure. I did not see the explosion. All I saw was the reflection on our own ship. I saw the *Hood* again. I came down off the catapult control platform and we carried on steaming ahead of the *Hood*, and all I recognised was the bows forepart. They appeared to be turned completely round.[40]

Ted Briggs, meanwhile, wrote:

A small patch of oil blazed where she [the *Hood*] was cremated. Several yards away I could see the stern of the *Prince of Wales* as she pressed on with her guns firing. She was being straddled by shells from the *Bismarck* and *Prinz Eugen,* and I did not give much of a chance to her survival.[41]

Weighing up the evidence that has been presented in this chapter, it may be concluded that the actual time for the *Hood* receiving the fatal hit from the *Bismarck* was not the traditionally accepted time of 6 a.m., but was in fact almost two minutes earlier—at or shortly after 5.58 a.m.

If this was the case, then given that the *Bismarck* and *Prinz Eugen* opened fire at 5.55 a.m., the *Hood* had been under enemy fire for a mere three minutes, not five. While the loss of the *Hood* sent a shockwave through the Royal Navy, it is quite possible that 6 a.m. was noted as a time to save face. The ship blowing up after being subjected to five minutes of enemy fire was less humiliating than blowing up after three minutes. On the Admiralty warship index, when one of the Wrens tasked with maintaining the index made the final entry on the card for the *Hood*, it was filled out incorrectly, the entry reading: 'At 0635 today blew up and sank in action in the Denmark Strait'.[12] If the Admiralty warship index was filled out incorrectly, it may be fair to assume that other official documents noting the time of the *Hood*'s loss (such as the plot of the *Prince of Wales*) could also be incorrect. After she exploded, the *Hood* sank within three or four minutes—a time frame more compatible with descriptions of the sinking process, especially that given by Ted Briggs:

As the *Hood* turned, 'X' turret roared in approval, but its Y twin stayed silent and then a blinding flash swept around the outside of the compass platform. Again I found myself being lifted off my feet and dumped head first on the deck. This time, when I got up with the others, the scene was different. Everything was cold and unreal. The ship which had been a haven for me for the last two years was suddenly hostile. After the initial jarring she listed slowly, almost hesitatingly, to starboard. She stopped after about ten degrees, when I heard the helmsman's voice shouting up the voice-pipe to the officer of the watch: 'Steering's gone, sir'. The reply of 'Very good' showed no signs of animation or agitation. Immediately Kerr ordered: 'Change over to emergency steering'.

Although the *Hood* had angled to starboard, there was still no concern on the compass platform. Holland was back in his chair. He looked aft towards the *Prince of Wales* and then re-trained his binoculars on the *Bismarck*. Slowly the *Hood* righted herself. 'Thank heaven for that', I murmured to myself, only to be terrorized by her sudden, horrifying cant to port. On and on she rolled, until she reached an angle of forty-five degrees. When everyone realized that she would not swing back to the perpendicular, we all began to make our way out in single file towards the starboard door at first. Then some turned towards the port door and attempted to break panes of reinforced glass in the foreport of the platform. But it was all done as if in drill. There was no order to abandon ship; nor was a word uttered. It just was not required. The *Hood* was finished and no one needed to be told that.

I was surprised by my cold yet uncontrolled detachment, as I made my way to the door. 'Tiny' Gregson was in front of me with the squadron navigation officer. As I reached the steel-hinged door, Commander Warrand stood aside for me and let me go out first. I looked back over my left shoulder and saw Holland slumped on his chair in total dejection. Beside him the captain tried to keep to his feet as the *Hood*'s deck turned into a slide. I began picking my way down the ladder from the compass platform to the admiral's bridge. Then the sea swirled around my legs and I was walking on the side of the bridge, instead of the ladder. I threw away my tin hat and gas-mask and managed to slip off my anti-flash gear, but my lifebelt was under my Burberry and I could not get at it to inflate it. There was no one else in sight, although I knew that at least two officers were nearby, as the water engulfed me with a roar.

Panic had gone. This was it, I realized. But I wasn't going to give in easily. I knew that the deckhead of the compass platform was above me and that I must try to swim away from it. I managed to avoid being knocked out by the steel stanchions, but I was not making any progress. The suction was dragging me down. The pressure on my ears was increasing each second, and panic returned in its worse intensity. I was going to die. I struggled madly to try to heave myself up to the surface. I got nowhere. Although it seemed an eternity, I was under the water barely a minute. My lungs were bursting. I knew that I just had to breathe. I opened my lips and gulped in a mouthful of water. My tongue was forced to the back of my throat. I was not going to reach the surface. I was going to die. I was going to die. As I weakened, my resolve left me ... My blissful acceptance of death ended in a sudden surge beneath me, which shot me to the surface like a decanted cork in a champagne bottle. I wasn't going to die. I wasn't going to die. I trod water as I panted in great gulps of air. I was alive. I was alive.

Although my ears were singing from the pressure underwater, I could hear the hissing of a hundred serpents. I turned and fifty yards away I could see the bows of the *Hood* vertical on the sea. It was the most frightening aspect of my ordeal and a vision which was to recur terrifyingly in nightmares for the next forty years. Both gun barrels of B turret were slumped hard over to port and disappearing fast beneath the waves. My experience of suction seconds before forced me to turn in sheer terror and swim as fast and as far as I could away from the last sight of the ship that had formulated my early years.[42]

A time of 5.58 a.m. for the fatal hit that resulted in the explosion of the *Hood* is compatible with the firing of five salvos from the *Bismarck*, which opened fire at 5.55 a.m. and would be compatible with the ten salvos fired by the *Hood* after opening fire at 5.52:30 a.m., as observed by Schmalenbach.

If the battle photographs are analysed and NH-69731 is interpreted in the manner put forward by Paul Cadogan and many other individuals in online forums who place the photograph at 6.03 a.m., when the distance travelled by the *Prince of Wales* between NH-69724 and NH-69731 is analysed, it may be deemed that the course of the *Prince of Wales* beyond the point of the *Hood*'s sinking was approximately one minute longer than that shown on traditional track charts. At the same time, it may be presented that the compass platform hit sustained by the *Prince of Wales* occurred one minute earlier than has previously been thought, thus allowing Captain Leach sufficient time to recover from the blast effect of the shell passing through the platform and to descend to the armoured conning tower.

As I wrote at the beginning of this chapter, the purpose of this chapter is not an attempt to change history but is a demonstration of the rational possibility that the officially accepted time of the fatal hit that detonated the *Hood*'s magazines and caused her to sink may not be accurate. While the evidence has been put forward over the course of this chapter, it is up to the reader to draw their own conclusions and to decide whether or not there is merit behind this possibility.

HMS *Prince of Wales*

Given that initially both the *Prinz Eugen* and the *Bismarck* concentrated their fire on the lead vessel (the *Hood*) before the *Prinz Eugen* was ordered to switch to the left-hand target (which was the *Prince of Wales*), the question naturally arises: Would it have made a difference to the *Hood* if the *Prince of Wales* had been the lead vessel? Would this have been enough to force both the *Bismarck* and the *Prinz Eugen* to concentrate their fire on her as opposed to the *Hood* in the first stages of the battle?

The Germans mistook the newly commissioned *Prince of Wales* for Admiral Tovey's flagship HMS *King George V*. The brand new *Prince of Wales* could have been the flagship in her own right. While a hypothetical question and one that is ultimately impossible to answer, it is not an idle question. Had the *Bismarck* concentrated her fire on the *Prince of Wales* like she did the *Hood*, then based on the fact that the *Prince of Wales* had thicker armour than both the *Bismarck* and the *Hood*, and given the damage she withstood following the loss of the *Hood*, then the *Prince of Wales* would not have sunk rapidly and deprived the British forces of its nominal superiority.

Admiral Tovey revealed later that he almost issued a signal to Holland stating that the *Prince of Wales* should lead the British formation into the attack. Tovey states that he decided against this because he felt that Holland was too senior a commander.[1] If this is indeed true, it is an interesting suggestion. In theory, it could have worked with the *Prince of Wales* having armour up to accepted modern standards. With the Germans believing that they were facing the *King George V* and the *Hood*, the *Prince of Wales* in the vanguard may have drawn the German fire. HMS *Prince of Wales* did assume guide of the squadron at 4.50 a.m. briefly before the *Hood* resumed the guide at 5.05 a.m., which in itself may suggest that Holland himself may have considered the idea.[2] If he did consider the idea, why did Holland not take this approach?

In the first instance, it would not have reflected well on Holland if the *Prince of Wales*, as new a ship as she was with a partially worked up crew and with known defects, were to suffer heavy damage and casualties because Holland put her in the line of fire while he followed behind in the *Hood*.[3] Second, it may have been the case that Holland thought that he could use the reputation of 'the Mighty *Hood*' to strike fear into the hearts of the German sailors if they saw the great battlecruiser sailing to engage them. Thirdly, since he was flying his flag in the *Hood*, Holland may have felt duty-bound to lead his ships into battle and as such made the decision not to put the *Prince of Wales* in the vanguard. While it would have been very reasonable to put the *Prince of Wales* at the front of the squadron going into battle, it is understandable why Holland may have been unwilling to do so.

Based on the events of the battle, a handful of criticisms may be levelled against Captain Leach and Admiral Tovey. In the first instance, one criticism that may be levelled against Captain Leach was his bold but unrealistic decision to declare the *Prince of Wales* fully operational on 21 May 1941. When he declared the *Prince of Wales* to be fully operational Leach was more than aware that, in addition to the teething troubles with the main battery armament that is so often cited by commentators of the battle, a significant portion of the ship's company had not received sufficient training while the ship as a unit needed to be fully worked up. According to Marco Santarini, 'It is likely that Leach's strong desire to make a contribution to the operations, added to the hope that the crew's commitment and the sturdy passive defences of his ship could counterbalance the existing deficiencies, accounted for his optimistic decision'.[4] As Santarini has himself noted, the King George V-class were considered unsinkable by some in Britain owing to the thickness of their armour.

Related to the above, Tovey himself may be criticised for taking Leach's declaration that the *Prince of Wales* was operational at face value and for deploying her immediately to intercept the *Bismarck* and her unidentified consort. Tovey could have taken the decision to move his flag to another vessel freeing up the *King George V* to sail with the *Hood*. However, at the same time, while one may be tempted to criticise Tovey for employing the *Prince of Wales*, Tovey's disposition made tactical sense. Uncertainty about the route that Lütjens and the ships under his command would take to break out into the Atlantic combined with the considerable overconfidence in the performance of the *Hood* made him optimistically choose to order the newer *Prince of Wales* to accompany the *Hood*.

Tovey had four heavy ships at his disposal—the *Hood, King George V, Prince of Wales*, and *Repulse*. As such, he divided his heavy units into two groups—the famed 'Mighty *Hood*' and the barely ready *Prince of Wales* under Holland then the *King George V* and the *Repulse* (which had thinner armour than the *Hood*) under his own command. As Dr Eric Grove has commented:

This made two fast forces effectively 'one and a half' capital ships strong for each exit. It was a logical deployment pattern. *Hood* with *KGV* and *Prince of Wales* with *Repulse* would have produced two highly unbalanced groups and Holland would have had to shift his flag to *Prince of Wales*, a highly disruptive event when he had a fully operational flagship already, and one into which he had only just moved. Tovey was too sensible to even consider it.[5]

It is only right that Lieutenant-Commander Colin McMullen of the *Prince of Wales* be commended for the way in which he organised the firing of the ship's guns. In spite of the evident troubles and difficulties that he faced with the numerous breakdowns of the main battery armament of the ship, he managed with great skill to hit the *Bismarck* on three occasions, employing a total of fifty-five shells, giving him an average of hitting the *Bismarck* with every 18.33 shells fired. The *Bismarck* by contrast, with her fully functioning main armament, scored a total of four or five hits on the British battleship and fired ninety-three shells producing a hit ratio of one hit for every twenty to twenty-five shells fired.[6]

In addition to this, the *Prince of Wales* scored her first hit on the *Bismarck* within three minutes of opening fire and after firing six partial salvos, totalling twenty shells. The *Bismarck* on the other hand took four minutes, five salvos, and thirty-eight shells to score a hit. Despite this, most commentators stress the defects in the guns of the *Prince of Wales* and comment on the supposedly exceptional performance of the *Bismarck*'s guns. Despite this, no great emphasis has been placed on the exceptional performance of the *Prince of Wales*, which inflicted much greater damage on the *Bismarck* than that which she herself suffered.

Two reasons account for this disparity. In the first instance, there is the loss of the *Hood*. 'The Mighty *Hood*' was struck by the fifth salvo fired by the *Bismarck* and disappeared in a cataclysmic explosion that was both so unexpected and so tragic with regards the loss of life that it captured the imagination and attention of everyone. As a result of this, the British were likely sure, and perhaps needed to believe, that the ship that was capable of causing the catastrophe that befell the most powerful and iconic ship in the Royal Navy, the showpiece of British naval power, must possess extraordinary capabilities when it came to waging war on the high seas. Based on this, it is likely that this is one of the reasons behind how the *Bismarck*'s guns grew to huge proportions in the collective imagination in Britain leading to her firing being remembered for its legendary efficiency. At the same time, exalting the efficiency of the gunnery of the *Prince of Wales* would have served to reinforce the doubts and reservations that existed within the minds of those who were dissatisfied with the results of the battle in particular Leach's decision to break off the engagement when he did.

In reality, the *Bismarck* was far from being as superior a battleship as she was and indeed has been made out to be. In fact, the *Bismarck* was not even the heaviest armoured or fastest German warship. While the *Bismarck* boasted 12.6-inch belt armour and 14-inch turret armour, the *Scharnhorst* boasted 13.8-inch belt armour and up to 14.2-inch turret armour. Only in deck armour was the *Bismarck* equipped with thicker armour—the *Bismarck* had between 3.9 and 4.7-inch-thick deck armour, while the *Scharnhorst*'s was 2 inches thick. In terms of speed, while the *Bismarck* was capable of sailing at 30 knots, the *Scharnhorst* was marginally faster, being capable of 31 knots. It was only with her armament that the *Bismarck* could boast a true superiority being armed with eight 15-inch guns against the nine 11-inch guns of the *Scharnhorst* and the *Gneisenau*. Being more heavily armed, the *Bismarck* packed a weightier punch when compared to other German battleships.

When compared to contemporary British, French, and Italian battleships, the *Bismarck* did not have overwhelming firepower. The *Bismarck*'s eight 15-inch guns fired a broadside with a weight of 6,400 kg. If rates of fire are set aside, this is less than the 7,030 kg fired by the First World War vintage battleships still in service with the Royal Navy in May 1941—the Royal Sovereign- and Queen Elizabeth-class vessels that were also armed with eight 15-inch guns. Even the King George V-class battleships, of which HMS *Prince of Wales* was one, fired a broadside with a weight of 7,212 kg. For balance, it may be noted that the King George V-class were the only battleships in the Royal Navy with a comparable speed to the *Bismarck*; the ships of the Royal Sovereign- and Queen Elizabeth-classes had a much slower speed.

Damage to the *Bismarck* and the *Prince of Wales*

Owing to the catastrophic loss of the *Hood*, the damage that was sustained by the *Prince of Wales* (with the exception of the hit that tore through her bridge and compass platform) and the damage that was sustained by the *Bismarck* (namely that which punctured the hull and trapped 1,000 tonnes of fuel in her bow) during the Battle of the Denmark Strait has been largely overlooked or brushed over. This chapter will detail the damage that was sustained by both the *Bismarck* and the *Prince of Wales* during the course of the battle on the morning of 24 May 1941.

During the course of the engagement, the *Prince of Wales* succeeded in hitting the *Bismarck* on three occasions. The first hit that the *Prince of Wales* scored against the *Bismarck* was to be found on the hull just above the forward edge of the fake bow wave that had not been covered up when the Baltic camouflage was painted over when the ship dropped anchor in Grimstadfjord. An analysis of the wreck conducted by James Cameron, William Jurens, and others shows that a shell entered on the port side and followed a trajectory through the bow with an angle of fall of approximately fifteen degrees. It is likely that the shell which passed through the bow here was fired by the *Prince of Wales* at a range of 16,000 metres. The path of the shell was oblique, passing from port to starboard across Compartments XX and XXI; the second, third, and fourth watertight compartments located aft of the forward perpendicular compartments were damaged by fragments caused by the passage of the projectile through the ship.

The entry hole is located above the *Bismarck*'s *Batteriedeck* and exited the ship above the deck or near the intersection of the deck with the side shell. The shell passed directly through the ship without exploding. The exit hole for the shell was in Compartments XX and XXI, slightly above the waterline but within the bow wave with the result that water flowed in and eventually succeeded in flooding compartments on the upper, middle, and lower platform decks. The trim down by the bow served to exacerbate this problem. Reserve fuel oil tanks were located on the trajectory of the shell. It is believed that none of the reserve tanks were affected by the trajectory taken by the shell, but that if a loss of fuel did occur in this area then it must have been the result of fragments from the shell or from fragments of the ship ripped apart as the shell passed through the bow, which severed pipes to the tanks and damaged the structure.

It is likely that when the *Bismarck* was refuelled in Gotenhafen on 18 May ahead of the mission, the reserve oil tanks would have been the last ones filled and that it would have been from these tanks that the 200 tons taking the battleship up to full capacity would have been pumped had the fuel hose not broken and had Lütjens decided to complete the refuelling operation. While the reserve fuel tanks were filled with fuel for the *Bismarck*'s consorts, the battleship could, in an emergency, have used the fuel herself.

Observers aboard the *Prinz Eugen* reported oil on both sides of the *Bismarck*'s wake prompting an order to be issued late in the morning of 24 May for the *Prinz Eugen* to take up a position astern of the *Bismarck* to try and disperse the oil slick to make it more difficult for shadowing aircraft or ships to follow. Some of the reserve fuel tanks could have been punctured by fragments caused by the hit sustained on the bow. While damage control parties on the *Bismarck* noted that the exit hole for the shell that struck the bow was in Compartments XX and XXI, it was noted that approximately a metre of water was to be found on *Batteriedeck* level ten. In addition to this the main bulkhead located between Compartments XX and XXI and Compartments XXI and XXII had been punctured with holes and were no longer watertight. A hole approximately 1 metre in diameter was to be found on the starboard hull, similar to that made in the port side plating. Counter-flooding voids were provided to allow counter-flooding to compensate for the list and trim resulting from the flooding and damage caused at the waterline.

The *Prince of Wales* also scored what Jurens *et. al* have described as an 'important hit' on the *Bismarck* abeam of the forward structure. A 14-inch shell from the *Prince of Wales* succeeded in penetrating the port side hull plating below the ship's armour belt when it passed in to the side protection system. The shell exploded near to the main transverse bulkhead between Compartments XIII and XIV. The shell detonated with great force against the 45-mm torpedo bulkhead outboard of Electrical Power Station No. 4, which affected the watertight boundaries between the aforementioned space and the adjacent No. 2 Port Boiler Room as well as the inboard auxiliary boiler room located inboard of Compartment XIV. Splinters from the shell passed into the double bottom tanks and wing fuel bunkers in Compartment XIV, which lead to the eventual flooding of those tanks and contaminated the feed water in the double bottom of the compartment. The damaged wing tank in Compartment

XIV began to leak oil on to the surface of the sea while saltwater gradually flowed in to replace the oil in the tanks. When the *Bismarck* sustained this particular hit, a number of observers on board the *Prince of Wales* witnessed a burst of black smoke from the funnel of the *Bismarck* while a number of German survivors recalled a slight shock response aboard the battleship from this hit.

According to survivors from the *Bismarck*, large cracks appeared in the welded seams in the outboard strakes of the main transverse bulkhead, which was also the forward boundary of the No. 2 Port Boiler Room in Compartment XIII. Seawater poured in through these cracks and caused the gradual flooding of this boiler room. While a damage-control party did attempt to plug the cracks with hammocks, their efforts only served to slow down the rate at which water entered the ship. For a short time, this boiler room was operational once more; Boiler III was lighted while Boiler IV was shut down owing to being contaminated by salt as a result of saltwater intrusion into the feed water system. By the mid-afternoon of 24 May, Boiler II would be shut down and evacuated.

Like the No. 2 Port Boiler Room in Compartment XIII, water entered the ship through the damaged wing tanks in Compartment XIV. Following the battle, a damage-control party attempted to seal off the leaks in the 45-mm torpedo bulkhead with the use of hammocks and matting, but again, their efforts only served to slow down the seepage of water into the boiler room. Eventually, the boiler room would be evacuated as the water reached chest deep. Steam from the other boilers would be rerouted through the turbine in the port engine room. Splinters from the shell that caused the damage severed the main steam line in the No. 4 Turbo Generator Room where five crewmen were scalded necessitating the shutdown of the generators. The turbo generator room also suffered from flooding.

The flooding in the bow, coupled with the displacement of fuel oil in Compartment XIV and the subsequent flooding of spaces there, caused the *Bismarck* to trim 3 degrees by the bow and to take on a 9-degree list to port.

During the course of the battle, HMS *Prince of Wales* was 'quite seriously damaged'.[1] In total, the *Prince of Wales* sustained seven hits. Four 15-inch shells from the *Bismarck* had struck the British battleship along with three 8-inch shells from the *Prinz Eugen*. While she had been struck by more 15-inch shells than 8-inch shells, it was the latter that caused the most visible damage. The damage sustained by the *Prince of Wales* allowed 400 tons of water to flood into the ship reducing speed to a maximum of 27 knots. With the influx of water, a number of compartments were flooded, including the steering compartment, but the steering gear remained operable.

One of the most reported hits sustained by the *Prince of Wales* was the hit on the compass platform. A 15-inch shell from the *Bismarck* struck the forward starboard corner of the compass platform, which the shell passed obliquely through without detonating. While it did not detonate, the passage of the shell created a storm of shrapnel, which killed or mortally wounded everyone on the compass platform with the exception of Captain Leach, the navigation officer, and the chief yeoman of the signals.

Having exited the compass platform, the shell continued through the port searchlight control position located at the base of the bridge superstructure. This shell severed electrical cabling, which rendered the high-angle control system unusable and flooded the chart room when it struck a water tank. Further casualties were caused among the ship's company in the nearby air defence platform.

Perhaps the most prominent hit sustained by the *Prince of Wales* during the course of the Battle of the Denmark Strait was another hit sustained by fire from the *Bismarck*. This hit was a 15-inch shell that had landed short of the target, coming down in the sea, but which had maintained enough velocity to penetrate the hull of the *Prince of Wales* below the waterline before crashing through the side of the ship leaving behind a trail of destruction of twisted metal and jagged holes before coming to a rest beside the armoured torpedo bulkhead in the immediate vicinity of the main engineering spaces.[2] This hit is perhaps the most prominent hit sustained by the *Prince of Wales* during the Battle of the Denmark Strait owing to the fact that the shell did not explode and was only found on 6 June 1941 when the ship was taken into dry dock at Rosyth to have her battle damage repaired.

The impact of this shell was felt, with one Admiralty report detailing the damage sustained by the *Prince of Wales* stating that the impact was felt as a 'heavy hit'. An inspection of the area around the starboard diesel room revealed the outer air spaces 184-196, the outer oil field tanks 184-206, and the starboard diesel tank to be filled to the crown with a mixture of oil and water.[3] When the damage was examined in the dry dock at Rosyth, a clean hole of 15 inches in diameter was found approximately 1 foot above the bilge keel with further perforations found in the light plating, which formed the sides of the outer fuel tank. Heavy marking was to be found on the protective bulkhead.

The shell came to rest between two frames at the bottom of the inner air space 184-194 pointing nose forward. With the fuse intact but missing its ballistic cap, the shell was removed by cutting a 4 foot by 2 foot hole in the keel through which it was lowered by chains, a quick action grab and lifting bands whereupon it was placed onto a rubber-tyred ammunition trolley and wheeled aft before being picked up by a dockyard crane and placed on a bomb disposal boat and removed.[4]

In addition to this damage, both of the ship's forward high-angle directors were disabled and the port circle was cut while the pedestal was canted and strained. The Supermarine Walrus that was carried on board was damaged while sitting on the catapult by a 15-inch shell that struck the starboard crane and exploded against the second funnel, which sent splinters across the boat deck. Such was the damage to the Walrus that the aircraft had to be jettisoned as in its damaged state it posed a fire risk.

In addition to the Walrus damaged by splinters from the shell, several of the ship's boats were also damaged. Further to this damage, the shrapnel from the hit penetrated the boat deck and caused several fatalities in the Type 284 radar office, which was located below. A list of those who lost their life aboard the *Prince of Wales* during the battle may be found in Appendix II. The after funnel was extensively punctured by shrapnel and shell fragments. Some of this damage was, however, caused by an 8-inch shell from the *Prinz Eugen*, which penetrated the boat deck. The shell passed obliquely through the superstructure and was ultimately deflected into the area beneath the port 5.25-inch mount P3—the third 5.25-inch gun on the port side of the ship—where it penetrated the working space of P3.

The *Bismarck* was not the only ship to score an underwater hit on the *Prince of Wales* as the battleship also sustained a hit from one of the 8-inch shells of the *Prinz Eugen*. The 8-inch shell penetrated the starboard side of the stern below the water line, which resulted in splinter damage and caused minor flooding. A 15-inch shell hit was sustained near frame 187 in one of the inner air spaces approximately one foot above the starboard bilge keel. While the shell did not detonate, its passage resulted in splinter damage which, combined with the 8-inch shell hit of the *Prinz Eugen* combined to cause severe damage to the air intake in 'X' Boiler Room, and to damage one boiler room fan impeller and an oil cooler.

16

Conclusions

Following the Battle of the Denmark Strait, Lütjens made the decision to cancel Operation Rheinübung and had the *Bismarck* make for the port of Saint Nazaire on the French Atlantic coast for repairs to the damaged flagship to be enacted with a view to resuming the operation at a later point in the company of the *Gneisenau* or the *Scharnhorst*. At the same time, Lütjens decided that the *Prinz Eugen* should be released to undertake cruiser warfare on her own. There followed an epic chase, which has been extensively documented in which the Royal Navy systematically hunted down and cornered the pride of the *Kriegsmarine* leading to her sinking three days later on 27 May 1941.

In the wake of the Battle of the Denmark Strait, two Boards of Inquiry were convened in order to try and determine how and why HMS *Hood* was lost with such a catastrophic loss of life. Despite the Boards of Inquiry attributing the loss of the *Hood* to the detonation of one or more of her after magazines, debate has raged as to what caused the loss of the ship. From the evidence that has been presented over the preceding pages, it becomes clear that while there exist a number of potential reasons behind why the *Hood* was lost, ranging from the detonation of her torpedoes, the boat deck fire, and even an issue with the handling of the ship's ammunition, the likely cause of the ship's loss remains the detonation of one of the ship's main 15-inch magazines. No doubt, however, debate on what caused the loss of the *Hood* will continue to rage as those who could categorically confirm what happened aboard the battlecruiser in the moments immediately preceding her sinking were all lost when the ship went down.

It is hoped that this work has gone some way to clarifying what occurred with regards the loss of the *Hood* and answering the question as to why so many of the crew were killed, and on the reverse, and perhaps more appropriately, how anyone survived. It would appear to be the case that Ted Briggs, William Dundas, and Robert Tilburn happened to be in the right place at exactly the right moment and that their survival of the sinking of the *Hood* came down to nothing more than pure chance for they were caught by the air bubbles escaping from the rapidly imploding hull, resulting from the explosion of the ship's boilers, which, in turn, propelled them to the surface. While managing to locate floats on the surface, meaning that they did not have to remain in the freezing water indefinitely, the three men, in particular Tilburn and Briggs, were fortunate that HMS *Electra* located them when she did as the arrival of the destroyer brought with it salvation, taking the men back from the brink of succumbing to hypothermia.

It is hoped also that this work has gone some way to absolving Admiral Holland of the criticism that he has endured since the loss of the *Hood* and his death on 24 May 1941. When Holland's approach to the battle is studied, a well-thought-out plan remains. Many of the criticisms that have been levelled against Holland are based on the benefit of hindsight and are unfair. Holland was unlucky, a commander blighted by fate. Holland was an able commander and made tactical decisions that were based on the best information available to him; he utilised his forces in order to maximise their potential. His decisions ahead of the battle during the night of 23 May and the early morning hours of 24 May and during the subsequent engagement with the *Bismarck* and *Prinz Eugen* were educated.

Furthermore Holland's decisions were also shrewd and served to cater for all of the responsibilities and limitations that his command was burdened with. By analysing Holland's decisions, such as the turn to the north, the decision to send his destroyers northwards, and the decision to close the distance to the *Bismarck*, when analysed against the tactical situation faced by Holland, they prove fair decisions to make and are tactically sound. It may be said that the action taken by Holland was the best of a bad bunch of options. While he has been criticised for initially ordering both the *Hood* and the *Prince of Wales* to engage the left-hand ship in the belief that it was the *Bismarck*, it is unfair to fully blame him for this error. Also, it is not wholly surprising that he made the error of issuing the order to engage the left-hand ship. This error was a mixture of human error combined with the distances involved, the angle of approach taken by the British ships and the far from ideal weather conditions. This was also combined with a failure aboard the cruisers HMS *Suffolk* and *Norfolk*, which shadowed the German formation as it transited the Denmark Strait, from picking up the change of positions ordered by Lütjens to compensate for the malfunctioning of the *Bismarck*'s forward radar when she fired her forward main battery guns.

While he failed to sink the *Bismarck*, Holland, it may be said, was ultimately successful in his mission—to take the *Hood* and the *Prince of Wales* and to prevent the *Bismarck* from raiding commerce. Holland succeeded in bringing Lütjens and the *Bismarck* into a battle that they could not avoid. Although the *Hood* was lost along with Holland, the *Prince of Wales* succeeded in scoring three hits, two of which ultimately served to curtail the commerce raiding sortie of the *Bismarck* before she broke out into the Atlantic. As such, in this respect, Holland was successful. While not perfect, Holland acted in a professional manner, meaning he was justifiably Mentioned in Dispatches for the skill and determination he showed during the Battle of the Denmark Strait.

This work has also shown that contemporary maps showing the movement of the *Prinz Eugen* relative to the *Bismarck* are incorrect and has shown that the *Bismarck* did not transit from the port side of the *Prinz Eugen* to the starboard side of the heavy cruiser as a number of historians have claimed or have simply overlooked and failed to question. In demonstrating this, the battle photographs were analysed and lead to the conclusion that, owing to the relative dispositions of the two opposing forces—the *Prinz Eugen* and the *Bismarck* on the one hand and the *Hood* and the *Prince of Wales* on the other—that it is the case that approximately half of the battle photographs have been printed in reverse. As such, Ludovic Kennedy, Jürgen Rohwer, and Robert J. Winklareth are correct in their assessments of the so-called 'reverse photo theory'.

At the same time, this book has shown that while many of these 'known' elements of the battle are incorrect or not quite as they appear, the possibility exists that events, namely the sinking of the *Hood* and the retreat of the *Prince of Wales* may have occurred sooner than has been previously thought. Whether or not there is full credence in these theories is open to debate.

The Battle of the Denmark Strait was one of the greatest naval engagements fought during the Second World War and of history. The battle was a watershed moment, marking the end of the big-gun capital ship era as the battleship gave way to air power and the aircraft carrier as the new mistress of the sea. It is an engagement that is likely to continue to inspire and enthral historians and one that will continue to be debated for many years to come.

ADM 239/268 Armour Protection (1939) Table No. 5

British capital ships—approximate immunity ranges to chance vital hits in magazines and speed hits in machinery spaces from foreign capital ships' gunfire

90° Inclination

1	2		3		4		5		6		7	
British, under fire from	16-inch (Japan, USA)		15-inch (Germany, Italy, France)		14-inch medium velocity (Japan, USA)		14-inch high velocity (USA)		12.6-inch (Italy)		11-inch (Germany)	
Class	C.V.H.	Speed.	C.V.H.	Speed.	C.V.H.	Speed.	C.V.H.	Speed.	C.V.H.	Speed.	C.V.H.	Speed.
King George V (5)	14-33	16-30	13-31	15-27	0-32	14-29	0-36	14-32	Immune	0-34	Immune	Immune
Nelson (2)	16-35	16-26	15-33	15-25	15-35	15-27	14-up	14-29	Immune	0-31	Immune	0-33
Royal Sovereign (4)	0	0	0	0	0	0	15-18	0	0-19	0-11	0-23	0-16
Royal Oak (1)	18-25	0	17-24	0	17-25	0	15-28	0	0-30	0-11	0-33	0-16
Warspite (3)	18-26	18-19	17-25	17-18	17-26	17-19	15-29	15-22	0-31	0-24	0-33	0-27
Barham (1)	18-26	0	17-25	0	17-26	0	15-29	0	0-31	0-12	0-33	0-16
Malaya (1)	18-26	0	17-25	0	17-26	0	15-29	0	0-31	0-12	0-33	0-16
Hood (1)	0	0	0	0	19-20	0	17-24	17-18	9-25	9-19	13-28	13-23
Renown (1)	0	0	0	0	0	0	0	0	13-30	13-22	18-33	18-25
Repulse (1)	0	0	0	0	0	0	0	0	13-32	0	18-up	0

Figures for C.V.H. are given in thousands of yards. The number next to the class name denotes the number of ships within that class.

The 'shut down' range for all ships is of the order of 12,000 yards at 90° inclination, and decreases as the inclination narrows. The perforation range for vertical armour decreases as the inclination narrows, thereby giving a broadening of the immunity zones.

The Lost Crew of HMS *Prince of Wales*

Below are the names of the fourteen members of the crew of the *Prince of Wales* who lost their lives as a result of the Battle of the Denmark Strait. All of those listed below died on 24 May 1941 unless otherwise indicated.

Leading Signalman Walter Graham Andrews
Ordinary Seaman Harold Barlow
Able Seaman Leslie Maddocks Deeds
Ordinary Seaman Edward Patrick Diamond
Midshipman Peter Tuthill Dreyer
Ordinary Seaman William John Fairbairn
Able Seaman Harry Halam
Able Seaman Arthur Molyneaux Harper
Leading Signalman Edward James Hunt
Midshipman John Bret Ince
Boy Signalman Norman Johnstone
Able Seaman Thomas Ronald Slater
Ordinary Seaman Thornton Smith
Leading Seaman Mervyn Tucker (died 25 May 1941)

Endnotes

Chapter 1

1. Müllenheim-Rechberg, B., *Battleship Bismarck: A Survivor's Story* (London: The Bodley Head Ltd, 1981), p. 21.
2. *Ibid.*, p. 24; Knowles, D., *Tirpitz: The Life and Death of Germany's Last Great Battleship* (Stroud: Fonthill Media, 2018), pp. 26–47; Gröner, E., *German Warships 1815–1945* (Annapolis: Naval Institute Press, 1990), pp. 33–35; Garzke, W. H. and Dulin, R. O., *Battleships: Axis and Neutral Battleships in World War II* (Annapolis: Naval Institute Press, 1985), p. 203; Williamson, G., *German Battleships 1939–45* (Oxford: Oxford University Press, 2003), p. 43.
3. Rico, J. M., 'Operation Rheinübung', kbismarck.com (2013), kbismarck.com/operheini.html, Accessed 28/06/2018.
4. Boyne, W., *Clash of Titans: World War II at Sea* (New York: Simon & Schuster, 1995), pp. 53–54.
5. Rico, *op. cit.*
6. Konstam, A., *The Bismarck 1941: Hunting Germany's Greatest Battleship* (Oxford: Osprey Publishing Ltd, 2011), pp. 30–31.

Chapter 2

1. Konstam, *The Bismarck 1941*, p. 31.
2. Winklareth, R. J., *The Battle of the Denmark Strait: A Critical Analysis of the Bismarck's Singular Triumph* (Oxford: Casemate Publisher, 2012), p. 104.
3. Bishop, P., *Target Tirpitz: X-Craft, Agents and Dambusters—The Epic Quest to Destroy Hitler's Mightiest Warship* (London: Harper Press, 2012), p. 21.
4. Coles, A. and Briggs, T., *Flagship Hood: The Fate of Britain's Mightiest Warship* (London: Robert Hale Limited, 1988), p. 198.
5. Ballantyne, I., *Killing the Bismarck: Destroying the Pride of Hitler's Fleet* (Barnsley: Pen and Sword, 2015), p. 28.
6. Rico, 'Operation Rheinübung'.
7. Konstam, *op. cit.*, p. 37.
8. Rico, *op. cit.*
9. *Ibid.*
10. Coles and Briggs, *op. cit.*, pp. 203–204.

11 Konstam, *op. cit.*, pp. 39–40.
12 Coles and Briggs, *op. cit.*, p. 204.
13 Norman, A., *HMS Hood: Pride of the Royal Navy* (Stroud: The History Press, 2009), p. 100.

Chapter 3

1   Rico, J. M., 'The Battle of the Denmark Strait', kbismarck.com (2013), http://www.kbismarck.com/denmark-strait-battle.html, Accessed 28/06/2018.
2   *Ibid.*
3   Konstam, *The Bismarck 1941*, p. 40.
4   Rico, 'The Battle of the Denmark Strait'.
5   ADM 116/4352.
6   Ibid.
7   Konstam, *op. cit.*, p. 44.
8   Rico, 'The Battle of the Denmark Strait'.
9   Coles and Briggs, *Flagship Hood*, pp. 214–215.
10 Müllenheim-Rechberg, *Battleship Bismarck*, pp. 109–110.
11 ADM 116/4351.
12 *Ibid.*
13 *Ibid.*
14 *Ibid.*
15 *Ibid.*
16 *Ibid.*
17 *Ibid.*
18 *Ibid.*
19 *Ibid.*
20 Coles and Briggs, *op. cit.*, pp. 215–216.

Chapter 4

1   Rhys-Jones, G., *The Loss of the Bismarck* (London: Cassell, 1999), p. 131.
2   *Kriegstagebuch Des Kreuzers Prinz Eugen* (*Prinz Eugen* War Diary) 18 May 1941–1 June 1941, p. 21.
3   Bishop, *Target Tirpitz*, p. 27.
4   Brooke, G., *Alarm Starboard!: A Remarkable True Story of the War at Sea* (Barnsley: Pen & Sword, 2009), p. 61.
5   Kennedy, L., *Pursuit: The Chase and Sinking of the Bismarck* (London: HarperCollins, 1974), p. 212.
6   *Sunday Pictoral*, 25 May 1941.
7   *Sunday Mirror*, 25 May 1941.
8   *Sunday News*, 25 May 1941.
9   *San Francisco Examiner*, 25 May 1941.
10 *The Capital Times*, 25 May 1941.
11 *Middlesboro Daily News*, 25 May 1941.

Chapter 5

1   Woodward, T., 'Putting VADM Holland's Actions During the Battle of the Denmark Strait into Context', *HMS Hood Association Website* (2014), http://www.hmshood.com/history/denmarkstrait/woodward.htm, Accessed 28/06/2018.

2   Taylor, B., *The End of Glory: War and Peace in HMS Hood, 1916-1941* (Barnsley: Seaforth publishing, 2012), p. 183.
3   Grenfell, R., *The Bismarck Episode* (New York: The Macmillan Company, 1949).
4   Kennedy, *Pursuit: The Chase and Sinking of the Bismarck* (London: HarperCollins, 1974).
5   Knowles, *Tirpitz*, p. 151.
6   Woodward, *op. cit.*
7   Ibid.
8   Page, C. (ed.), *German Capital Ships and Raiders in World War II: Volume I From Graf Spee to Bismarck, 1939–1941* (Oxon: Routledge, 2012).
9   Woodward, *op. cit.*
10 Ibid.
11 Roskill, S., *The War at Sea 1939–45 Volume 1: The Defensive* (London: Majesty's Stationary Office, 1954), p. 404.
12 Coles and Briggs, *Flagship Hood*, p. 243; Woodward, *op. cit.*
13 Howse, D., *Radar at Sea: The Royal Navy in World War 2* (Annapolis: Naval Institute Press, 1993), p. 11, p. 26; Ballantyne, I., *HMS Rodney: Slayer of the Bismarck and D-Day Saviour* (Barnsley: Pen and Sword, 2016), p. 101.
14 Woodward, *op. cit.*
15 Coles and Briggs, *op. cit.*, p. 243.
16 ADM 116/4352.
17 Waddingham, S., 'Decision in the Denmark Strait: VADM Holland—Blunderer or Blighted by Fate, *HMS Hood Association Website* (2014), http://www. hmshood.com/history/denmarkstrait/holland.htm, Accessed 28/06/2018.
18 Ash, B., *Someone Had Blundered: The Story of the Repulse and Prince of Wales* (London: Michael Joseph, 1960), p. 60; Howse, *op. cit.*, p. 26.
19 Ash, *op. cit.*, p. 59; Woodward, *op. cit.*
20 Roskill, *op. cit.*, pp. 401–402.
21 Rhys-Jones, *The Loss of the Bismarck*, p. 115.
22 Ballantyne, *op. cit.*, p. 66; Knowles, D., *HMS Hood: Pride of the Royal Navy* (Stroud: Fonthill Media, 2019), pp. 325-326; Norman, *HMS Hood*, p. 100.
23 Woodward, *op. cit.*
24 *Ibid.*
25 Müllenheim-Rechberg, *Battleship Bismarck*, p. 104.
26 See Knowles, *Tirpitz: The Life and Death of Germany's Last Great Battleship*.
27 Woodward, *op. cit.*
28 *Ibid.*
29 Norman, *op. cit.*, p. 100.
30 ADM 234/509.
31 Ballantyne, *op. cit.*, p. 66.
32 ADM 116/4352.
33 *Ibid.*
34 Woodward, *op. cit.*
35 *Ibid.*
36 Bradford, E., *The Mighty Hood* (London: Hodder & Stoughton, 1977), p. 147.
37 Woodward, *op. cit.*
38 Ash, *op. cit.*, p. 59.
39 Woodward, *op. cit.*
40 Ash, *op. cit.*, p. 60.
41 Kennedy, *op. cit.*, p. 72.
42 Winton, J., *Death of the Scharnhorst* (London: Cassell, 2001), p. 82.
43 ADM 116/4352.

44 Coles and Briggs, *op. cit.*, p. 204.
45 Woodward, *op. cit.*
46 Müllenheim-Rechberg, *op. cit.*, pp. 104-105.
47 Grenfell, *op. cit.*, p. 63.
48 Bradford, *op. cit.*, p. 170.
49 Friedman, N., *Naval Firepower: Battleship Guns and Gunnery in the Dreadnought Era* (Barnsley: Seaforth Publishing, 2008), p. 154; Woodward, *op. cit.*
50 Knowles, 2019, *op. cit.*, pp. 66–67.
51 ADM 293/268.
52 Knowles, 2019, *op. cit.*, p. 276.
53 Waddingham, *op. cit.*; Woodward, *op. cit.*; ADM 234/509.
54 Levy, J. P., *The Royal Navy's Home Fleet in World War II* (Basingstoke: Palgrave Macmillan, 2003), p. 92; Woodward, *op. cit.*
55 Knowles, 2018, *op. cit.*, p. 72.
56 Coles and Briggs, *op. cit.*, p. 240.
57 *Ibid.*
58 Taylor, B., *The Battlecruiser HMS Hood: An Illustrated Biography 1916–1941* (Barnsley: Seaforth Publishing, 2015), p. 216; Robertson, L. G., 'HMS Hood: Battle-Cruiser 1916–1941' in Windgate, J. (ed.), *Warships in Profile Volume II* (Windsor: Profile Publications, 1973), p. 165.
59 Taylor, 2015, *op. cit.* p. 216.
60 Müllenheim-Rechberg, *op. cit.*, p. 104; *Kriegstagebuch Des Kreuzers Prinz Eugen* (*Prinz Eugen* War Diary) 18 May 1941–1 June 1941, p. 20; *Kriegstagebuch Des Schlachtschiffes Bismarck 24 August 1940–27 Mai 1941* (Battleship *Bismarck* War Diary 24 August 1940–27 May 1941), p. 131.
61 Bercuson, D. J., and Herwig, H. H., *Bismarck: The Story Behind the Destruction of the Pride of Hitler's Navy* (London: Pimlico, 2003), p.101.
62 *Ibid.*, p. 102.
63 ADM 234/325.
64 ADM 116/4309.
65 *Ibid.*
66 Woodward, *op. cit.*
67 Pope, D., *The Battle of the River Plate: The Hunt for the German Pocket Battleship Graf Spee* (New York: McBooks Press, 2005), p. 109.
68 Woodward, *op. cit.*
69 Grenfell, *op. cit.*, p. 62.
70 Knowles, 2019, *op. cit.*, p. 26; ADM 1/8408/6.
71 Müllenheim-Rechberg, *op. cit.*, p. 107.
72 ADM 116/4352.
73 Knowles, 2019, *op. cit.*, p. 330.
74 Coles and Briggs, *op. cit.*, p. 296.
75 Ballantyne, *op. cit.*, p. 74.
76 *Ibid.*; see also Ash, *op. cit.*, p. 63.
77 Santarini, M., *Bismarck and Hood: The Battle of the Denmark Strait A Technical Analysis for a New Perspective* (Stroud: Fonthill Media, 2013), p. 44.
78 Coles and Briggs, *op. cit.*, p. 243.
79 Woodward, *op. cit.*
80 *Kriegstagebuch Des Kreuzers Prinz Eugen* (*Prinz Eugen* War Diary) 18 May 1941–1 June 1941, p. 20.
81 Müllenheim-Rechberg, *op. cit.*, pp. 103-107.
82 Woodward, *op. cit.*

Chapter 6

1   Rose, L. A., *Power at Sea: Volume 2 The Breaking Storm, 1919-1945* (Columbia: University of Missouri Press, 2007), p. 156.
2   Winklareth, *The Battle of the Denmark Strait*, p. 308.
3   *Kriegstagebuch Des Schlachtschiffes Bismarck 24 August 1940–27 Mai 1941* (Battleship *Bismarck* War Diary, 24 August 1940–27 May 1941), p. 131.
4   Winklareth, *op. cit.*, pp. 307–308.

Chapter 7

1   Jurens, W., 'The Loss of HMS Hood: A Re-Examination', *Warship International*, Vol. 24, No. 2 (1987), p. 123.
2   *Ibid.*, pp. 139-154; Knowles, *HMS Hood*, pp. 361–362.
3   ADM 116/4352.
4   Coles and Briggs, *Flagship Hood*, p. 215.
5   Ballantyne, *HMS Rodney*, pp. 78–79.
6   ADM 116/4351.
7   *Ibid.*
8   *Ibid.*
9   *Ibid.*
10 Winklareth, *The Battle of the Denmark Strait*, pp. 244–245.
11 ADM 116/4351.
12 *Ibid.*
13 *Ibid.*
14 *Ibid.*
15 Ballantyne, *op. cit.*, pp. 204–205.
16 Jurens, *op. cit.*
17 ADM 116/4351.
18 *Ibid.*
19 *Ibid.*
20 *Ibid.*
21 *Ibid.*
22 *Ibid.*
23 *Ibid.*
24 Taylor, *The Battlecruiser HMS Hood*, p. 224.
25 Mearns, D. and White, R., *Hood and Bismarck: The Deep-Sea Discovery of an Epic Sea Battle* (London: Channel 4 Books, 2002), pp. 206–207.
26 ADM 116/4351.
27 *Ibid.*
28 Coles and Briggs, *op. cit.*, p. 215.
29 ADM 116/4351.
30 Müllenheim-Rechberg, *Battleship Bismarck*, p. 110.
31 Mearns and White, *op. cit.*, p. 207.
32 Jurens, W., Garzke, W. H., Dulin, R. O., Roberts, J., and Fiske, R., 'A Marine Forensic Analysis of HMS Hood and DKM Bismarck', *Society of Naval Architects and Marine Engineers*, 110 (2002), p. 146.
33 ADM 116/4351.
34 *Ibid.*
35 *Ibid.*
36 Schmalenbach, P., *Schwerer Kreuzer Prinz Eugen* (Munich: Heyne, 2003), p. 139.
37 Jurens, *op. cit.*

Chapter 8

1 ADM 116/4351.
2 *Ibid.*
3 *Ibid.*
4 *Ibid.*
5 *Ibid.*
6 *Ibid.*
7 *Ibid.*
8 Hodges, P., *The Big Gun: Battleship Main Armament, 1860-1945* (Annapolis: Naval Institute Press, 1981), p. 133.
9 Raven, A. and Roberts, J., *British Battleships of World War Two: The Development and Technical History of the Royal Navy's Battleships and Battlecruisers from 1911 to 1946* (Annapolis: Naval Institute Press, 1976), p. 411.
10 *Ibid.*, p. 60.
11 Burt, R. A., *British Battleships 1919–1939* (Annapolis: Naval Institute Press, 2012), p. 135; Rohwer, J., *Chronology of the War at Sea 1939–1945: The Naval History of World War Two* (Annapolis: Naval Institute Press, 2005), p. 118.
12 Jones, G. P., *Battleship Barham* (London: William Kimber, 1979), pp. 258–259.
13 Knowles, *HMS Hood*, p. 18.
14 *Ibid*, p. 26.

Chapter 9

1 Jurens, 'The Loss of HMS Hood: A Re-Examination', p. 155.
2 Lenihan, D. J., *Submerged Cultural Resources Study: USS Arizona and Pearl Harbour National Historic Landmark* (Santa Fe: Southwest Cultural Resources Center, 1989), www.nps.gov (2001), https://www.nps.gov/parkhistory/online_books/usar/scrs/scrs2h.htm, Accessed 08/05/2018.
3 Jurens, *op. cit.*, pp. 155–157.

Chapter 10

1 Ballantyne, *HMS Rodney*, p. 77.

Chapter 13

1 ADM 234/509; Cadogan, P., *The Sinking of H.M.S. Hood: An Examination of the Timing of Her Fatal Hit*, p. 3.
2 Konstam, *The Bismarck 1941*, p. 9; Taylor, *The Battlecruiser HMS Hood*, p. 242.
3 Knowles, *Tirpitz*, p. 27.
4 Müllenheim-Rechberg, *Battleship Bismarck*, p. 108.
5 ADM 234/509.
6 ADM 116/4352.
7 Chesneau, R., *Hood: Life and Death of a Battlecruiser* (London: Cassell Publishing, 2002), p. 180.
8 ADM 116/4351.
9 ADM 234/509.
10 Brooke, *Alarm Starboard!*, p. 60.
11 ADM 116/4352.
12 *Ibid.*
13 ADM 116/4351.

14 ADM 53/114888.
15 *Kriegstagebuch Des Kreuzers Prinz Eugen* (*Prinz Eugen* War Diary) 18 May 1941–1 June 1941, p. 21.
16 Busch, F. O., *Prinz Eugen im Ersten Gefecht* (Gütersloh: Verlag C. Bertelsmann, 1943).
17 Müllenheim-Rechberg, *op. cit.*, pp. 110–111.
18 ADM 234/509.
19 Müllenheim-Rechberg, *op. cit.*, pp. 105–107.
20 *Ibid.* pp. 109–110.
21 ADM 116/4351.
22 *Kriegstagebuch Des Kreuzers Prinz Eugen*, p. 20; HMS *Prince of Wales* salvo plot.
23 *Kriegstagebuch Des Kreuzers Prinz Eugen*, p. 20.
24 Müllenheim-Rechberg, *op. cit.*, p. 108.
25 Taylor, *The Battlecruiser HMS Hood*, pp. 216–217.
26 ADM 116/4352.
27 Cadogan, *op. cit.*, p. 10.
28 Admiralty, *The Gunnery Pocket Book* (London: The Admiralty, 1945), p. 51.
29 *Kriegstagebuch Des Kreuzers Prinz Eugen*.
30 *Ibid.*, p. 45.
31 ADM 116/4352.
32 Coles and Briggs, *Flagship Hood*, p. 214.
33 Cadogan, *op. cit.*, p. 12.
34 *Ibid.*, p. 212.
35 ADM 234/509.
36 IWM 10751.
37 ADM 116/4351.
38 *Ibid.*
39 *Kriegstagebuch Des Kreuzers Prinz Eugen*, pp. 44–45.
40 ADM 116/4351.
41 Coles and Briggs, *op. cit.*, pp. 217–218.
42 *Ibid.*, pp. 215–217.

Chapter 14

1 Ash, *Someone Had Blundered*, p. 58.
2 ADM 116/4352.
3 Coles and Briggs, *Flagship Hood*, p. 241.
4 Santarini, *Bismarck and Hood*, p. 52.
5 Mearns and White, *Hood and Bismarck*, pp. 64–65.
6 Santarini, *op. cit.*, p. 53.

Chapter 15

1 Ballantyne, *HMS Rodney*, p. 100.
2 *Ibid.* pp. 204–205.
3 ADM 267/111.
4 *Ibid.*

Bibliography

Archival Material

ADM 1/8408/6 (Kew: The National Archives).
ADM 53/114888 (Kew: The National Archives)
ADM 116/4309 (Kew: The National Archives)
ADM 116/4351 (Kew: The National Archives)
ADM 116/4352 (Kew: The National Archives)
ADM 234/325 (Kew: The National Archives)
ADM 234/509 (Kew: The National Archives)
ADM 267/111 (Kew: The National Archives)
ADM 293/268 (Kew: The National Archives)
IWM 10751 (London: Imperial War Museum)
Kriegstagebuch Des Kreuzers *Prinz Eugen* (*Prinz Eugen* War Diary) 18 May 1941-1
    June 1941
Kriegstagebuch Des Schlachtschiffes *Bismarck* 24 August 1940-27 Mai 1941
    (Battleship *Bismarck* War Diary 24 August 1940-27May 1941)

Literature

Admiralty, *The Gunnery Pocket Book* (London: The Admiralty, 1945)
Ash, B., *Someone Had Blundered: The Story of the Repulse and Prince of Wales*
    (London: Michael Joseph, 1960)
Ballantyne, I., *HMS Rodney: Slayer of the Bismarck and D-Day Saviour* (Barnsley:
    Pen and Sword, 2016)
Ballantyne, I., *Killing the Bismarck: Destroying the Pride of Hitler's Fleet* (Barnsley:
    Pen and Sword, 2015)
Bercuson, D. J., and Herwig, H. H., *Bismarck: The Story Behind the Destruction of
    the Pride of Hitler's Navy* (London: Pimlico, 2003)
Bishop, P., *Target Tirpitz: X-Craft, Agents and Dambusters – The Epic Quest to
    Destroy Hitler's Mightiest Warship* (London: Harper Press, 2012)
Boyne, W., *Clash of Titans: World War II at Sea* (New York: Simon & Schuster, 1995)
Bradford, E., *The Mighty Hood* (London: Hodder & Stoughton, 1977)
Brooke, G., *Alarm Starboard!: A Remarkable True Story of the War at Sea*
    (Barnsley: Pen and Sword, 2009)

Burt, R. A., *British Battleships 1919-1939* (Annapolis: Naval Institute Press, 2012)

Busch, F. O., *Prinz Eugen im Ersten Gefecht* (Gütersloh: Verlag C. Bertelsmann, 1943)

Cadogan, P., *The Sinking of H.M.S. Hood: An Examination of the Timing of Her Fatal Hit* (Online, 2014)

Chesneau, R., *Hood: Life and Death of a Battlecruiser* (London: Cassell Publishing, 2002)

Coles, A., and Briggs, T., *Flagship Hood: The Fate of Britain's Mightiest Warship* (London: Robert Hale Limited, 1988)

Friedman, N., *Naval Firepower: Battleship Guns and Gunnery in the Dreadnought Era* (Barnsley: Seaforth Publishing, 2008)

Garzke, W. H., and Dulin, R. O., *Battleships: Axis and Neutral Battleships in World War II* (Annapolis: Naval Institute Press, 1985)

Grenfell, R., *The Bismarck Episode* (New York: The Macmillan Company, 1949)

Gröner, E., *German Warships 1815-1945* (Annapolis: Naval Institute Press, 1990)

Hodges, P., *The Big Gun: Battleship Main Armament, 1860-1945* (Annapolis: Naval Institute Press, 1981)

Howse, D., *Radar at Sea: The Royal Navy in World War 2* (Annapolis: Naval Institute Press, 1993)

Jones, G. P., *Battleship Barham* (London: William Kimber, 1979)

Jurens, W., 'The Loss of HMS Hood: A Re-Examination', *Warship International*, Vol. 24, No. 2 (1987), pp. 122-180.

Jurens, W., and Garzke W. H. (et. al), 'A Marine Forensic Analysis of HMS Hood and DKM Bismarck', *Society of Naval Architects and Marine Engineers*, No. 110 (2002)

Kennedy, L., *Pursuit: The Chase and Sinking of the Bismarck* (London: HarperCollins, 1974)

Knowles, D., *HMS Hood: Pride of the Royal Navy* (Stroud: Fonthill Media, 2019)

Knowles, D., *Tirpitz: The Life and Death of Germany's Last Great Battleship* (Stroud: Fonthill Media, 2018)

Konstam, A., *The Bismarck 1941: Hunting Germany's Greatest Battleship* (Oxford: Osprey Publishing Ltd, 2011)

Levy, J. P., *The Royal Navy's Home Fleet in World War II* (Basingstoke: Palgrave Macmillan, 2003)

Mearns, D., and White, R., *Hood and Bismarck: The Deep-Sea Discovery of an Epic Sea Battle* (London: Channel 4 Books, 2002)

Müllenheim-Rechberg, B., *Battleship Bismarck: A Survivor's Story* (London: The Bodley Head Ltd, 1981)

Norman, A., *HMS Hood: Pride of the Royal Navy* (Stroud: The History Press, 2009)

Padfield, P., *The Battleship Era* (London: Pan Books, 1975)

Page, C. (ed.) *German Capital Ships and Raiders in World War II: Volume I From Graf Spee to Bismarck, 1939-1941* (Oxon: Routledge, 2012)

Pope, Dudley,*The Battle of the River Plate: The Hunt for the German Pocket Battleship Graf Spee* (New York: McBooks Press, 2005)

Raven, A., and Roberts, J., *British Battleships of World War Two: The Development and Technical History of the Royal Navy's Battleships and Battlecruisers from 1911 to 1946* (Annapolis: Naval Institute Press, 1976)

Rhys-Jones, G., *The Loss of the Bismarck* (London: Cassell, 1999)

Robertson, L. G., 'HMS Hood: Battle-Cruiser 1916-1941' in Windgate, John (ed.), *Warships in Profile Volume II* (Windsor: Profile Publications, 1973)

Rohwer, J., *Chronology of the War at Sea 1939-1945: The Naval History of World War Two* (Annapolis: Naval Institute Press, 2005)

Rose, L. A., *Power at Sea: Volume 2 The Breaking Storm, 1919-1945* (Columbia: University of Missouri Press, 2007)

Roskill, S., *The War at Sea 1939-45 Volume I: The Defensive* (London: Her Majesty's Stationary Office, 1954)

Santarini, M., *Bismarck and Hood: The Battle of the Denmark Strait A Technical Analysis for a New Perspective* (Stroud: Fonthill Media, 2013)

Schmalenbach, P., *Schwerer Kreuzer Prinz Eugen* (Munich: Heyne, 2003)

Taylor, B., *The Battlecruiser HMS Hood: An Illustrated Biography 1916-1941* (Barnsley: Seaforth Publishing, 2015)

Taylor, B., *The End of Glory: War and Peace in HMS Hood, 1916-1941* (Barnsley: Seaforth publishing, 2012)

Williamson, G., *German Battleships 1939-45* (Oxford: Oxford University Press, 2003)

Winklareth, R. J., *The Battle of the Denmark Strait: A Critical Analysis of the Bismarck's Singular Triumph* (Oxford: Casemate Publisher, 2012)

Winton, John, *Death of the Scharnhorst* (London: Cassell, 2001)

Webpages

Allen, Frank, Bevand, Paul, 'The Pursuit of Bismarck & the Sinking of H.M.S. Hood Part 1', *HMS Hood Association Website* (2018), http://hmshood.com/history/denmarkstrait/bismarck1.htm, Accessed 23/02/2020.

Allen, Frank, Bevand, Paul, 'The Pursuit of Bismarck & the Sinking of H.M.S. Hood Part 2', *HMS Hood Association Website* (2018), http://hmshood.com/history/denmarkstrait/bismarck2.htm, Accessed 23/02/2020.

Allen, Frank, Bevand, Paul, 'The Pursuit of Bismarck & the Sinking of H.M.S. Hood Part 3', *HMS Hood Association Website* (2018), http://hmshood.com/history/denmarkstrait/bismarck3.htm, Accessed 23/02/2020.

Lenihan, Daniel J., *Submerged Cultural Resources Study: USS Arizona and Pearl Harbor National Historic Landmark* (Santa Fe: Southwest Cultural resources Center, 1989), www.nps.gov (2001), https://www.nps.gov.parkhistory/online_books/usar/scrs2h.htm, Accessed 23/02/2020.

Rico, José M., 'The Battle of the Denmark Strait', kbismarck.com (2013), http://www.kbismarck.com/denmark-strait-battle.html, Accessed 23/02/2020.

Rico, José M., 'Operation Rheinübung', *kbismarck.com* (2013), http://www.kbismarck.com/operheini.html, Accessed 23/02/2020.

Waddingham, Sean, 'Decision in the Denmark Strait: VADM Holland – Blunderer or Blighted by Fate, *HMS Hood Association Website* (2014), http://www.hmshood.com/history/denmarkstrait/holland.htm, Accessed 23/02/2020.

Woodward, Tim, 'Putting VADM Holland's Actions During the Battle of the Denmark Strait into Context', *HMS Hood Association Website* (2014), http://www.hmshood.com/history/denmarkstrait/woodward.htm, Accessed 23/02/2020.

Newspapers

The Capital Times, 25 May 1941.
Middlesboro Daily News, 25 May 1941.
San Francisco Examiner, 25 May 1941.
Sunday Mirror, 25 May 1941.
Sunday News, 25 May 1941.
Sunday Pictorial, 25 May 1941.

Index